The Social Structures of
the Economy

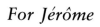
For Jérôme

The Social Structures of the Economy

PIERRE BOURDIEU

Translated by Chris Turner

polity

Every effort has been made to trace all copyright holders, but if any have been inadvertently overlooked the publishers will be pleased to include any necessary credits in any subsequent reprint or edition.

First published in 2005 by Polity Press

Reprinted 2008 (three times), 2010

Polity Press
65 Bridge Street
Cambridge CB2 1UR, UK

Polity Press
350 Main Street
Malden, MA 02148, USA

ISBN: 978-0-7456-2540-9 (pbk)
ISBN: 978-0-7456-2539-3 (hbk)

A catalogue record for this book is available from the British Library.

Typeset in Sabon in 11pt on 12pt
by BookEns Ltd, Royston, Herts.
Printed and bound in Great Britain by
MPG Books Ltd, Bodmin, Cornwall

Contents

While economics is about how people make choice, sociology is about how they don't have any choice to make.

Bertrand Russell

Introduction

> It takes centuries of culture to produce a utilitarian such as John Stuart Mill.
>
> Henri Bergson

The science called 'economics' is based on an initial act of abstraction that consists in dissociating a particular category of practices, or a particular dimension of all practice, from the social order in which all human practice is immersed. This immersion, some aspects or effects of which one finds in Karl Polanyi's notion of 'embeddedness', obliges us (even when, for the purposes of increasing knowledge, we are forced to treat it otherwise) to conceive every practice, beginning with the practice which presents itself, most obviously and in the strictest sense, as 'economic', as a 'total social fact' in Marcel Mauss's sense.

The individual studies I carried out more than forty years ago in Algeria on the logic of the economy of honour and 'good faith' or on the economic and cultural determinants of practices of saving, credit or investment or, in the mid-1960s with Luc Boltanski and Jean-Claude Chamboredon, on banks and their customers or, more recently, with Salah Bouhedja, Rosine Christin, Claire Givry and Monique de Saint-Martin, on the production and marketing of single-family houses[1] differ from economics in its commonest form in two essential respects: they attempt in each case to bring to bear all the available knowledge relating to the different dimensions of the social order – which we may list, in no particular order, as the family, the state, the school system, the trade unions, grassroots organizations, etc. – and not merely knowledge relating to banking, firms and the market; and they deploy a system of concepts, developed in response to observational data, which might be presented as an alternative theory for understanding economic action: the concept of *habitus*, which was developed as part of an attempt to account for the practices of men and women who found themselves thrown into a strange and foreign economic cosmos imported and imposed by colonialism, with cultural equipment and dispositions – particularly economic dispositions – acquired in a precapitalist world; the concept of *cultural capital* which, being elaborated and deployed at more or less the same time as Gary Becker was putting into circulation the vague and flabby notion of 'human capital' (a notion heavily laden with sociologically unacceptable assumptions), was intended to account for otherwise inexplicable differences in the academic performance of children with unequal cultural patrimonies and, more generally, in all kinds of cultural or economic practices; the concept of *social capital* which I had developed, from my earliest ethnological work in Kabylia or Béarn, to account for residual differences, linked, broadly speaking, to the resources which can be brought together *per procurationem* through networks of 'relations' of various sizes and differing density, and which – often associated today with the name of James Coleman, who was responsible for launching it on the highly protected market of American sociology – is frequently used to correct the implications of the dominant model through the effect of 'social networks';[2] the concept of *symbolic capital*, which I had to construct to explain the logic of the economy of honour and 'good faith' and which I have been able to clarify and refine in, by and for the analysis of the economy of symbolic goods, particularly of works of art; and lastly, and most importantly, the concept of *field*, which has met with some success, in an unattributed and often rather watered-down form, in the 'New Economic Sociology'.[3] The introduction of these notions is merely one aspect of a more general shift of language (marked, for example, by the substitution of the lexicon of dispositions for the language of decision-making, or of the term 'reasonable' for 'rational'), which is essential to express a view of action radically different from that which – most often implicitly – underlies neoclassical theory.

In having recourse to concepts that have been developed and applied to objects as diverse as ritual practices, economic behaviours, education, art or literature, I would not wish to appear to be indulging in that kind of reductionist annexationism, ignorant of the specificities and particularities of each social microcosm, to which certain economists are increasingly addicted today, in the conviction that the most general concepts of the most highly refined economic thought are adequate for the analysis, outside of any reference to the work of historians or social anthropologists, of social realities as complex as the family, intergenerational exchanges, corruption or marriage. In fact, I start out with quite the opposite conviction: because the social world is present in its entirety in every 'economic' action, we have to equip ourselves with instruments of knowledge which, far from bracketing out the multidimensionality and multi-functionality of practices, enable us to construct *historical models* capable of accounting, with rigour and parsimony, for economic actions and institutions as they present themselves to empirical observation. Clearly, this is achieved at the expense of a prior suspension of one's ordinary commitment to the preformed notions and assumptions of common sense. As is shown by so many deductive models produced by economists, which are mere mathematical formalizations – and formularizations – of a commonsense insight, this break with ordinary practice is perhaps never so difficult as when what is to be questioned, such as the principles underlying economic practices, is inscribed in the most ordinary routines of everyday experience.

I can give an idea of the labour of conversion needed to break with the primal vision of economic practices only by referring to the long string of surprised, astonished and disconcerted reactions that led me to *experience* quite tangibly the contingent character of so many behaviours which form part of our normal daily round: calculation of cost and profit, lending at interest, saving, credit, the creation of a reserve, investment or even work. I remember spending many an hour peppering with questions a Kabyle peasant who was trying to explain a traditional form of the loan of livestock, because it had not occurred to me that, contrary to all 'economic' reason, the lender might feel an obligation to the borrower on the grounds that the borrower was providing for the upkeep of an animal that would have had to have been fed in any case. I also remember all the tiny anecdotal observations or statistical findings I had to put together before gradually realizing that I, like everyone else, had an implicit philosophy of work, based on an equivalence between work and money: the behaviour, deemed highly scandalous, of the mason who, after a long stay in France, asked that a sum corresponding to the cost of the meal laid on for the workers at the end of the job – a meal he had refused to attend – should be added to his wages or the fact that, despite working an objectively identical number of hours or days, the peasants of the southern regions of Algeria, where emigration has had less of an impact, were more likely to say they were 'working' than the Kabyles, who tended to describe themselves as unemployed or jobless. This philosophy which to me (and all those like me) seemed self-evident was something that some of those observed, in particular the Kabyles, were just *discovering*, wrenching themselves with enormous effort from a vision, which I found very difficult to conceive, of activity as *social occupation*.[4] And I can also remember feeling a kind of amused stupefaction at the extraordinary story of the children of Lowestoft in Norfolk, England, who, as the French newspapers of 29 October 1959 reported, had set up a scheme of insurance against punishment which meant that for a beating the insured party received four shillings and who, in response to attempts to abuse the system, had gone so far as to add a supplementary clause to the effect that no payment would be made to those incurring punishment deliberately.

Since they lacked these 'predispositions', which the spontaneously Millian schoolchildren of Lowestoft had imbibed with their mother's milk, the economic agents I was able to observe in Algeria in the 1960s had to learn or, more exactly, *reinvent,* with greater or lesser success depending on their economic and cultural resources, everything economic theory considers (at least tacitly) as a given, that is to say, everything it regards as an innate, universal gift, forming part of human nature: the idea of work as an activity procuring a monetary income, as opposed to mere occupation on the lines of the traditional division of activities or the traditional exchange of services; the very possibility of impersonal transactions between strangers, linked to a market situation, as opposed to all the exchanges of the economy of 'good faith', as the Kabyles call it, between relatives and acquaintances or between strangers, but strangers 'domesticated', so to speak, by the provision of guarantees from close relations and intermediaries capable of limiting and averting the risks associated with the market; the notion of long-term investment, as opposed to the practice of putting in reserve, or the simple anticipation that forms part of the directly felt unity of productive cycles; the modern conception, which has become so familiar to us that we forget that it once gave rise to interminable ethical and legal debates, of lending at interest and the very idea of a contract, with its previously unknown strict deadlines and formal clauses, which gradually supplanted the honourable exchange between men of honour that excluded calculation and the pursuit of profit, and involved an acute concern with fairness etc. These are all so many partial innovations, but together they form a system because they are rooted in a representation of the future as a site of 'possibles' that are open and susceptible to calculation.[5]

I was able to verify in this way, in quasi-experimental conditions, that there are economic and cultural preconditions to the transformation of worldview demanded of those who, equipped with dispositions shaped by the precapitalist world, are thrown into the economic universe imported and imposed by colonization. Only a very particular form of ethnocentrism, which assumes the guise of universalism, can lead us to credit economic agents universally with the aptitude for rational economic behaviour, thereby making disappear the question of the economic and cultural conditions in which this aptitude (here elevated into a norm) is acquired, and the question of what action is indispensable if these conditions are to be universalized. It is, in fact, by breaking radically with the anti-genetic prejudice of a so-called pure science, that is to say, a profoundly de-historicized and de-historicizing science, because it is based (like the Saussurian theory of language) on the initial bracketing out of any social rootedness of economic practices, that one can once more present in their proper light (that is to say, as historical institutions) social realities whose apparent self-evidence is ratified and consecrated in economic theory.

Everything economic science posits as given, that is, the range of dispositions of the economic agent which ground the illusion of the ahistorical universality of the categories and concepts employed by that science, is, in fact, the paradoxical product of a long collective history, endlessly reproduced in individual histories, which can be fully accounted for only by historical analysis: it is because history has inscribed these *concomitantly* in social and cognitive structures, practical patterns of thinking, perception and action, that it has conferred the appearance of natural, universal self-evidence on the institutions economics claims to theorize ahistorically; it has done this by, among other things, the *amnesia of genesis* that is encouraged, in this field as in others, by the immediate accord between the 'subjective' and the 'objective', between dispositions and positions, between anticipations (or hopes) and opportunities.

Against the ahistorical vision of economics, we must, then, reconstitute, on the one hand, the genesis of the economic dispositions of economic agents and, especially, of their tastes, needs, propensities or aptitudes (for calculation, saving or work itself) and, on the other, the genesis of the economic field itself, that is to say, we must trace the history of the process of differentiation and autonomization which leads to the constitution of this specific game: the economic field as a cosmos obeying its own laws and thereby conferring a (limited) validity on the radical autonomization which pure theory effects by constituting the economic sphere as a separate world. It was only very gradually that the sphere of commodity exchange separated itself out from the other fields of existence and its specific *nomos* asserted itself – the *nomos* expressed in the tautology 'business is business'; that economic transactions ceased to be conceived on the model of domestic exchanges, and hence as governed by social or family obligations ('there's no sentiment in business'); and that the calculation of individual gain, and hence economic interest, won out as the dominant, if not indeed exclusive, principle of business against the collectively imposed and controlled repression of calculating inclinations associated with the domestic economy.

The word 'conversion', which may seem inappropriate or excessive, forces itself upon us once we realize that the universe into which the newcomers must enter is also, just as much as the one they are leaving behind, a universe of belief: paradoxically, the universe of reason is rooted in a worldview which, though it has the principle of reason (or, if one prefers, the principle of economy) at its centre, does not have reason as its central principle. Observing the enforced conversions, often very costly and painful, which the newcomers to the strictly 'economic' economy have by force of necessity to undergo, doubtless enables us to form a rough idea of what happened during the origins of capitalism, when dispositions were being invented at the same time as the field in which they were to find scope for deployment was gradually being established. The *spirit of calculation*, which is in no way implied in the no doubt universal capacity to submit behaviour to calculating reason, gradually wins out in all fields of practice over the logic of the domestic economy, which was based on the repression, or more precisely the denial, of calculation: to refuse to calculate in exchanges between members of the household is to refuse to obey the principle of economy, as aptitude and propensity to 'economize', to 'make economies' (of effort, trouble and, subsequently, work, time, money, etc.), a refusal which may no doubt eventually promote a kind of withering away of the propensity and aptitude for calculation. Whereas the family provided the model for all exchanges, including those we regard as 'economic', it is the economy, now constituted as such and recognized as such, with its own principles and its own logic – the logic of calculation, of profit, etc. – which, to the horror of the Kabyle father whose son demands a wage from him, now claims to govern all practices and exchanges, including those within the family. It is from this inversion of the scale of values that economics as we know it was born. (And whose implications some particularly intrepid economists, like Gary

Becker, are merely following out – their very thinking being its unreflected product – when they apply models constructed in accordance with the postulate of calculating rationality to the family, marriage or art.)

In a kind of confession to itself, capitalist society stops 'deluding itself with dreams of disinterestedness and generosity': registering an awareness, as it were, that it has an economy, it constitutes the acts of production, exchange or exploitation as 'economic', recognizing explicitly as such the economic ends by which these things have always been guided. The ethical revolution that enabled the economy eventually to be constituted *as such*, in the objectivity of a separate universe, governed by its own laws (the laws of self-interested calculation and unfettered competition for profit), finds its expression in 'pure' economic theory, which registers the social dissociation and practical abstraction that give rise to the economic cosmos by inscribing them tacitly at the heart of its construction of its object.

Paradoxically, this process is itself inseparable from a new form of repression and denial of the economy and the economic that establishes itself with the emergence of all the fields of cultural production based on the repression of their economic and social conditions of possibility.[6] It is only by accepting a break that tends to consign certain practices to the inferior world of the economy – formed, as we have seen, by divesting productive acts and relations of production of their properly symbolic aspect that the various universes of symbolic production were able to assert themselves as closed and separate microcosms in which wholly symbolic, pure, disinterested actions (from the standpoint of the economic economy) are carried out. The emergence of these universes which, like the scholastic worlds, offer positions from which one can feel justified in apprehending the world from a lofty distance as spectacle, and in organizing it as an entity solely intended for knowledge, goes hand in hand with the invention of a scholastic worldview that finds one of its most perfect expressions in the myth of *homo oeconomicus* and in 'rational action theory', the paradigmatic form of the scholastic illusion, which leads the scholar to project his thinking into the minds of the active agents and to see as underlying their practice (that is, as informing their 'awareness') his own spontaneous or elaborated representations or, worse, the models he has had to construct to account for their practices.

A number of observers, alerted by such especially perceptive economists as Maurice Allais, have noted that a systematic discrepancy exists between theoretical models and actual practices,[7] and various works of experimental economics (themselves not always entirely free from the scholastic illusion) have shown that, in many situations, economic agents make choices systematically different from those predicted in the economic model: either they do not play the game in accordance with the predictions of game theory, or they resort to 'practical' strategies, or they evince a concern to act in conformity with their sense of fairness or justice and to be treated in the same way themselves. This empirically observed discordance is merely the reflection of the structural discrepancy I have analysed from my earliest work as a social anthropologist, between the logic of scholastic thought and practical logic or, to use the phrase Marx used of Hegel, which I find bears considerable repetition, 'between the things of logic and the logic of things'. There can be no doubt that the dispositions and schemas shaped by immersion in a field which, like the economic, is distinguished from other fields in several respects, and particularly by an exceptional degree of 'formal rationalization',[8] can engender practices that show themselves to be (at least roughly) in accordance with rationality without our being able to suppose for all that that they always have reason as their underlying principle. It is true that the penalties imposed in this field are stringent and unambiguous (prices represent a 'harsh reality') and that behaviour here can be openly directed to the maximization of individual gain without attracting the label 'cynical' or 'opportunist'. Economic interest, to which we erroneously tend to reduce any kind of interest, is merely the specific form assumed by investment in the economic field when that field is perceived by agents equipped with adequate dispositions and beliefs – adequate because they are acquired in and through early and protracted experience of its regularities and necessity. The most basic economic dispositions – needs, preferences, propensities – are not exogenous, that is to say, dependent on a universal human nature, but *endogenous* and dependent on a history that is the very history of the economic cosmos in which these dispositions are required and rewarded. This means that, against the canonical distinction between ends and means, the field imposes on everyone, *though to varying degrees depending on their economic position and capacities*, not just the 'reasonable' means, but also the ends, of economic action, that is to say: individual enrichment.

It is not 'decisions' of the rational will and consciousness or mechanical determinations resulting from external powers that underlie *the economy of economic practices* – that reason immanent in practices – but the dispositions acquired through learning processes associated with protracted dealings with the regularities of the field; apart from any conscious calculation, these dispositions are capable of generating behaviours and even anticipations which would be better termed *reasonable* than *rational*, even if their conformity with calculative evaluation tends to make us think of them, and treat them, as products of calculating reason. Observation shows that, even in this world where the means and ends of action, and the relationship between the two, are to a very high degree explicitly expressed, agents are guided by intuitions and anticipations arising out of a practical sense which very often leaves the essential factors implicit and which, on the basis of experience acquired in practice, engages in strategies that are 'practical' in the dual sense of implicit – i.e. non-theoretical – and expedient – i.e. adapted to the exigencies and urgent pressures of action.[9]

(By virtue of the fact that the 'economic' logic of interest and calculation is inseparable from the constitution of the economic cosmos in which it is generated, strictly utilitarian calculation cannot fully account for practices that remain steeped in the non-economic; and, above all, it cannot explain what makes the object of calculation possible, that is to say, the formation of the value on which calculation is to be performed, or – and this amounts to the same thing – the production of what I shall term the *illusio*, the fundamental belief in the value of the stakes and of the game itself. This can be clearly seen in the case of fields such as the religious or the artistic, where the social mechanisms of production of non-'economic' – in the narrow sense – interests obey laws that are not those of the economic field: they may conform locally to the principle of economy – for example, in recourse to the prayer wheel or in applying the '*do ut des*' formula ('I give that you may give') to exchanges with supernatural powers – without there being any hope of understanding their working, even very partially, on the basis of that principle alone. Similarly, no amount of calculation regarding the calculations which take place in the art market – or, *a fortiori*, the world of science or even bureaucracy – will contribute one jot to an understanding of the mechanisms which constitute the work of art as a value that can be subject to economic calculation and transactions. And the same is not untrue, though this is much less clearly evident, in the economic field: if, in fact, we set aside certain historical situations, such as those I was able to observe in Algeria, or some relatively extraordinary social conditions – for example, the condition of adolescents from working-class backgrounds who, having acquired through schooling, even where this was not a happy experience, dispositions which are less strictly matched to probable positions than those of their elders, resorted to various means to

avoid simple reproduction – everything conspires to make us forget
the socially constructed, and hence arbitrary and artificial, character
of investment in the economic game and its stakes: the ultimate
reasons for commitment to work, a career or the pursuit of profit in
fact lie beyond or outside calculation and calculating reason in the
obscure depths of a historically constituted habitus, which means
that, in normal circumstances, one gets up every day to go to work
without deliberating on the issue, as indeed one did yesterday and
will do tomorrow.)

The 'scholastic bias' I have just described is doubtless not the only
cause of the distortions currently affecting economics. Unlike
sociology, a pariah science that is always under suspicion for its
supposed political leanings, and from which the powerful expect
nothing but a minor, generally somewhat ancillary knowledge of
techniques of manipulation or legitimation, and which, as a result, is
less exposed than other disciplines to demands likely to threaten its
independence, economics is always more of a state science and is, as
a result, haunted by state thinking: being constantly preoccupied
with the normative concerns of an applied science, it is dependent on
responding politically to political demands, while at the same time
defending itself against any charge of political involvement by the
ostentatiously lofty character of its formal, and preferably mathematical, constructions.

It follows from this that, between economic theory in its purest,
that is to say, most formalized, form, which is never as neutral as it
wishes to believe or make out, and the policies implemented in its
name or legitimated through it, agents and institutions are
interposed that are steeped in all the assumptions inherited from
immersion in a particular economic world, which is the product of a
singular social history. Neoliberal economics, the logic of which is
tending today to win out throughout the world thanks to
international bodies like the World Bank or the International
Monetary Fund and the governments to whom they, directly or
indirectly, dictate their principles of 'governance',[10] owes a certain
number of its allegedly universal characteristics to the fact that it is
immersed or embedded in a particular society, that is to say, rooted
in a system of beliefs and values, an ethos and a moral view of the
world, in short, an *economic common sense*, linked, as such, to the
social and cognitive structures of a particular social order. It is from
this particular economy that neoclassical economic theory borrows
its fundamental assumptions, which it formalizes and rationalizes,
thereby establishing them as the foundations of a universal model.

That model rests on two postulates (which their advocates regard as proven propositions): the economy is a separate domain governed by natural and universal laws with which governments must not interfere by inappropriate intervention; the market is the optimum means for organizing production and trade efficiently and equitably in democratic societies. It is the universalization of a particular case, that of the United States of America, characterized fundamentally by the weakness of the state which, though already reduced to a bare minimum, has been further weakened by the ultra-liberal conservative revolution, giving rise as a consequence to various typical characteristics: a policy oriented towards withdrawal or abstention by the state in economic matters; the shifting into the private sector (or the contracting out) of 'public services' and the conversion of public goods such as health, housing, safety, education and culture – books, films, television and radio – into commercial goods and the users of those services into clients; a renunciation (linked to the reduction in the capacity to intervene in the economy) of the power to equalize opportunities and reduce inequality (which is tending to increase excessively) in the name of the old liberal 'self-help' tradition (a legacy of the Calvinist belief that God helps those who help themselves) and of the conservative glorification of individual responsibility (which leads, for example, to ascribing responsibility for unemployment or economic failure primarily to individuals, not to the social order, and encourages the delegation of functions of social assistance to lower levels of authority, such as the region or city); the withering away of the Hegelian–Durkheimian view of the state as a collective authority with a responsibility to act as the collective will and consciousness, and a duty to make decisions in keeping with the general interest and contribute to promoting greater solidarity.

Moreover, American society has no doubt pushed to the extreme limit the development and spread of the 'spirit of capitalism', the product of an ethical revolution which Max Weber saw as paradigmatically personified in Benjamin Franklin, with his extolling of the increase of capital elevated into a 'calling' [*Beruf*]; and also the cult of the individual and 'individualism', the basis of the whole of neoliberal economic thinking, which is one of the pillars of the *doxa* on which, as Dorothy Ross argues, the American social sciences were built;[11] or, again following Dorothy Ross, the extolling of the dynamism and flexibility of the American social order, which, in contrast to the rigidity and risk-aversiveness of European societies, leads to linking efficiency and productivity with a high degree of flexibility (by contrast with the constraints imposed by a high level of social security) and even to elevating *social insecurity* into a positive principle of collective organization, capable of producing more efficient and productive economic agents.[12]

This is to say that, of all the characteristics of societies in which the economic order is 'immersed', the most important for contemporary societies is the form and force of its state tradition, which one cannot ignore, as certain hurried and eager-to-please politicians do, without running the risk of proposing as progressive advances measures that are potentially terribly regressive, such regressions being currently invisible, but inescapable in the more or less long term. Not unlike the French politicians and senior civil servants who, in imposing, doubtless in good faith, a new policy of housing subsidy in the 1970s, a policy inspired by a neoliberal vision of the economy and society, did not know that they were preparing the ground for the conflicts and dramas that were later to bring the inhabitants of the large public estates, now deserted by their better-off occupants, into a long-lasting opposition to the inhabitants of petit-bourgeois suburban housing.[13]

The state is the culmination and product of a slow process of accumulation and concentration of different species of capital: a capital of physical force, in the form of the military and the police (which is evoked by Weber's definition of the state as exercising the 'monopoly of legitimate physical violence'); economic capital (which is necessary, among other things, to provide the funding for the physical force); cultural or informational capital, accumulated in the form of statistics, for example, and also in the form of instruments of knowledge endowed with universal validity within the limits of its competence, such as weights, measures, maps or land registers; and, lastly, symbolic capital. In this way, it is able to exert a determining influence on the way the economic field functions (and also, though to a lesser extent, on the other fields). This is the case chiefly because the unification of the market of economic goods (and also of symbolic goods, the marriage market being one dimension of this) accompanied the construction of the state and the concentration of different species of capital it brought about. This means that the economic field is, more than any other, inhabited by the state, which contributes at every moment to its existence and persistence, and also to the structure of the relations of force that characterize it. This it does mainly through the different, more or less circumstantial 'policies' it implements as and when it sees fit (for example, its 'family policies' which, through inheritance laws, the tax regime, family allowances and social assistance, have their effect on consumption – particularly on the consumption of houses – and standards of living) and, at a deeper level, through the structural effects produced by budgets, expenditure on infrastructure, particularly in the fields of transport, energy, housing and telecommunications, the taxation (or exemption from tax) of investment, control of the means of payment and credit, training of labour and the regulation of immigration, and the definition and imposition of the rules of the economic game, such as, for example, the labour contract – all these being so many political interventions which make the bureaucratic field a macroeconomic stimulator, playing its part in ensuring the stability and predictability of the economic field.

It is evident, then, that the immersion of the economy in the social dimension is such that, however legitimate the abstractions made for purposes of analysis, we must keep clearly in mind that the true object of a real economics of practices is nothing other, in the last analysis, than the economy of the conditions of production and reproduction of the agents and institutions of economic, cultural and social production and reproduction or, in other words, the very object of sociology in its most complete and general definition. The very immensity of the task means that we have to resign ourselves to forfeiting a measure of elegance, parsimony and formal rigour, that is to say, to abdicating the ambition of competing with the purest economics, without for all that ceasing to propose models, but models based on description rather than deduction alone, and capable of offering effective antidotes to that *morbus mathematicus* (mathematical sickness) which the thinkers of the Cambridge School already saw in the Cartesian temptation of deductive reason.[11] And afford ourselves the pleasure of discovering that there can perhaps be the beginnings of solutions to some of the problems which so vex economists, such as why rich people do not spend all their wealth before they die or why, more simply, the young help the old or vice versa, once we leave behind the rarefied atmosphere of pure theory.

Part I

The House Market

There is no critique of the assumptions of economics, no challenge to its shortcomings and limitations, that has not been expressed somewhere or other by an economist. This is why, rather than follow so many other writers and indulge in ineffective, sterile questionings of economic principles that are certain in the end to appear either ignorant or unjust, I have ventured here to confront an object that is typically assigned to the economy, namely, the production and marketing of single-family houses, and to do so using the weapons of social science, causing to emerge in the process, *over and above these immediate concerns, as it were,* a set of questions relating to the anthropological vision the majority of economists deploy in their practice.

Economic choices in respect of housing, whether to buy or to rent, whether to buy an old house or a new one and, in the latter case, whether to buy a traditionally built house or an 'industrial' one, depend, on the one hand, on the (socially constituted) economic *dispositions* of the agents – particularly on their tastes – and the economic resources they can summon and, on the other, on the *state of supply* of dwellings. But the two terms of the canonical relationship, which neoclassical economic theory treats as uncondi-tioned givens, depend in turn, more or less directly, on a whole set of economic and social conditions produced by 'housing policy'. In effect, the state – and those who are able to impose their views through it – contributes very substantially to *producing the state of the housing market*, doing this largely through all the forms of regulation and financial assistance aimed at promoting particular ways of bringing tastes to fruition in terms of housing, through assistance to builders or private individuals, such as loans, tax exemptions, cheap credit, etc. And it does this, particularly, by directly or indirectly guiding the financial – and also emotional – investments of the various social categories in respect of housing. For example, every measure aimed at diminishing the supply of accessible rented property – by reducing the funds allotted to the production of low-cost social housing – redirects a section of potential tenants towards home ownership, which is itself varyingly attractive depending on the level of personal financial assistance available and the cost of credit. Similarly, a policy such as that laid down in the French housing law of 1977 was the culmination of a whole set of initiatives aimed at steering towards ownership the 'choices' of those social categories who were up to that point the least inclined to satisfy their housing needs in this way, and at making access to the ownership of their dwellings a major form of financial investment for them. (In the minds of some who were behind this policy, who associated social housing with collectivism or socialism, this also meant directing them towards a lasting attachment to the established order and hence towards a form of conservatism.)

In short, the market in single-family houses is (as all markets no doubt are to varying degrees) the product of a *twofold social construction* to which the state contributes crucially: the construction of demand, through the production of individual dispositions and, more precisely, of systems of individual preferences – most importantly regarding ownership or renting – and also through the allotting of the necessary resources, that is to say, state assistance for building or for housing, as defined in laws and regulations whose genesis can also be described; the construction of supply, through the policy of the state (or the banks) in respect of credit to building companies, which contributes, together with the nature of the means of production used, to defining conditions of access to the market and, more precisely, a company's position within the structure of the – highly dispersed – field of house builders and, hence, the structural constraints applying to the decisions made by each of them with regard to production and advertising. And one has only to take the analysis a step further to discover that demand is only specified and defined fully in relation to a particular state of supply and also of social (and, particularly, legal) conditions (building regulations, planning permissions, etc.) which allow it to be satisfied.

One can hardly fail to see, particularly where the purchase of a product so laden with meaning as a house is concerned, that the 'subject' of economic action has about it nothing of the pure consciousness of the subject of orthodox theory, a consciousness wholly devoid of a past, and that economic strategies, which, through the dispositions responsible for them, are very deeply rooted in the individual and collective past, are most often integrated into a complex system of strategies of reproduction and are thus laden with the whole history of that which they aim to perpetuate – namely, the domestic unit, itself the product of a work of collective construction which is once again largely attributable to the state; and that, correlatively, economic decisions are not taken by isolated economic agents, but by a collective, group, family or enterprise functioning as a field.

It must be the aim of analysis, then, to describe the structure of the field of production and the mechanisms that determine its functioning (instead of being content with the mere recording, which would itself require explanation, of statistical co-variations between variables and events) and also the structure of the distribution of economic dispositions and, more especially, of tastes in respect of housing; not forgetting to establish, by a historical analysis, the social conditions of the production of this particular field and of the dispositions able to find more or less complete fulfilment in it.

1

Disposition of the Agents and the Structure of the Field of Production

Many of the particularities of the production of dwellings and of the relationships formed between construction firms result from the particular characteristics of this product, which has a particularly substantial symbolic component. As a material good which (like clothing) is exposed to the general gaze, and is so *on a lasting basis*, this form of property expresses or betrays, in a more decisive way than many other goods, the social being of its owners, the extent of their 'means', as we say; but it also reveals their taste, the classification system they deploy in their acts of appropriation and which, in assuming objective form in visible goods, provides a purchase for the symbolic appropriations of others, who are thereby enabled to situate the owners in social space by situating them within the space of tastes.[1] Moreover, it is the occasion of particularly substantial *investments*, both economic and affective:[2] as a consumer good which, by its high cost, constitutes one of the most difficult economic decisions of a whole domestic life-cycle, a decision fraught with enormous consequences, it is also an 'investment' in the sense of being a non-financial form of saving and an investment good, and as such is expected to retain or enhance its value, while at the same time affording immediate satisfactions.[3] In this regard, it is the central element in a *patrimony*, which is expected to last at least as long as its owners, and even to survive them as a transmissible heritage.

The mythology of the 'house'

However, one can fully understand the investments of all kinds made in the house – in money, labour, time and emotion – only when one sees, as the double meaning of the word 'house' reminds us, referring as it does both to the dwelling and the totality of its inhabitants, that it is inseparable from the *household* as a durable social group and from the collective project of perpetuating that household. We know, indeed, that in some cultural traditions, particularly in peasant and aristocratic usage, the word 'house' refers both to the material residence and to the family which lived, lives or will live there, a social entity whose transcendence in relation to individual persons asserts itself precisely in the fact that it has at its disposal a patrimony of material and symbolic goods – and, particularly, a name, which is, in many cases, different from that of its members – handed down directly from one generation to the next.[4] In many societies, building a new house is, as in old Kabylia, a collective enterprise, mobilizing the entire agnatic group in a voluntary *corvée* (particularly, for the transporting of the beams) that coincides with the founding of a new family. And even today, a 'building' project is almost always associated with the project of 'starting a home' (or enlarging one), of building a house in the sense of a household – in other words, the creation of a social group united by bonds of alliance and kinship, reinforced by the ties of cohabitation.[5]

So, to treat the house as a mere capital good, characterized by a particular rate of amortization, and to view the purchase of a house as an economic strategy in the narrow sense of the term, ignoring the system of reproduction strategies of which it is one instrument, would be to strip the product and the economic act of all the *historical properties*, effective in certain historical conditions, which they owe to their insertion in a historical fabric, and which ought to be written into the science, because they are built into the reality in which its object is steeped. What is being tacitly asserted through the creation of a house is the will to create a permanent group, united by stable social relations, a lineage capable of perpetuating itself over time in a manner similar to the durable, stable, unchangeable *residence*. It is a collective project for, or wager on, the future of the domestic unit, that is, on its cohesion, its integration or, if one prefers, on its capacity to resist break-up and dispersal. And the very undertaking that consists in choosing a house together, fitting it out, decorating it and, in short, making it a 'home' that feels to be truly a 'home of one's own' – among other reasons because one loves in it the sacrifices of time and effort it has cost, and also because, as a visible attestation of the success of a shared project carried out in common, it is the ever renewed source of a shared satisfaction – is a product of affective cohesion which in its turn intensifies and reinforces that cohesion.

An anthropological analysis of what is invested in houses should also take into account the inherited fund of collective or private (and particularly literary) mythologies which attaches to them and which, as we shall see, is constantly evoked, revived and reactivated by the rhetoric of advertising.[6] However, in reminding ourselves of the anthropological constants which, even today, underlie the dominant representation, we should also not forget the variations of signification and function of houses depending on the milieu and the moment. The social use of the house as the stable, long-standing residence of the household presupposes the tradition of *settlement* (as opposed to all the various forms of temporary or permanent nomadism) specific to agrarian economies, favouring rootedness to a particular piece of land and immutability over time. This ties in with a conservative view of the world that values all forms of rootedness (the *Heimat* and the *heimlich*, which *völkisch* ideology contrasts with 'wandering' and rootlessness) and extols the enchanted social relations, conceived on the model of an integrated family, of the idealized agrarian 'community' (*Gemeinschaft*).

The purchase of a house, being connected with the family as *household*, and with its permanence over time, which it presupposes and also aims to guarantee, is both an economic investment – or at least a form of accumulation of capital as an element of a lasting, transmissible patrimony – and a social one, in so far as it contains within it a wager on the future or, more exactly, a biological and social *reproduction project*. The house is inextricably linked with the family as a social unit oriented towards its own biological reproduction: it is an element, as a necessary, but not sufficient condition, in child-rearing plans; and as a unit oriented also towards its social reproduction: it is one of the chief means by which the domestic unit ensures that a certain transmissible heritage is accumulated and preserved. It follows that changes in the traditions by which the domestic unit is constituted or dissolved (in particular, the rise in the divorce rate and a decline in the practice of different generations living under one roof) are liable to affect, more or less directly, strategies with regard to housing – particularly the choice between home ownership and renting.

The more or less unconscious dispositions which lead to the house being constituted in practice as the stable residence of a permanent household mean that, where houses are concerned, no doubt by a metonymic contamination of container by content and mode of production by product, most economic agents have a preference for a technology of manufacture that has no equivalent except in some food products and, more generally, in all luxury goods. Being attached to a so-called traditional mode of production, conceived as a guarantee not just of technical quality but also of symbolic *authenticity*, they are almost always inclined to favour the 'handmade' house, built in the old style, either in reality or in imitation mode (the 'mason-built house'[7] made of breeze blocks, produced on industrial lines), individually owned and situated in an authentically or fictively rural setting (housing estate), over the industrially built house (or accommodation in a jointly owned block). And, as we shall see below, this socially constituted housing need is particularly developed among the consumers most imbued with successoral traditions, whose aim is to perpetuate the 'house', particularly through the privilege accorded to the eldest of the descendants.

A full definition of the properties of the product requires an appreciation of the relationship between its objective characteristics, both technical and formal, and the inseparably aesthetic and ethical patterns of the habitus that structures the perception and appreciation of it. It is this which defines the *real demand* with which producers have to contend. And the economic constraints or attractions that lead to the observed purchasing decisions are established as such only in the relationship between a certain state of supply proposed by the field of production and a certain state of the requirements registered in the dispositions of the buyers, who thus contribute to the constraints to which they are subject. As a consequence, we have to conceive supply and demand, and the relationship between them, in entirely new terms. At a given moment, *supply* presents itself as a *differentiated and structured space of competing suppliers whose strategies depend on the other suppliers* (and not as an aggregated total of independent suppliers). And it is because it is itself structured (particularly by state intervention) that supply can satisfy and exploit the *demand*, also differentiated and structured, which it has in part contributed to creating.

Though it is not incorrect to say that production produces consumption, supply, by the very fact that it tends to eliminate some or all of the other possible ways of satisfying housing need (for example, the renting of single-family houses), contributes to imposing a particular way of satisfying this need, while apparently respecting the rights of the sovereign consumer; and, similarly, the firms capable of organizing their activity in such a way as to confer the appearance of traditional craft work on industrial mass production can succeed only to the extent that they manage to make consumers pay very dearly for their more or less phantasmic desire for a detached, durable, transmissible, 'hand-made' house. (It is no doubt in this respect that the housing market shares in the characteristic logic of the art market, in which there is also a preference for a technology dominated by the cult of the authenticity of *'manifattura'*, as guaranteed by the signature, which affords proof that the work is made by the hand of the 'master' and is, consequently, 'master-built').

Advertising is so effective only because it panders to pre-existing dispositions in order the better to exploit them, subjecting the consumer to its demands and expectations in the guise of serving those dispositions (by contrast with a political policy, which might be said to use a realistic knowledge of dispositions to work to transform them or displace them on to other objects).[8] To this end it uses effects which we must, at the risk of shocking the reader, term 'poetic'. Like poetry, and with quite similar means, it plays on the *connotations* of the message, systematically drawing on the power of poetic language to evoke lived experiences, 'specific to all individuals, variable between individuals, and variable also in the same individual between one moment and another'.[9] It mobilizes words or images capable of summoning up the experiences associated with houses, which we may describe, without contradiction, as both shared and individual, commonplace and unique. They are shared in as much as they owe something to cultural tradition, and, in particular, to inherited cognitive structures, such as those brought out by the structural analysis of the internal space of houses or of the relationship between domestic and public space. They are unique in what they owe to the socially specified form which the encounter with domestic words and entities has assumed for each of us over the course of a singular history.

This can be seen very clearly from the analysis Marc Augé offers us of his experience as a reader of real estate advertisements.[10] In making explicit the subjective experiences advertisements evoke in his mind (that of an educated, male town-dweller), he reveals the mechanisms on which advertising discourse (and, more generally, all poetic discourse) relies in order to summon up the world of private connotations: on the one hand, the enchanted memory of primal experiences, which are both situated in time and place, and hence unique, and translocal and trans-historic (in so far as every childhood contains something of all childhoods); on the other hand, the range of literary associations which are at least as creative of the seductive power of evocative words and suggestive images as they are expressive of that power. The symbolic effect of the advertisement is the product of a collaboration between the writers, who draw on their inherited cultural fund of words and images capable of awakening unique experiences in their readers, and the readers, who contribute to conferring on the inductive text the symbolic power it exerts on them or, better, the *spell* it casts over them. The readers, armed with their previous experiences, both of the ordinary, and also the literary, world, project onto the text/pretext the aura of correspondences, resonances and analogies which make it possible for them to recognize themselves in it. And it is because they *feel at home*, as we say, in the little, private mythology of the domestic world offered to them that they can make it their own; that they can both appropriate it and at the same time allow themselves to be possessed by it. 'The system of adverts overall', writes Augé, 'operates as a selective trap whose mechanisms might be said to work to guide the different categories of victim towards the chambers specifically designated for them.'[11] The magic and charm of the words partake directly of the magic and charm of the things they evoke: the pleasure the reader feels in inhabiting his or her houses of words − 'ancient priories', 'old mills', 'post houses' or 'eighteenth-century manor houses' − is merely a symbolic anticipation of the pleasure of inhabiting (of feeling 'at home' in) a world of things that remains indissociable from the world of words necessary to name and dominate − in a word, to *domesticate* − them.

The house is the object of a whole set of activities which (using an adjective borrowed from Ernst Cassirer) we might term 'mythopoetic', whether these are verbal activities, such as the exchanges of delighted comments on improvements accomplished or to be accomplished,[12] or practical activities, such as 'do-it-yourself', this latter the site of genuine poetic creation, its ultimate expression being the palais du Facteur Cheval:[13] these demiurgic interventions contribute to transmuting the mere technical object, which is always neutral and impersonal, and often disappointing and inadequate, into a kind of irreplaceable, sacred reality − into one of those *churingas* in which, as in family portraits, albums or tombs, the lineage affirms and celebrates its unity and continuity.[14]

The space of the buyers and the social genesis of preferences

However, there is a danger that the anthropological − or phenomenological − analysis of the signification of the house will lead us to forget that, in this field as elsewhere, experiences and expectations are differentiated, and are so according to a principle which is simply that of the position occupied in social space.[15] The desire for possession, within the context of which the enchanted representation of the house as residence is effected, does not itself have the universality tacitly accorded to it by phenomenological (or ethnological) analysis. And it is quite noticeable that the ways in which it is satisfied have undergone a profound change. In fact, the link between house and patrimony, and hence, also, family, has weakened: whereas the levels of direct transmission of that category of heritage that is the house are declining (among recent home-owners, in 1984 those who owed their housing to inheritance or settlement represented only 9 per cent of the total[16]), purchase through borrowing represents the most common mode of acquisition of a main residence, and the burden of average credit repayments weighs increasingly on the budgets of households in which people are becoming homeowners at an ever younger age and are not waiting to inherit their parents' dwelling, which is indeed, in the great majority of cases, ultimately sold off.

Unlike what was observed in earlier generations, where it was almost always by inheritance or a slow accumulation of savings that property ownership was achieved, the homeowners of more recent generations see the acquisition of property as a means of meeting their housing needs, while at the same time building up a patrimony in terms of real estate. At the same time, saving has been falling steadily (from 18 per cent in 1970 to 12 per cent in 1987, without any corresponding increase in household credit, which has remained stable over the same period).[17] But, at a deeper level, statistics show clearly that preferences vary according to different factors: economic capital, cultural capital, the structure of overall capital, social trajectory, age, marital status, number of children, position in the family life-cycle, etc.

The concern to take into account the *system of determining factors* here compels us to free ourselves from the limitations inherent in monographs devoted to *preconstructed* populations (low-income households, the retired, the self-builders known as '*castors*',[18] 'new entrants') and the simplifications typical of the *partial explanations* with which statistical analyses most often content themselves. For example, the survey which is carried out at regular intervals by INSEE (Institut National de la Statistique et des Études Économiques – National Institute for Statistics and Economic Studies), using substantial samples (29,233 households in 1984, 23,606 in 1978), covers the current housing situation and present trends within it, the system of housing finance, the main characteristics of households, etc., but it leaves out such important explanatory factors as social trajectory over several generations (or, at least, father's occupation); and the analysis offered does not accord proper weight to such factors as cultural or technical capital (where, indeed, the division of labour between researchers concentrating on different factors or populations – 'new entrants' for one, the rented sector for another etc. – does not prevent any comparison and overall synthesis).[19]

From the secondary analysis of a set of tables produced at our request using the data from the housing survey carried out by INSEE in 1984, it emerges that one's chances of entering the property market depend on the *volume of capital* possessed, which undoubtedly operates as a necessary, but not sufficient condition, but that the propensity to buy rather than to rent depends above all on the *structure of that capital*, that is to say on the relative proportions of economic and cultural capital.[20]

The rate of owner-occupation of houses does not increase very greatly with income: it ranges from 35.2% for the lowest income group to 43.1% for the highest. By contrast, the rate of flat ownership varies a great deal: it rises from 8.1% for the lowest income group to 22.1% for the highest. When one looks not at the whole range of owners and tenants, but at those who, at the time of the survey, had moved into their present dwelling within the last three years, the proportion of homeowners in 1978 ranges from 8.9% among the lowest income group to 35.4% among the highest, with the proportion of flat owners growing just as greatly, as incomes increase.[21]

It seems as though a minimum volume of capital is required before the decision to become a homeowner is taken, or home ownership seems too bold an undertaking below a certain threshold: when asked the various reasons for not buying a house or a flat, 45% of white-collar workers and 42% of blue-collar workers cite lack of financial resources as the main reason, as against only 24% of members of intermediate occupations, higher executives and professionals.[22] The fear of falling into debt, in a situation in which one does not know 'what the future holds', is also mentioned more often by white-collar workers (15%) than by the other categories (8%). Many more (18%) craftsmen, shopkeepers and entrepreneurs/corporate managers than higher executives and intermediate occupations (2%) or blue-collar workers (1%) indicate that investment in property is no longer a good enough economic proposition.

Everything inclines us, then, to conclude that the *structure of capital* plays a determining role in the choice between purchasing and renting: if we leave aside the retired, it is among the categories appreciably richer in economic than cultural capital, and which

Percentages owning and renting houses and flats by socio-occupational category of head of household, 1984

	Owned			Rented				
	House	Flat	Total	House	Flat	Total	Other	Total
Farmers	61.3	3.7	65	8.9	7.6	16.5	18.5	100
Semi-skilled workers	28.3	3.8	32.1	14.7	47.3	62	5.9	100
Skilled workers	39.1	6.4	45.5	10.4	38.8	49.2	5.3	100
Foremen	55.3	9.3	64.6	8.9	19.8	28.7	6.7	100
Service employees	21.7	7.6	29.3	5.3	47.6	52.9	17.9	100
Retired blue-collar	47.4	7.9	55.3	8.7	25.2	33.9	10.8	100
Craftsmen	54.6	11.5	66.1	6.6	22.4	29	4.8	100
Shopkeepers	44.4	14.1	58.5	9	25.9	34.9	6.6	100
Retired craft/shopkeepers	50.2	19.5	69.7	3.1	19.3	22.4	7.9	100
Police	25.8	4.5	30.3	8.7	37.5	46.2	23.4	100
Commercial employees	21.5	6.1	27.6	5.6	57.2	62.8	9.6	100
Clerical, private sector	23.9	13.2	37.1	5.6	50.4	56	6.8	100
Clerical, public sector	28.4	8.4	36.8	5	51.6	56.6	6.6	100
Retired white-collar	39.1	13.1	52.2	4.8	34	33.8	9	100
Intermediate occupations, private	36.3	15.4	51.7	6.6	35.7	42.3	6	100
Intermediate occupations, public	36	11.2	47.2	6.9	38.5	45.4	7.4	100
Technicians	43.4	13.7	57.1	6	32.2	38.2	4.6	100
Primary teachers	39.8	13.8	53.6	5.2	30.5	35.7	10.8	100
Retired intermediate occupations	52.0	18.2	70.2	3.9	20.8	24.7	5.1	100
Entrepreneurs, corporate managers	50	26.3	76.8	1.9	16.7	18.6	4.6	100
Executives, private	36.1	22.4	58.5	8.8	27.7	36.5	5	100
Engineers	41.8	18.3	60.1	9.7	25.4	35.1	4.8	100
Executives, public	32.5	17.4	49.9	10.1	29.6	39.7	10.5	100
Teachers	33.9	15.8	49.7	6.5	32.7	39.2	11.1	100
Professionals	42.3	23.5	65.8	6.5	24.1	30.6	3.6	100
Artistic	20.6	16.6	37.2	9.1	44.7	53.8	8.9	100
Retired executives	46.6	31.1	77.7	3.3	16.3	19.6	2.8	100
Other	27.2	9.5	36.7	5.8	38.3	44.1	19.3	100
Total	39.7	11.1	50.8	7.8	32.9	40.7	8.6	100

Source: INSEE survey, 1984; table produced at our request.

depend mainly on economic capital for their reproduction, that the proportion of homeowners is highest. For example, in 1984 the figures are as follows: entrepreneurs/corporate managers 76.8 per cent, craftworkers 66.1 per cent, farmers 65 per cent. We know that, generally, the proprietors of industrial and commercial concerns invest (in all senses of the term) more than all other categories in the *possession of material goods*: houses and luxury cars. There is every reason to suppose that the fact that these categories, where levels of occupational heredity are very high, depend very greatly on the *economic heritage* for their reproduction predisposes them to regard the dwelling as an element of transmissible patrimony and as the most important of all *family investments* (and also, in some cases, to see it as a genuinely speculative investment).

By contrast, the proportion of homeowners is distinctly lower in the categories with high cultural capital. Within the field of power, in keeping with a logic already observed in many other areas, entrepreneurs/corporate managers, who are more often home-owners, stand opposed to the teachers, artistic occupations and public sector managers, who are more often tenants, the inter-mediate position being occupied by private sector executives, engineers (closer to public sector managers and teachers) and professionals (closer to the employers). Within the middle strata, one finds an analogous structure, with craftsmen and shopkeepers, who are more often homeowners, at one end of the scale and, at the other, primary school teachers and intermediate occupations in the public sector (the white-collar workers in companies and the civil service being homeowners much less often than the other categories).

Whereas among the fractions richer in economic than cultural capital the rate of home ownership is hardly dependent on income at all, it is closely linked to it among the fractions richer in cultural than economic capital, who we know have resorted more than others to credit to finance their acquisition of property: 88 per cent of entrepreneurs/corporate managers with less than 100,000 francs of annual income in 1984 are house owners, as against 44.5 per cent of those who have between 100,000 and 200,000 francs (this is undoubtedly linked to the fact that the lowest income entrepreneurs/corporate managers live more often in rural areas or small towns).[23] Similarly, among craftsmen, the proportion of homeowners is 56.5 per cent for those with incomes below 50,000 francs, 54 per cent for those in the middle income range, and 54.5 per cent for those with incomes above 100,000 francs. The small traders and farmers with the highest incomes own their own houses a little more often than those with the lowest incomes (among professionals, who combine economic with cultural capital, the fact of being a homeowner or a tenant is not dependent on income level). By contrast, there are particularly strong variations among primary school teachers and intermediate occupa-tions in the public services: fewer than 10% of the lowest paid primary school teachers (who are also the youngest) own a house, as against more than 60 per cent of those earning more than 150,000 francs, and similar variations are also found among intermediate occupations in the public services. Similarly, among engineers and managers (in both the public and private sectors) the rate of home ownership increases greatly with income.

As for *cultural capital*, this has practically no visible effect on the level of ownership within each social category, whatever the income. However, in the lower categories, it seems that a minimum of educational capital, characterized by possession of a CEP or a CAP,[24] is the necessary condition for access to property (there is no doubt also a link here with ascetic dispositions, indicated by a low rate of fertility), the probability of ownership being lower among blue- and white-collar workers and technicians or intermediate occupations with no educational qualifications than among those with a CEP or CAP, who are themselves more likely to be homeowners than the members of the same categories who have a BEPC or baccalaureate.[25]

The category of holders of the CEP or CAP enables us to grasp the effects of a particular kind of cultural capital which finds a particularly visible point of application in accession to home ownership: *technical capital* (the capital of the DIYer), partly acquired at school and reasonably well attested by the possession of a CAP (see in appendix I to this chapter, 'Technical capital and ascetic dispositions', pp. 78–81). Thus, standing at the top of the hierarchy of manual workers, whose technical capacities they doubtless possess in the highest degree, foremen and supervisors[26] can commit the capacities partly acquired at school (certified by academic qualifications such as the CAP or the BEP), and developed over their careers, to the service of the ascetic dispositions which doubtless explain their career advancement and incline them to make many sacrifices to acquire a house built in part, or wholly (in the case of the '*castors*') by themselves, often with the help of work colleagues or members of their families.

Among new house-buyers who are the first owners of the dwellings they occupy, unskilled industrial workers and craftsmen, skilled storage/handling workers, white-collar workers in the commercial sector and intermediate occupations in the public services (all categories situated in the 'left-hand' sector of social space, on the 'public' side) more often (according to the INSEE survey of 1984) say that they chose a house model from a catalogue (more than 48 per cent in each of these groups); fewer farmers, craftsmen, small traders, entrepreneurs/corporate managers and professionals (categories which depend, for their reproduction, on economic capital) use this mode of construction (fewer than 25 per cent in each of these categories).

Moreover, we know that the propensity to attach greater importance to the technical, and less to the symbolic, aspect of the house increases as we move down the social hierarchy. Analysis of the data produced by the study carried out in 1984 by the Institut

Mode of house construction (new owners)

	Total self-build	Planned by self or professional	Catalogue house	Developer	Total
Farmers	4.2	75.8	18.3	1.7	100
Semi-skilled workers	8.4	31.8	48.1	1.7	100
Unskilled workers	9.4	34.9	43.6	12.1	100
Foremen	12.5	36.8	35.9	14.8	100
Retired blue-collar	9.9	55.5	29.2	6.3	100
Craftsmen	25.5	49.3	19.7	5.4	100
Shopkeepers	10.6	56.0	24.0	9.5	100
Retired craftworkers, shopkeepers	9.9	52.7	27.9	9.4	100
Police, military	3.6	35.7	38.8	21.9	100
Commercial employees	5.1	36.1	49.9	8.9	100
Clerical staff, civil service, private sector	3.2	33.2	46.1	17.6	100
Clerical staff, public sector	4.8	36.5	38.3	20.4	100
Retired white-collar	3.3	60.0	34.9	1.8	100
Intermediate occupations, private sector	3.2	40.7	38.6	17.4	100
Intermediate occupations, public sector	1.5	27.3	48.4	22.8	100
Technicians	6.2	41.7	34.1	18.0	100
Teachers, primary	4.3		26.9	16.1	100
Retired, intermediate occupations	4.1	52.8	43.0	5.0	100
Entrepreneurs, corporate managers	18.1	49.5	21.6	10.8	100
Executives, private	0.9	47.7	33.1	18.3	100
Engineers	5.8	39.3	32.9	21.9	100
Executives, public	1.3	40.0	38.8	19.9	100
Teachers, secondary and higher	8.0	47.8	25.9	18.3	100
Professionals		75.1	19.0	5.9	100
Retired executives	2.3	72.2	22.7	2.8	100
Total	7.6	42.0	37.1	13.2	100

We have left out of the calculations those households which are not the first owners of their houses. *Source:* INSEE survey, 1984; table produced at our request.

Français de Démoscopie on a representative sample of 998 persons brings out a particularly marked opposition where ideas about prefabricated houses are concerned between individuals at the top of the economic, social and cultural hierarchies on the one hand (respectively, the persons with the highest incomes; higher executives and professionals; and individuals with the highest educational qualifications and university backgrounds) and, on the other, those with the lowest incomes, blue-collar workers or unemployed, who have received only a primary education.[27] The former have the most negative representation of prefabricated houses: they are the readiest to believe that people build such houses only because they cannot afford a traditional house, or wish to avoid all the administrative formalities. The latter most often express the view that one may have good reason to choose a prefabricated house and that those who make that choice are showing a taste for modern ways; they believe this type of house is more solid and easier to personalize. Everything seems to confirm that, as we have seen in other areas of practice, the most economically and, in particular, culturally deprived adhere, without of course developing this into a conscious theory, to an aesthetic we might term *functionalist*, which is free (by default) of the prejudices associated with cultural level: considering houses as instruments which have to be comfortable, safe, solid, readily available and open to further development if need be, they have a technicist view of houses, a view bolstered by the technical skill they can commit to their transformation. And everything suggests that, among wage-earners, it is skilled workers, technicians or engineering workers, no doubt because they are further removed from the dominant representation of the house, either by dint of their technical culture or of their social origins, or both, who are the most susceptible to the attractions of industrial houses and, in any case, are (relatively) the least sensitive to the blandishments of the developers of evocatively named 'residences'.

The effect of *size of settlement* is well known. The main point, however, is that this has specific effects according to the volume and structure of capital possessed. The gap between social classes increases as we pass from rural districts to large conurbations, both in terms of home ownership and of the occupation of single-family houses.[28]

Nicole Tabard has shown that the discrepancies between managers or professionals and blue-collar workers are more marked in the Essonne département than in France as a whole.[29] The apparent 'democratization' of access to the ownership of single-family houses is essentially attributable to the fact that the upper strata of the working class most often live in rural areas or, when they live in a conurbation, in the outer suburbs. Analysis of the 1984 survey confirms that within each category the proportion of single-family houses varies inversely with size of settlement. It is practically only in rural areas that blue-collar workers can become homeowners. By contrast, supervisory staff can be homeowners, even in the Parisian conurbation (to the tune of 31.6 per cent).

Generally, the proportion of homeowners, which is still low among the under-35s, increases with *age*. Everything seems to indicate that access to ownership arrives at a later age as one moves down the social scale, with the exception of supervisory staff, in which category 50 per cent home ownership is achieved in the 30–34 age group. For example, it is only among the over-50s that there are more owners than tenants among unskilled workers, home owner-ship often coinciding with retirement. In fact, age itself assumes meaning only as a point in the *domestic life-cycle*: the question of house purchase arises with particular force at certain stages of that cycle, which relate to the concern to 'start a family', as the expression goes, that is to say, at marriage or, in the following years, in connection with the arrival of children.

According to the INED survey, married couples are those who, at any age, most often 'choose' to own their main residence and borrow to do so (nine-tenths of new entrants are married couples). By contrast, when the unmarried (among whom one finds only half as many homeowners at 50 as among married couples) become owners, they do so mainly through inheritance or by buying a property outright. The level of homeowners among divorcees is also low, divorce often being accompanied by recourse to the rented sector.[30]

In the generation of Parisians born between 1926 and 1935, the majority of those who bought their dwellings had already formed their families before acquiring property. That acquisition occurred earlier in the family life-cycle for senior managers than for blue- or white-collar workers. It seems to be the case that the former are more able to cope simultaneously with the costs associated with child-rearing and with mortgage repay-ments.[31] It seems probable that, for later generations, home-buying, occurring at an earlier and earlier age, has forced couples, including those in the working and middle classes, to carry the burden of child-rearing and loan repayments at the same time.

The proportion of the members of the waged fractions of the middle classes (white-collar workers, middle managers, and also supervisory staff) and of the better-off sections of society who are house owners increases in most cases with the number of dependent children. By contrast, among unskilled, semi-skilled and skilled workers and white-collar workers in the commercial sector, the relationship is more complex, in so far as the propensity to acquire a house is indissociable from an ambition to ascend the social ladder, which is inseparable from the restriction of fertility: so we see that in these categories, the households in which there are two children are more commonly owner-occupiers than those with no children or one child, and those with three children or more.[32]

In fact, as applies across the entire range of consumption, one could account more fully for the differences observed in terms of housing only by bringing in, not just the volume and structure of capital (which govern the effect of factors such as the degree of urbanization of the area of residence, or family size), but also the *development over time* of these two characteristics, which can be apprehended from, among other things, social and geographic origins, and which often express themselves in changes of residence or of housing status. Though we have practically no statistical data on the effects of social origin (hardly ever taken into account in the surveys), apart from the indications provided by the interviews, it would seem reasonable to suppose that those acquiring property (most often by way of credit) have largely been the newly rich, who were also 'newcomers' in urban society, 'provincials' who had gone to live in Paris or the other cities and acquired houses in the inner or new outer suburbs (whereas long-standing residents are more likely to live, often as tenants, in the old city-centre areas).[33]

The chances of being an owner or a tenant differ between those with home-owning parents and those whose parents rent their main residence. The comparative study of tenants and property buyers from a single generation (those aged 39 at the date of the survey) living in the département of Alpes-Maritimes shows that daughters of homeowners have a two-in-three chance of becoming owners themselves (by the age of 39), whereas daughters of tenants have a little less than a one-in-two chance.[34] (The distribution of sons of homeowners and tenants is roughly the same.) Social origin (indirectly and crudely captured here) undoubtedly contributes to structuring the residential strategies of households, but only through a whole set of mediations such as type of settlement, point in the life-cycle, occupation and origin of spouse, etc.

The wage-earning fractions of the middle classes, who are great users of bank credit, and the upper fractions of the working class represent a significant proportion of recent 'new entrants' to home ownership. According to the survey carried out by INSEE in 1984, of all house owners primary school teachers, public sector managers, technical staff, those in intermediate occupations in the public and private sectors and skilled workers are the most frequent occupants of relatively new houses (built in 1975 or later). If recourse to credit to buy a house has become widespread, it is, according to this same survey, within these same categories (to which we must add engineers and supervisory staff) that it is most frequent (cf. the table p. 35).

The wage-earning fractions of the middle-classes are also among those who, if not already house owners, are most desirous of becoming so or, where they own flats and are planning to move, are most likely to state that they wish to buy a house. Thus, access to house ownership has grown most markedly in that region of social space defined by the primacy of cultural over economic capital, that is to say, in all the higher (engineers, senior managers) and middle-ranking categories (technical staff, middle managers, white-collar workers) of salaried staff in the public or semi-public sector (with the exception, however, of the intellectual and artistic occupations) and also in the higher regions of the working class (supervisors, skilled workers) and even among an appreciable fraction of semi-skilled or unskilled workers.

It follows that the overall process of increase in the rate of ownership is accompanied by an *homogenization* of the two sectors which stand at opposite ends of the horizontal dimension of the social space or, in other words, stand opposed in terms of the structure of their capital: categories previously disinclined to see the purchase of their dwelling as a major form of financial investment and who would have represented a natural clientele for a policy aimed at promoting the building of public housing for rent (single-family houses or blocks of flats) have, thanks to credit and government assistance, come to subscribe to the logic of the accumulation of an economic heritage, thus creating a role in their reproductive strategies for the direct transmission of material goods; while at the same time categories that had previously relied solely on the economic heritage to reproduce their position have had to have recourse to the education system to make the adaptations forced upon them by the rigours of competition. (These two complementary and convergent movements have undoubtedly contributed to reducing the gap between the 'right' and the 'left' of the social space, and of the political field, by replacing the various oppositions which divided reality and the representation of the social world – ownership and tenancy, the free market and state provision, private and public – with attenuated oppositions between mixed forms. This means, as we may note in passing, that one can understand individual choices, both in political and also in economic matters – for example, increased investment in education or increased cultural consumption – only if one takes into account objective structures and their transformation.)

In the first high-growth period in house building, which ran from 1950 to 1963–4, senior and middle managers turned in very large numbers to home ownership, while the proportion of homeowners increased almost as rapidly among blue- and white-collar workers (though starting from a much lower base) and appreciably less quickly among professionals and large- or small-scale employers.[35] After a decline in the years 1964–8, which affected all social categories, but blue-collar workers in particular, the

'First owners' of houses, 1984

	First owner	Not first owner	Total
Farmers	31.2	68.8	100
Semi-skilled workers	49.8	50.2	100
Unskilled	63.9	36.1	100
Foremen	67.6	32.4	100
Domestic and maintenance	50.1	49.9	100
Retired blue-collar	33.8	66.2	100
Craftsmen	59.2	40.8	100
Shopkeepers	53.8	46.2	100
Retired craftworkers, shopkeepers	39.7	60.3	100
Police, military	62.3	37.7	100
Commercial employees	48	52	100
Clerical, civil service, private sector	56.9	43.1	100
Clerical, public sector	59.1	40.9	100
Retired white collar	38	62	100
Intermediate occupations, private sector	63.9	36.1	100
Intermediate occupations, public	62.5	37.5	100
Technicians	68.3	31.7	100
Teachers, primary	61.7	38.3	100
Retired, intermediate occupations	44.7	55.3	100
Entrepreneurs, corporate managers	63.2	36.8	100
Executives, private sector	56.9	43.1	100
Engineers	66.6	33.4	100
Executives, public	66.6	33.4	100
Teachers, secondary and higher education	46	54	100
Professionals	28.8	71.2	100
Artistic	24.1	75.9	100
Retired executives	47.1	52.9	100
Other	30.5	69.5	100
Total	50.5	49.5	100

Source: INSEE survey, 1984; table produced at our request.

spread of home ownership again grew relatively quickly (though less rapidly than in the 1950s), particularly among senior and middle managers, and also among supervisory staff and skilled workers (whereas white-collar, semi-skilled and unskilled workers remained at a very low level, and ownership among employers and professionals grew at a slower rate than among all other categories). After 1974, the rise in home ownership again slowed down, whereas ownership of *single-family houses* remained constant and even increased a little during the 1980s. This can be explained by the fact that in the late 1970s, a wave of new products arrived on the market, created by new forms of subsidy and credit: these products, developed by the large industrial or semi-industrialized construction companies, were of a kind to attract new entrants, who were drawn in the main from among skilled blue-collar workers, white-collar workers and middle managers.[36]

Mode of accession to ownership of a house or flat

	House owners					Flat owners				
	Inheritance gift	Cash purchase	Loan	Other*	Total	Inheritance gift	Cash purchase	Loan	Other*	Total
Farmers	37.5	22.9	38.8	0.8	100	54.1	18.3	27.6	—	100
Semi-skilled workers	13.2	13.1	71.9	1.8	100	16.1	15.2	65.2	3.5	100
Skilled workers	7.6	4.7	84.1	3.6	100	8.2	10.3	75.7	5.8	100
Foremen	5.5	4.7	85.8	4	100	6.9	9.3	76.1	7.8	100
Service workers	19.4	19	61.7	—	100	22.2	22.3	53.1	2.4	100
Retired blue-collar workers	21.1	35.1	39.3	4.4	100	17.2	42.2	35.9	4.7	100
Craftsmen	10.9	11.7	75.8	1.6	100	13.7	11.2	68.6	6.5	100
Shopkeepers	9.5	16.1	72.7	1.8	100	25.2	16	53.4	5.3	100
Retired craft workers, shopkeepers	19.5	46.2	31.3	3	100	20.5	49.85	28.6	1.2	100
Police, military	5.3	10.1	81.4	3.2	100	8	12.4	75.2	4.4	100
Commercial employees	12.1	13.8	69.7	4.4	100	11.8	35.7	52.5	—	100
Clerical, private sector, civil service	9.4	9	78.3	3.3	100	7.2	11.5	78.6	2.7	100
Clerical, public sector	7.4	9.8	80.8	2	100	14.2	8.3	74.9	2.6	100
Retired white-collar workers	20.8	37.3	38.9	3	100	7.5	49.1	40.6	2.8	100
Intermediate occupations, private sector	5.5	5.2	86.4	2.9	100	6.5	6.8	85.3	1.4	100
Intermediate occupations, public	5.7	7.1	85.1	2.1	100	7.4	10.3	78.5	3.8	100
Technicians	4.2	3.9	87.9	4	100	1.8	7.4	86	4.7	100
Teachers, primary	2.9	7.5	89	0.6	100	11.6	11.5	76.9	—	100
Retired, intermediate occupations	15.8	33.1	48.9	2.2	100	7.5	40.5	48.7	3.3	100

Entrepreneurs, corporate managers	3.1	11.3	83.1	2.5	100	14.2	29.5	56.3	–	100
Executives, private	2.8	8.1	88.2	0.9	100	7.1	9.7	81.4	1.8	100
Engineers	4.4	4.7	88.9	2	100	1.5	12.8	83.3	2.3	100
Executives, public	5.5	5.5	88.4	0.6	100	3.2	7.9	85.5	3.4	100
Teachers, secondary and higher education	6.8	11.4	78.3	3.5	100	4.1	10.8	83.2	1.9	100
Professionals	7.7	15.8	76	0.5	100	4	9.8	84.2	2	100
Artistic	2.3	10.2	87.5	–	100	7.6	17.9	74.5	–	100
Retired executives	16.6	34.6	47.4	1.4	100	5	43.1	50.6	1.3	100
Other	28.6	37	31.2	3.2	100	21.9	34.1	42.6	1.4	100
Total	14.1	18.7	64.4	2.8	100	10.8	23.6	62.5	3.1	100

*Includes *achat en viager* (purchase by instalments providing the seller with a life annuity) and various other types of rental-purchase scheme.
Source: INSEE survey, 1984; table produced at our request.

The apparent democratization of access to property suggested by the increase in the rate of home ownership (which rose from 35 per cent in 1954 to 45.5 per cent in 1973 and 46.7 per cent in 1978, subsequently reaching 51.2 per cent in 1984) conceals considerable differences that depend on the siting of the dwelling (the opposition between suburbs and town centres having supplanted the old rural/urban opposition) and on the actual characteristics of that dwelling (level of comfort etc.). These factors, when combined, determine enormous discrepancies in *modes of life* associated with the type of housing or enforced by it. The differences relate, first, to real costs, not merely in money (the costs of credit), but also *in time*: in time spent working on the house to improve it, in the case, for example, of the supervisory staff who spend their evenings and weekends in do-it-yourself activities; in waiting time to become owners, or to 'settle in'; and lastly, and most importantly, in the *journey time* spent getting to work.

In the Paris region, the acquisition of residential property has often been accompanied by a move to the outer suburbs. For example, in the generation born between 1926 and 1935 living in the Paris region, 25 per cent lived in Paris before acquiring property, as against only 14 per cent after the purchase of their dwellings. Among those who left Paris, nearly two-thirds (63 per cent) miss the district they formerly lived in and would prefer to have stayed there.[37] It is distance from the city centre (more than the distance they have to travel to work) that house owners increasingly complain about. Between 1978 and 1984, the proportion of owners of single-family houses disgruntled at being a long way from the city centre more than doubled, rising from 10 to 20 per cent of new entrants and 11 to 24 per cent of other homeowners, whereas the figure remained relatively stable for owners of flats (rising from 9 to 10 per cent for new entrants and from 7 to 10 per cent for the other flat owners).[38]

If transport expenses are particularly high for the homeowners among the wage-earning fractions of the middle and upper classes, costs in working time to 'finish' the house or maintain it by performing various kinds of work are particularly high for blue-collar workers.[39] The forms of energy consumed among the working classes in single-family houses are less expensive than for flats because they 'incorporate domestic labour'. By contrast, for the other social classes, domestic energy expenditure increases twofold in the move from flat to house, and the figure is even higher among the better-off.[40]

The differences relate also to *profits* from use and from potential resale. The houses owned are clearly very unequal in value, both in terms of technical or aesthetic quality and, above all, of location: they are also unequal in terms of space and comfort; they are very differently appointed and situated at very unequal distances *from public or private amenities,* such as schools, cultural institutions, commercial outlets, etc. and from workplaces. For example, agricultural workers, unskilled industrial workers and craftsmen own the smallest houses, while entrepreneurs/corporate managers and professionals have the most spacious ones. In 1984, 73 per cent of professionals and 71.5 per cent of entrepreneurs/corporate managers who owned their houses occupied a property with more than 120 square metres of floor space, as against 14 per cent of unskilled workers, 16 per cent of agricultural workers and 17.5 per cent of supervisory staff who owned their own homes. The differences between the various different social categories are of the same order where the number of rooms is concerned. In 1975 the proportion of cramped dwellings among those occupied by homeowners from the manual working class was 8.6 times higher than for the members of the professions and senior managers of the same housing status.[41]

In spite of the limitations inherent in the way these statistical data are collected, this analysis allows us to sketch out an initial picture of the system of explanatory factors which, with varying weights (which could be specified only by a regression analysis of the relevant data gathered by a special survey of a single representative population), guide the choices economic agents may make within the limits set on their dispositions by, on the one hand, the state of housing supply (linked to the operation of the field of production) and, on the other, the economic means at their disposal – limits which, like the state of supply, themselves depend very largely on 'housing policy'.

The specific logic of the field of production

To understand the logic of the single-family house market, we have to state two methodological principles of object construction, which are, at the same time, hypotheses about the very nature of the reality being studied.[42] First, the objective relations established between the different construction companies competing to win shares of this market constitute between them a field of force, the structure of which, at a given moment, provides the basis for the struggles to conserve or transform that field. Second, the general laws of operation which apply in all fields, and, more especially, in all fields of economic production, assume specific forms depending on the characteristic properties of the product.

Better than the notions of 'sector' or 'branch of industry', which commonly designate *aggregates* of companies producing the same product and are sometimes viewed as a single agent oriented towards a common function, without questioning either the homogeneity of the totalities considered or – a more serious omission – the relations between their components, the notion of field allows us to take into account differences between firms (the magnitude of which no doubt varies very widely between different branches of industry) and the objective relations of complementarity-in-rivalry that both unite and oppose them. It thus enables us better to understand the logic of competition operating within the field and to determine the differential properties which, functioning as *specific market assets* or 'strengths', defined in their very existence and effectiveness in relation to the field, determine the position each firm occupies within the space of the field, that is to say, in the structure of the distribution of these 'strengths'.

Of the specific properties which make houses very particular products, it is doubtless the very high symbolic charge invested in them and their crucial relation to space that explain the particular characteristics of the field of production and, in particular, the overwhelming predominance of 'national' firms (in spite of the presence of a very small number of international companies) and the persistence of small craft-based firms alongside the big industrial producers. By virtue of the symbolic dimension of the product, house production stands at a midpoint between two opposite forms of productive activity: on the one hand, the production of art works, in which the share of productive activity devoted to the manufacture of the material product is relatively low and is assigned to the artist himself or herself, while the share objectively devoted to the symbolic promotion-creation of the work (by critics, dealers, etc.) is much greater; on the other hand, the production of material goods like oil, coal and steel, in which the manufacturing apparatus assumes a preponderant place, while the proportion of symbolic investment remains very low. We clearly have here a continuum; and we could determine a whole series of intermediate positions such as, for example, where the production of art works is concerned, haute couture, a semi-artistic activity which already has a division of manufacturing labour and promotional and sales strategies that are quite close to those pertaining in the area of the production of dwellings, or where heavy industry is concerned, car production, in which the activity of symbolic production of the product – with the design and creation of marques and models etc. – plays a more substantial role.

The house is also a product *doubly linked to space* and to a particular place in space: conceived as 'immovable' property, it is a dwelling which must be built *in situ* (not 'prefabricated'); it is, moreover, caught up in local traditions both through the architectural and technical norms imposed by administrative regulation and, above all, through the tastes of potential buyers for regional styles. All this means that *locally based micro-markets*, partially removed from general competition, may perpetuate themselves, because, among other things, at least in rural areas, which are still very firmly attached to the traditional representation of the house, and no doubt far beyond those areas, preference is given to local craftsmen. Given this state of affairs, as we have seen, the purchase of an 'industrially built' house can only seem an effect of indigence or incomprehensible eccentricity.

The particular characteristics of the product and of the dispositions which go into shaping it, into its very reality, by imposing the dominant definition of how it must be, mean that, in this geographically sectorized market, one finds side by side a small number of very large industrial or semi-industrial companies selling houses from catalogues (amounting to only 10 per cent of the single-family house market in 1981), a number of large developers building residential 'villages' (alongside offices, shopping centres and blocks of flats), a large number of medium-sized companies building between 20 and several hundred houses a year in one or, sometimes, more regions, and a whole host of small and medium-sized companies (on average one per canton) building a few houses every year and, in some cases, small housing estates.[43]

According to another source (the survey carried out in 1983 by UCB[44] on house builders), firms producing at least 20 houses a year in 1982 built 38 per cent of houses, while property development companies (private and public) built 26 per cent of houses (in the form of grouped settlements) along with other buildings (offices, shopping centres, etc.). The rest of house building (36 per cent) was produced by small building firms and small local craftsmen building a few houses a year, by individuals using the services of an architect or a design consultancy or engaging in a self-build project (alone or organized on 'mutual' lines like the so-called *castors*) or self-building with the help of craftsmen – sometimes within the black economy (almost 10 per cent of houses produced are self-build projects).[45]

The builders of single-family houses, building firms, design consultancies and specialist builders, often referred to as 'catalogue' house builders, are also highly differentiated by the geographical area of their markets: 69 per cent of them are confined to one or two départements; 28 per cent operate in around ten départements (two or three regions in the INSEE classification), 4 per cent in four to nine regions and only 1 per cent across the whole of France. Forty-five per cent of builders engage in some other form of economic activity (improvement and restoration work, property development, the development of building plots) aside from direct construction. As a result, it is not easy to see what common ground there is between a large Parisian property developer with connections to large banking groups, a franchiser who sends out technicians on a daily basis to help small local craftsmen, a big builder whose sales teams draw up credit arrangements while the actual building work is contracted out, the subsidiary of a large construction group which mass-produces shells of buildings, the regionally based family firm which covers all aspects of the houses it builds, and the small local firm which, among other activities, builds a few houses.

There can undoubtedly be few 'sectors' of economic production in which the differences between firms are so marked: first, in terms of size, which ranges from large production units pouring thousands of houses on to the market each year (on average more than 4,000 in 1984 in the case of the four largest companies) to small craftsmen whose annual production is in single figures (at the beginning of the 1980s, 93 per cent of companies had fewer than 10 employees and fewer than 100 companies had 1,000 or more employees); in terms of the mode of financing, which ranges from large building concerns more or less completely in the control of banks to self-employed master builders; and in terms of the modes of construction and marketing strategies, etc. However, these producers, who are apparently not at all comparable, are engaged in the same field and compete with one another on a less unequal basis than one might think (especially because competition between them is limited by effects of geographical distance, which favours the development of local markets, and also by the differentiation of demand).

The structure of the field of builders

Since it has not been possible to gather all the necessary data relating to house producers as a whole, we initially limited the analysis to the companies building single-family houses and the developers with the highest levels of turnover.[46] To this end, we drew on the roll of honour compiled by the *Moniteur des travaux publics et du bâtiment* of 18 October 1985, which presents the top 400 building and amenities firms (of which only some 40 are construction and property development companies) ordered by turnover, and on the yearbooks of the Union Nationale des Constructeurs de Maisons

Individuelles (UNCMI) and the Fédération Nationale de la Promotion et de la Construction (FNPC). We have also introduced five smaller firms into the analysis, as representative examples and for purposes of comparison.

Apart from the four large groups, Phénix, Maison Bouygues, Bruno-Petit and Groupe Maison Familiale (GMF) and their subsidiaries, Maison Évolutive, Alskanor and Bâti-Volume (all Phénix), France Construction, STIM SA and Bâtir (all Maison Bouygues), Pavillon Moderne de Sologne, SIF et Cie (all Bruno-Petit), we have selected the following builders and developers for analysis: Cogedim, Seeri, Sinvim et Cie, Promogim SA, Férinel, Meunier-Promotion, Kaufman and Broad, SACI, Laguarrigue-Le Clair Logis, Bâti-Service Promotion, Lemoux Bernard, Ast Construction, Sonkad, Établissements Émile Houot, Kiteco, Maisons Mondial Pratic, EPIB-SA, Prisme, Entreprise Vercelletto, Iéna Industrie, Bâti Conseil, Socarel, GTM-MI, GTM et Cie and Breguet. The five small builders selected were Nord France Habitation, Sergeco, Maison Occitane, AMI and OMI-France. (Interviews were carried out with officials and salespeople from the following companies: Phénix, Maison Bouygues, Nord France Habitation, Sergeco, Kaufman and Broad, and Bruno-Petit.)

We have attempted to assemble as much objective data as possible on these firms from the two associations of which they are members (UNCMI and FNPC), from the firms themselves and from the specialized press (in particular the surveys carried out by the 'Performance and Strategies' team of the *Moniteur des travaux publics et du bâtiment*). It has not been possible to include Ribourel in the analysis, as insufficient information was available on that company. Moreover, alongside the 26 construction or development companies included in the analysis as active elements, we have had to treat as supplementary elements 18 companies for which the available information was insufficient.

For each of these 44 companies, we have gathered information on the age of the company (date of foundation); its legal status (public limited company, private limited company, franchise company) and the organization of the firm (main sector of activity – property development or grouped settlement, building of single houses; existence of subsidiaries; number of brands represented – not to be confused with the number of models, since one company may have a single brand, in the most usual case, or several); site of head office (Paris, Paris region, provinces) and the scale of its geographical presence and sales area (whole of France, one or more regions, etc.); overall staff numbers; the scale and quality of economic activity (capital; turnover; net profit for 1984; number of start-ups – the figure for the number of houses handed over being a more reliable guide, but unobtainable; proportion of turnover in exports); the mode of control of the company (control exercised by the family, by banks, by large building concerns) and the diversification of that control.[47] All the information was collected for the reference year 1984. We made efforts to gather data

enabling us to measure the relative dynamism of the different companies:
the rise or fall in the number of building start-ups and in the turnover
between 1983 and 1984 or (and this was only as supplementary elements)
the rise or fall in the turnover between 1979 and 1984 and the rise or fall in
the number of housing start-ups between 1983 and 1984, together with the
number of subsidiaries and the proportion of company turnover
representing exports (not generally a significant activity). This information
was not available for a relatively large number of the companies.

A certain amount of information one would regard as strictly necessary
for building a model of the field proved to be unobtainable – on the
structure of the staff employed, recruitment of the senior management and
the board, type of product and mode of manufacture, and the proportion of
investment devoted to research, both in the commercial sector and in
production.

We ran up against all the issues, which specialists in research on firms
know well, regarding the definition and limits of enterprises and the
treatment of subsidiaries: should we, for example, include subsidiaries born
out of a need for commercial diversification, or enterprises which, like
France-Terre in the case of Bruno-Petit (Bruno Petit is its chief executive) or
France-Lot in the case of GMF, enable building firms to circumvent the law
that prevents builders from selling both the land and the house (without
having any legal connection to the holding company)? How were we to
treat franchisers (there are three in the sample: Lemoux Bernard, Sonkad
and Kiteco) who exploit a brand name, but use small local firms, providing
them with technical assistance? Each of the indicators gathered poses
problems, which often arise from the difficulty of determining the identity
of the enterprise: for example, date of foundation raises the question of
how to treat mergers and takeovers (with the brand name passing from one
unit to another). More generally, we ran up against the problem of the
comparability of data: for example, some builders work in terms of number
of houses sold, others in terms of numbers of houses actually handed over
or built. In other words, even after an enormous labour of sifting through
the yearbooks of industry bodies, company accounts, lists of top companies
in the press, an effort complemented by direct questioning of the firms
themselves and the questioning of journalists, administrative services, etc.,
the data assembled are very incomplete and there is an enormous
discrepancy between the effort deployed and the results obtained from
the analysis.[48]

The major opposition in terms of size of firm, measured by a
variety of roughly correlated indicators – turnover, capital, number
of house start-ups, numbers of staff employed, which matched up,
broadly speaking, with an opposition in terms of area of activity
(national, regional or local) and location (in Paris or the provinces) –
masked a secondary opposition, orthogonal to the preceding one,
which a second set of analyses, based on data taken from the survey

carried out by INSEE in 1987 on the structure of the personnel employed by the various construction firms, enables us to bring out. The structure of employment – particularly, the relative proportion of building workers, craftsmen, technicians and engineers or of white-collar workers and managers – is a quite reliable indicator of the firm's orientations and the primacy accorded either to the production or the marketing of the product.

Rather than simply amass more or less disparate indicators (as in the foregoing analysis), we decided to perform a new analysis on the same sample of construction companies (described above), but to do so limiting ourselves to information on the overall figures for personnel employed and their distribution within the division of labour and in geographical space which is gathered in the Employment Structure Survey carried out annually by the Research and Statistics Service of the French Ministry of Social Affairs and Employment, a survey managed by INSEE. Since such data are covered by the regulations on statistical secrecy, we were able to have access to them only after making a formal request and appearing before the Committee on Statistical Secrecy and after having rediscovered or reconstituted (by what was sometimes very difficult research work) the accession numbers of the files of each of the firms we chose to include in our study. In order to respect the commitment we made not to publish any data relating to a particular firm referred to by name, we have replaced the names of the firms in the diagram by the order number given to them in the statistical tables. We do, however, make reference in our commentary on this diagram to the other properties of the firms distributed according to the basic factors taken into account by the analysis.

The main opposition this analysis reveals is between large national companies developing or building single-family houses, all of them linked to banking groups, or franchise companies specializing mainly in design and distribution, and small and medium-sized firms established regionally or locally with family capital (and hence not tied in to any great extent with the financial market), building 'industrial' houses or timber/metal-framed houses and employing workers from all the various building trades. On the one hand (*on the right of the diagram*), we have firms that have substantial finance, research and advertising departments, as shown by their employment structures, from which blue-collar workers and craftsmen are almost completely absent and in which there are very few engineers and technicians, but a large number of managers and white-collar workers. These are, principally, commercial and financial firms, contracting out the building work. The builders situated at this end of the scale, though at first sight very disparate in

The field of single-family house builders

subsidiaries of building firms and/or companies with standardized production

S.S.W.#

2(24.06)

17

S.W.#

32

22 *Other*

places

Building sites

FOREMAN

45

NOEL 42

1(38.94)

S.S.W.*1

40

5

S.W.*   PHÉNIX

18 27   33   4

2

GTM.MI

FOREMAN   16

12

MIDDLE MANAGER 10 43   48
CLERICALTECH.   23 29 25 BOUYGES 47
28 30 44—26-37— 9 20 —14 46—

34   39 36 EXEC. 38   49
13 ENGINEER   8 15

ENTREP./CORP.MAN.   LEMOUX 21
Offices   3 50

Workshops

7   6

tertiary sector staff and/or subcontracting

secondary sector staff and/or no subcontracting

companies with diversified production and/or independent companies

Factorial analysis of correspondences

Table of 50 lines (*builders*), 5 of them illustrative (*property developers*) and 50 columns (*jobs*: entrepreneurs/corporate managers, executives, engineers, middle managers, technicians, foremen, clerical workers, skilled workers (SW) in industry, skilled craftsmen, semi-skilled workers (SSW) in industry, semi-skilled workers (SSW) in industry, semi-skilled craftsmen; *places of work*: workshops, factories, building sites, offices, other places).

Factors
	eigenvalues	percentages
1 − 0.31684		38.94
2 − 0.19577		24.06
3 − 0.09830		12.08

Main contributions

1st factor		2nd factor		3rd factor	
builders					
24	20.1	17	63.6	8	18.9
8	10.8	32	11.9	3	16.2
40	8.9	41	9.9	21	12.2
41	5.1	11	6.6	24	7.6
3	4.9			15	5.4
38	3.9			44	4.0
26	2.9			26	3.4
34	2.7			32	3.9
14	2.6			38	3.3
				29	2.9
variables					
SW, craft	37.9	SW, ind.	52.6	Exec.	50.8
Exec.	17.0	SSW ind.	33.2	Mid. man	17.5
Clerical	11.9	SW, craft	12.6	Engineer	8.9
Mid. man	10.4				

nature, both as regards capital structure and legal status (subsidiaries of large financial or construction/engineering groups, large family concerns) and in terms of the number of housing start-ups, which ranges from 30 in the case of Gestion Immobilière to more than 4,000 in the case of GMF and Maison Bouygues, share an employment structure that has a large number of white-collar workers and (senior and middle) managers and engineers (rather than blue-collar workers and craftsmen), which can be explained by their extensive recourse to subcontracting, itself based on the return to so-called traditional building methods, associated with an extremely highly developed commercial function. Further common factors are that their head offices are in the Paris region (except for Férinel, which has a head office at Roubaix and a subsidiary in the Paris region), that they were created between 1965 and 1975 – with the exception of SACI (Société Auxiliaire de la Construction Immobilière, 1951) – and they are linked in terms of their capital (which is in the middle reaches for the firms in the sample) with banking groups, insurance companies and large construction firms (in the case of Kaufman and Broad, with American companies).

The most significant example is that of Bruno-Petit Construire. Shortly before the survey was carried out, Bruno-Petit gave up its industrialized building methods, based on the use of prefabricated panels of honeycombed concrete, to go back to breeze blocks (while retaining, in its house-building subsidiary, Maison Bruno-Petit, part of the highly skilled in-house workforce required by the old procedure, a move which enabled it to reduce the time taken between the different sequences involved in constructing the building shells); at the same time, the company developed its commercial department and increased the number of its small regional subsidiaries. More generally, the tightening of the market in the early 1980s and intensified competition from the small craftsmen, prompted the producers to increase their sales forces (to the detriment of technical research and innovation) and attempt to move closer to their clients.

Very similar characteristics are also found among the franchise companies, which have very small workforces (between 10 and 15 in the three companies in our sample), all of them managers or technicians. Having a capital which, by comparison with the volume of production, is extremely small (and, in most cases, held by the owner), these commercial firms 'first and foremost provide finance' and their products are entirely traditional.

All the companies at the opposite end of the scale (*on the left of the diagram*) have a regional presence of varying degrees of magnitude and their head offices are often in the provinces (Ast's head office is at Metz and Vercelletto's at Mamers, while Laguarrigue is based at Alençon and Houot at Gérardmer). These are independent small and medium-sized companies, which are, in many cases, firms of long standing (Vercelletto was founded in 1903, Houot in 1927, Laguarrigue and André Beau in 1957) and have no connections whatever with financial groups or large building firms. They are based on family capital and often bear the name of the owner. All of them shun the use of subcontractors for the outer shell of the building and all use industrialized construction methods (prefabricated panels, concrete slabs, timber or metal frames, etc.), which in some cases they have invented themselves and which require a specialist workforce ('in-house workers') kept at stable levels, which rules out subcontracting or the recruiting of workers as and when needed. If we add that these firms are highly dependent on others supplying construction components, then we see that these very rigid organizations, of which Phénix is a typical example, are not well placed to offer 'personalized' products, and even less to adjust to the random fluctuations of the market. However, it is among them that *technical innovations*, and even new aesthetic developments, take place.

For example, Houot, a limited liability family company founded in 1927, is a long-established, highly integrated industrial joinery firm, which began building timber-framed houses using a construction procedure of its own in 1957. Vercelletto, another limited liability family company founded in 1903, is a long-established building firm that operates under the brand name Ouest-Construction and employs a construction procedure based on reinforced concrete cast in a metal formwork, which requires the employment of a highly skilled workforce for assembling the building shell. Socarel, a limited liability company founded in 1967, uses a proprietary building system, a superstructure built of cement blocks, and has a high proportion of in-house blue-collar workers among its staff. Phénix itself, a public limited company founded in 1945, the oldest of the firms producing only single-family dwellings and also the most industrialized (with its subsidiaries), employs an industrialized system using metal frames and concrete slabs that can only be erected on site by 'in-house' workers, which rules out any recourse to subcontracting.

The second factor differentiates between two categories of firm where the first makes no distinction: on the one hand (*at the top of the diagram*), subsidiaries of the exclusively regionally based large groups, that is to say, integrated subcontractors (as opposed to the external subcontractors of Maison Bouygues, for example) specializing entirely in the construction of single-family houses and, on the other (*at the bottom of the diagram*), small, local, integrated firms of a family type with a more diversified range of production. Whereas the former have a high proportion of industrial workers or craftsmen (depending on the building procedure), whose job it is to manufacture or build the shells of the buildings, and a small proportion of white-collar staff, commercial functions being performed by the parent companies, the latter are integrated companies, small and medium-sized, which themselves take care of all phases of production from the building of the shell to after-sales service.

The analysis of the *employment structures* of the different firms, a positive indicator of the most basic economic options, enables us to distinguish between three broad classes of house production firms, which, having very unequal 'strengths', are destined to experience very different futures in the competition that pits them against each other. First, the companies (*at the bottom right of the diagram*) which, thanks to a whole series of organizational innovations, dominate the market in single-family houses: by the remarkable feat of producing 'mason-built houses' with no masons of their own, they have managed industrially to manufacture products that are traditional in appearance; moreover, thanks to heavy investment in the commercial sector and, most especially, in advertising, they know how to dress up the industrial manufacture of mass-produced products as traditional craft-production and to exploit the myth of the house as 'residence' by using genuine characteristics of the traditional mode of construction, but diverted from their original meaning. (This system, based on subordinating traditional production to a modern structure, is reminiscent of the mode of production based on the subordination by farm-produce firms – particularly dairy-produce or cheese-making firms – of very small peasants, who are, in this way, subjected to 'industrial' discipline and converted into *de facto* subcontractors.)

The Maison Bouygues firm, which is typical of this category, was founded on 5 February 1979. It grew extremely quickly, rising in the space of ten years to first place in the single-family house market. From its beginnings in 1979, when it built three houses and had a turnover of 31,000,000 francs, it had by 1987 expanded to 3,500 houses and a turnover of 1,200,000,000 francs. Throughout this period, its exceptional commercial success was underpinned by a relatively simple, but highly coherent advertising strategy developed by the Synergie agency. During the first years of Maison Bouygues's existence, the emphasis in its advertising was on achieving product awareness and brand recognition. Hence the very first advertisement, produced in February 1979, saw the logo to the fore, together with the plain red colour and the slogan 'Maison de maçons': a mason-built house. To the left of the logo, we see, even at this point, the outline (a black-and-white line drawing) of the mason, standing in a familiar pose with his foot resting on two breeze blocks (illustration 1 on p. 51). This advertisement also stresses the specificity of a 'traditional' product, as opposed to the 'industrial' houses of the main competitors, Phénix chief among them, and clearly asserts the company's 'positioning' in the market as a 'mid-to-lower range' producer. In the years 1980–1, the figure of the mason assumes increasing importance: he is now a real 'honest Joe' and not just an outline; the figure now appears in colour and has grown to the size of the logo; he seems friendly and inspires confidence. The 'Maison de maçons' slogan is given prominence and encompasses all the other messages (illustration 2 on p. 51). The definitive formula has been found: red logo, slogan, mason and white text on a royal blue background. These will become the permanent features of brand recognition. The opening of a seventh subsidiary in 1980 justifies the appearance of advertisements in the glossies (*Télé 7 jours*, *Match*, *Parents*, *Maison individuelle*). Since then, every stage of the firm's life has had its own targeted 'media strategy': 1981 saw the creation of a new subsidiary (Maison Bouygues now covered more than 75 per cent of the nation) and radio campaigns. In 1982, the turnover reached 1 billion francs, the thirteenth subsidiary was opened and Maison Bouygues embarked on national poster advertising. In 1983 a new theme was broached, the company's 'newly weds' campaign being aimed at young couples, a significant proportion of its target market (illustration 3 on p. 52). Here the mason was replaced by the young husband (adopting the same pose); the slogan remained, but the emphasis was now on accessibility. By 1984, the brand was well established and Maison Bouygues had moved into second place in the single-family house building market. After devoting five years to developing product awareness and brand recognition, Maison Bouygues launched a new range: the 'Grand Volume' house. Here the advertising strategy changed: the consumer was sent off on flights of fancy with the 'Cathedral' living room and the mezzanine. With sales of 'Grand Volume' in full flow, 1985 was declared the year of 'Imagination' (after the name of one of the models on offer). This campaign was based on the use of photographs of interiors, but national posters still showed the mason, now in close-up, and indeed looming increasingly large, holding a trowel in his right hand and making a 'thumbs up' gesture with his left (illustration 4 on p. 52).

With television allowing advertising for housing for the first time, and the TF1 channel being purchased by Bouygues, the activities of the marketing department became focused on the small screen. In the field of radio and TV advertising, in spite of investment at a level only half that of Phénix, Maison Bouygues scored a success on TV with a film, 'L'Ami de la famille' (The Family Friend), which was very much oriented towards the product (a detailed visit of a house) and strongly identified with the brand ('honest Joe' sitting with the family and in the attitude and role of a friend; logo; music etc.) (illustration 5 on p. 52). With the takeover of TF1 by Bouygues, a strong advertising presence on that channel naturally ensued, together with the creation of a competition organized by TF1 and *Télé-Star*. This strong television presence increased with the sponsorship, from 1986 onwards, of Bernard Tapie's Marseille football team, whose matches were broadcast in the specialist slots and on news programmes. The orange Bouygues logo on the Marseille players' shirts was recognizable from a distance and clearly readable in close-up. Having become the leading builder of single-family houses in France, in 1987 Maison Bouygues employed the RSCG advertising agency (Roux, Séguéla, Cayzac et Goudard) to handle its account.

As for the second class, that of firms integrated and organized around the implementation of a method of industrial manufacture, whether similar to the preceding companies in terms of the scale and scope of their activity, like Phénix, the oldest and most powerful firm in this category, or smaller, both in terms of numbers of houses produced and volume of capital or personnel, they were subject to the extremely rigid technical constraints of integrated production, which translated into social constraints on account of the need to maintain a highly specialized in-house workforce on a permanent basis. Being forced always to run counter to the tide of ordinary demand for villa residences, they were in a sense hostage to the organizational conditions which at one stage gave them their lead at the technological level. Being the least well prepared to respond to the new situation created by the crisis in – and shrinkage of – the market, they were often in difficulties. And, though the largest of them have retained the 'strengths' relating to economies of scale and diversification of risk that their size affords them, a great many of these companies, particularly among the smallest, have been reduced to the status of subsidiaries of large groups.

There remain, lastly, all the small and medium-sized family-owned, integrated companies, building houses by traditional methods. These companies, offering a product 'hand-made' by masons and carpenters who are craftsmen, the group most traditionally associated with the idea of 'authenticity', in materials representative of the idea of permanence and stability – stone, wood, breeze blocks, cement, etc. – and using techniques of manufacture that are tried and tested, as are their 'plans' (which, though imposed by clients acting as spontaneous architects, almost always reproduce unconscious models), have all the traditional logic of the most traditional demand in their favour. But we may wonder whether, in a sphere where the art of producing appearances plays such an important role, the big firms oriented towards the industrial production of the *appearance* of the traditional house will not succeed, in this area as in others, in winning out over these small firms which actually make a (more or less adulterated) traditional product (a significant proportion of the elements they use are industrial products) and which will be able to survive only by accepting integration (as subcontractors or franchisees) into huge firms capable of the industrial fabrication of the image of the

A brand making its mark

1

2

3

5

4

'traditional' products their clients expect. Having said this, the small craft firms are in a sense essential to the operation of the whole system, which they provide with its symbolic justification. Through the '*maisons bourgeoises*' which they often build in a local style that is the product of a more or less approximate historical reconstruction – manor houses, *mas*, villa residences, etc. – they continue to breathe life into, and give concrete presence to, the dominant model of the traditional house, which so many buyers harbour in the unconscious as a kind of ideal – and which extends far beyond the customers who can actually afford it.

Advertising strategies

The relative weight a firm accords to the commercial function is undoubtedly one of the most potent and significant indicators of its position in the field of building companies. These companies are, in effect, faced with the following alternatives: on the one hand, to work to transform the socially constituted schemas of perception or appreciation (tastes) that potential buyers will apply to their product, to its physical reality as an object presented to perception, and also to the materials of which it is made and the manufacturing procedures that its perceptible configuration reveals, or betrays, to the inspection of an anxious or worried client – particularly by disarming prejudices against industrially built houses and by breaking down the customary associations of the house with the old and the traditional, in order to substitute associations with the modern and the avant-garde, technical research, comfort, etc.; or, conversely, to strive to bridge the gap between the impression spontaneously inspired by the product and the image that is to be produced for it. Since the big industrial firms have never truly chosen the path of subversion and outright modernism, they are particularly noteworthy for the scale of the symbolic campaigns of transfiguration mounted by their commercial departments (particularly their advertising departments, but also their sales forces) in order to make good the potential gap between the product as actually supplied and perceived and the expectation of that product, and to convince clients that the product on offer is made for them and they are made for that product.

Increased company size brings with it greater bureaucratization and an increase in the proportion of commercial staff. Staff working on building sites fall into the minority, the number of administrative workers increases slightly and the number of commercial employees grows greatly (by 10.5% for those firms building 20–50 houses; 12.5% for those building 50–100; 18% for those building between 100 and 250; 21.5% for those between 250 and 1,000; and 23.2% for firms building more than 1,000 houses). The more the company grows, the more it seems necessary to develop a large network of salespeople: word of mouth is no longer sufficient, and greater emphasis has to be put on advertising and prospecting for business. However, with company size, the number of sales made by each salesperson falls, while the number of orders cancelled increases (in 1984, almost 40 per cent of the orders registered by the salespeople in the largest companies were rescinded by clients, as opposed to a figure of a little under 10 per cent in the smallest firms). One can understand why the issue of recruiting and training salespeople becomes a priority for the largest construction companies, particularly as sales staff are extremely mobile (spending, on average, between six and eight months with the same building company, according to the *Moniteur des travaux publics et du bâtiment*). Several construction companies (Bruno-Petit, Phénix) have set up internal sales training centres. Others have attempted to improve their recruitment methods.

As the relative weight of the commercial sector increases with company size, so also does the use of the various methods of commercial prospection and publicity. For example, in the UCB survey of 1983, the percentage of construction companies saying they made frequent use of newspaper advertising ran from 48% for the smallest (those building 20–49 houses) to 69% for the builders of 50–99 houses, 72% for those building 100–249 houses and 74% for those building 250 or more; for the same categories, the figures for those taking stands at trade fairs and exhibitions were, respectively, 26%, 44%, 59% and 74%. We would see much more significant discrepancies between companies if we could also take into account the percentages of firms advertising in the major weeklies or on radio and television. The largest sized companies mount large-scale 'advertising campaigns' and use a very broad range of methods of prospection: leaflets delivered door-to-door, prospectuses, catalogues, brochures, advertising in regional and national dailies, weekly newspapers and magazines, poster campaigns, stands at exhibitions and fairs, 'show houses' either at their own centres or within housing 'developments' or at strategic points (big stores, stations, etc.), radio and, more recently (since 1985) television commercials (it is among the clients of the largest construction enterprises that the numbers who first heard of the company through advertising – and, in particular, through the newspapers or radio – are highest). By contrast, the small firms rely largely on networks of personal relations and advertisements in local newspapers.

We know that, like all symbolic action, advertising is most successful when it plays on, stimulates or arouses pre-existing dispositions, which it expresses and provides with an opportunity for acknowledgement and fulfilment. We can see why all companies draw more or less equally on the storehouse of words and themes best suited to induce in their audience the most traditional ideas of the house and the household, referring, for example, to the advantage of owning over renting ('it's cheaper to buy than to rent') or to the charms of *nature*; this they do, no doubt, in an effort to link the house to a set of attractive associations, but it may also, and may mainly, be done to deflect attention from the distance of the particular housing on offer from the town centre or the workplace, by making a virtue of necessity and transforming exile to a distant suburb into an active decision to return to the countryside (illustration 3 on p. 63).

The procedures employed are almost always the same. One of the commonest consists in comparing two radically opposing situations, that of the new entrant to ownership and the non-entrant. In another, use is made of a fictional dialogue between the potential client and the professional presenting his product, giving an illusory impression of a direct, personal relationship. Yet another, much employed to conceal the undesirable characteristics of the product, consists in using what we might term sleight of hand, which aims to attract the attention to real or presumed advantages, qualities or facilities offered, etc., in order to hide the disadvantages or unpleasant features. And property advertising is not always above engaging in some dubious technical or financial arguments or crude misrepresentations where the house itself or its environs are concerned. Several large construction companies have fallen foul of the law on false advertising (27 December 1973), of which article 44.1 forbids 'any advertisement including ... allegations, indications or claims that are false or such as to mislead when they relate to one or more elements of the product'. In 1983, for example, Maison Bouygues was found guilty of distributing a catalogue advertising 'houses made to measure' when in reality only houses corresponding to 'determinate types' were on offer, and of promising a 'frame truly built by craftsmen,' when 'the materials used were manufactured industrially and prefabricated, and the frames were not assembled following age-old techniques'.

The different firms also have less need to resort to advertising and to the rhetoric of ancestrality and security when their products and building methods are closer to these things in reality. And if advertising strategies increase in intensity with increased company size, it is, above all, their form that changes when we pass from those which, even if they have to make concessions to appearances – such as the imitation of roughcast on prefabricated panels – base themselves principally on the technical qualities of their product, and those which, like Maison Bouygues, base their strategies on the production of the appearances of a 'traditional' product and mode of production. The use of different themes and rhetorical procedures varies, in fact, according to position within the field. The strategy that consists in attributing to the product sold the qualities of the producer is without doubt more frequent in the advertisements of the largest and oldest companies. Building on the assumption that only a solid company can build solid houses, or that a solid company cannot build anything but solid houses, and hence that the houses built by a company of long standing will necessarily themselves be solid and long-standing, every effort is made, by resorting to a logic of magical contamination, to have the producer 'rub off' on to the product. For example, since Maison Bouygues is a recently formed company, reference is actually made to the many years' standing of the Bouygues Group as a guarantee of the quality of the houses of the same name, on the assumption that the buyer is highly unlikely to notice the slippage between the two: 'Maison Bouygues has the 30 years' experience of the Bouygues Group behind it, with all the purchasing power of that group to call on. As a result Maison Bouygues has been able to bring down the cost of a mason-built house.'[49]

The large construction companies seek, above all, to break down the resistance or quell the anxieties of their least well-off clients ('Becoming the owner of a Grand Volume house is easier than you think'). By playing up their services, their financial, legal and administrative assistance and the like, and stressing the guarantees they provide, they seek to generate confidence. 'Whatever your problem – credit (new PAP and APL loans), plot (plot advice service), administrative or other difficulties – our specialists will provide you with the precise information you need. You will see at a glance your chances of acquiring a single-family house in the area of your choice' (Maisons Alskanor, 1979). If at times they tend to dramatize the act of house purchase somewhat ('This is the most serious purchase of your life' – GMF; 'When you decide to build a house, you're putting something of your life into it' – Bruno-Petit), this is done to bring out more clearly their ability to take care of everything and have the client put themselves entirely in their hands, as is justified by their reputation: 'Everyone is well aware that there is nothing quite like a mason-built house. In addition, Maison Bouygues brings you all the advantages of a large construction company and dispels any worries you may have over prices, guarantees or quality' (Maison Bouygues, 1984). The 'Phénix Charter', the 'Bruno-Petit Law' or the guarantees offered by GMF or Maison Bouygues are supposed to protect customers, 'come what may'.

It is, paradoxically, because advertising strategies are determined to a large extent by competition that they tend to come to resemble each other: almost at the same moment, the different building companies launch campaigns deploying more or less the same arguments ('the personalized house'; 'become a homeowner', etc.). It is not possible, for example, to understand a number of the arguments used by Maison Bouygues if one is unaware that Bouygues, in its effort to wrest first place from Maison Phénix, has firmly resolved to mass-produce traditional houses, whereas Maison Phénix continues to appeal to more or less 'modernist' technical and financial arguments, while making concessions, both in its houses and its advertising, to traditional demands: 'Maison Bouygues's diligence and efficiency mean that it can provide houses within everyone's reach today – even for those with limited financial resources. Your Maison Bouygues house will not be prefabricated [subtext: like the ones built by Maison Phénix]. It will be a mason-built house, built by the best craftsmen in your region.'[50]

The advantage the most modern firms derive from the use of industrial techniques of lightweight prefabrication and of industrialized components (such as internal walls or door and window frames) is balanced out, and hence limited, by their clients' enthusiasm for traditional modes of manufacture which, even if they increasingly include the use of industrialized elements, afford a reassuring image of solidity. The image of the mason-built house has such resonance that the builders of industrial houses all have to resort to camouflaging strategies aimed at concealing the industrial components both in the reality of the houses (with purely decorative brick or masonry façades or prominence accorded to beams and all those characteristics which designate a traditional house) and the language used to promote them, which draws on the rhetoric of the 'local', the 'traditional', 'regional style' and the like.

So long as the distribution of technical 'strengths' between firms (linked to the degree of industrialization) varied in inverse proportion to the distribution of symbolic 'strengths' (linked to degree of conformity to the model of craft-building and the craft-built product), the situation was, in a sense, relatively clear. A decisive breakdown of this equilibrium, which had afforded the small craft-based and family firms every chance to compete, occurred with the organizational innovation that consisted in the creation of construction firms capable of producing mock-traditional houses industrially – particularly by turning to symbolic advantage one feature of their organization (massive recourse to subcontracting or franchising), thereby reconciling previously irreconcilable elements: the technical

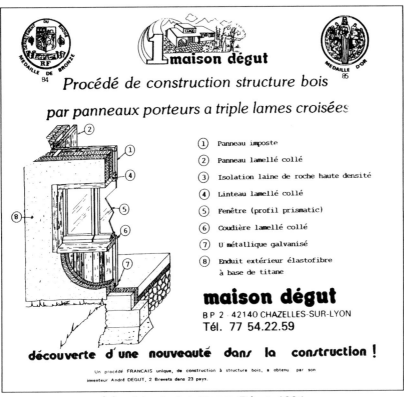

Advertising leaflet, Maison Dégut, 1986

advantages of mass production and the symbolic advantages of craft manufacture.[51]

The difficulties presented by the contradiction between industrial manufacturing procedures and client expectations show up very clearly in the advertising discourse and images of the medium-sized, locally based firms that offer products based on an industrial process. For example, Maison Dégut bases its advertising largely on technical arguments, such as the strength of 'triple laminate loadbearing panels' ('a panel 2.5 × 1 metres can withstand 17 tonnes before buckling'). These are shown in cross-section and the process of their manufacture is described in detail. Or the emphasis is on their efficiency in terms of insulation and ventilation, and also psychological and biological comfort ('the A. Dégut timber-framed house is healthy because it does not destroy the continuous field of atmospheric radiations required for the individual's biological equilibrium'). But, on another tack, it also appeals to the prestige of the old and the venerable to justify a process which has been rewarded with gold and bronze medals and is decked out with certificates of approval: 'The A. Dégut process takes its inspiration from the traditions of yesteryear (château-style woodwork), which have proved themselves over 500 years.' And it guarantees 'a tough exterior, thanks to the titanium-based, elastomeric fibre coating'. The collision of two semantic universes is patent here and the product promotion exercise has no other recourse available than to

Advertising leaflet, Maisons Houot, 1986

project itself into the distant future where today's technological advance will have turned into 'tomorrow's tradition'.

We find the same contradiction, this time in the raw state, as it were, without euphemism or transfiguration, in the advertising material of Maisons Émile Houot. This small family firm, founded in 1957, has its head office at Gérardmer and builds village developments and single-family houses in Lorraine and the northern Alps. Here the image presents the truth of the process most starkly (the firm has no actual advertising slogan): the house, produced in a factory by an industrial technique (the Houot process), arrives 'straight from the factory'. It is, in fact, shown descending from the heavens, fully complete, with lines running outward from its four corners to express the speed of its flight, as in a Superman cartoon. It is greeted with a hearty cheer ('Hooray for Maisons Houot!') by the family circle which, dog included, awaits it in the conventional decor of a petit-bourgeois lounge oddly suspended in mid-air. There could be no clearer expression of the contrast between the industrial product from another world (which must both be referred to and, by its transfiguration, blotted from memory) and the 'family' dimension, which is asserted in the foreground in its most standard social definition: the father wedged in his armchair; the mother seated on the chair arm, in a pose that might have come from a photo-novella, with her arm (no doubt) around his shoulder; the two children – a boy standing, his arm raised towards the flying object, as herald of modernity, and a girl sitting – the mirror image of the parental couple from which they are separated by a low table and a vase of flowers, the symbol, in many traditions, of the revival of life's springtime ... The iconographic construction here is that used to express *miracles* and, if we might be allowed what, for a cheap cartoon-strip illustration, may seem a rather overblown reference, we could make a link here to Erwin Panofsky's analysis of Roger van der Weyden's *Three Magi* altarpiece: the Émile Houot house occupies more or less the place of the little child surrounded by a halo of golden rays which we know immediately, because we bring a perspectival vision of space to the perception of the picture, that it is hovering in mid-air, like an apparition.[52]

The contradiction, which is symbolically resolved in the rhetoric of miracles, a rhetoric perfectly suited to the aims of the advertising message, leads in many cases to confusion of the expressive intention. Advertisements for Maisons de l'Avenir, for example, a small regional building firm formed in 1967 at Rennes (Brittany), which uses a heavy industrial manufacturing process, mingles the usual images of the completed house, surrounded by trees and peopled with children, with photographs of the manufacturing operation that evoke industry rather than traditional craft production. The industrial process, which is intended to appear traditional, as its oddly constructed name ('Superparpaing' – super breeze block) indicates, appears only on the hidden inside page of the leaflet.

All these contradictions, and the semantic collisions they generate within discourse, disappear when we come to those firms employing traditional building processes, whether through a form of organization that involves mass production on the basis of subcontracting, or through more or less modernized forms of traditional craft-based construction. A firm like Sergeco, founded in Paris in 1962, which offers so-called 'mid-range' single-family houses, built to measure by the most traditional methods and using traditional materials (hollow brick, copper piping, etc.), can without difficulty mobilize the whole symbolic arsenal of the villa residence: from the slogan 'our houses are built to last' to the cover page entitled, no doubt with deliberate ambiguity, 'a house for loving', and depicting a house growing, picture-book style, inside a flower, the way babies are born under gooseberry bushes (illustration 1 on p. 63).There is perfect harmony

Advertising leaflet, Maisons de l'Avenir, 1986

1   2

Advertising leaflet, Sergeco, 1986   Advertising leaflet, Maisons Sprint,
1986, p. 12

3

Catalogue, Sergeco, 1983–4, p. 5

here between the evocation of the construction process – two masons building a brick wall – and the evocation of the completed house (not reproduced here), the former being presented as a guarantee of the 'long life' of the latter or, in other words, a guarantee of the 'family's prosperity' and the long-term return on the wise financial investment it has made.

As for the advertisements for Maisons Sprint, a small regional firm created at Marseille in 1966, there is nothing in them (except the name, which speaks of rapidity) that runs counter to the enchanted evocation of the most traditional image of a house: on the one hand, the assurances which the idea of a 'big firm' brings with it are provided, and not just in the form of 'experience' and rational management ('software tools to manage the sites, coordinate the work and optimize purchasing'), but also of 'multidisciplinary' activity, bringing together specialists with titles that smack of scientificity ('concrete engineer, heat engineer, geologist, surveyor') and not just in being a member of the UNCMI and being overseen by SOCOTEC (Société de Contrôle Technique du Bâtiment), but also having the backing of a major bank and the protection of a large insurance group; on the other hand, the company gives all the guarantees associated with traditional building methods, from the 'genuine skill of the craftsman', whom we see at work laying floor tiles, to 'tasteful, harmonious finishing touches' (illustration 2 on p. 63). The illustration is able to give their due to the craftsmen, tilers, plasterers, roofers and masons, and to the so-called 'noble' materials they use; the accompanying text can speak of the rarity value of the product offered ('every year we build a limited number of houses') and its perfect alignment to the client's tastes ('an art of living made to measure'); and it can draw unrestrainedly in praising these 'master-built houses' on the storehouse of mock-poetic stereotypes that make up the 'literary' language of housing: mystery, charm, nature, proportions, tradition, region, native heath, residence, spaces, volumes, patio, mezzanine, pergola, barbecue, inglenook, beams, terracotta, curved tiles, fireside, history, soul, etc.

The recession and the field effect

The relations of force between firms depend on the overall economic situation, which, incidentally, they *refract* according to their own specific logic. The field effect was never so clearly seen as during the recession that hit the single-family house market around 1980: because, in their manufacturing and marketing strategies, they had to deal with a demand for 'traditional', 'personalized' constructions, a demand the small craft producers are supposedly best placed to satisfy, the big industrial construction firms, which can lower their costs only by increasing production through a standardization of the product, had to use an ever greater range of technical, organizational and symbolic strategies to limit or conceal the effects of mass production (diversification of models; large-scale organization of 'craft' building methods; recourse to a rhetoric based on tradition, origins and uniqueness). Many national firms came in this period to abandon their policy of integrated, industrialized production, to adopt production strategies that were those of small craft-based or semi-craft-based companies and to return to traditional building methods, using subcontractors to do the work.

The largest national builders, Phénix foremost among them, were the first to be affected; for the most part, they saw a decline in their activity (Phénix's level of business fell particularly sharply, from 16,000 houses per year in the late 1970s to only 8,000 in 1984, 7,200 in 1985 and 6,200 in 1986). The rapid turnover of firms is doubtless one of the major characteristics of this field: according to the survey of 80 per cent of the builders with at least 20 housing start-ups in 1982, carried out by UCB in spring 1983, 59 per cent were newcomers whose businesses had been set up within the last ten years (that is, since 1976) or who, more unusually, built fewer than 20 houses in 1976. These were almost always local, small or medium sized firms, the largest producers being also the oldest (for example, Phénix, founded in 1945, or GMF, established in 1949); there were, however, also some cases of very rapid advance: Maison Bouygues, for example, founded in 1979, was in second place in the 'catalogue' house market by 1982; similarly, the Architectes-Bâtisseurs, created in 1981, had by 1984 managed to bring together some 400 architects organized in small companies. But if there were many company start-ups, particularly in the 1970s and even in the 1980s, closures and bankruptcies were even more common since, according to the UCB survey, there were 1,100 house-building firms in 1976, but the figure had fallen to just 800 by 1982. After a boom period (the number of house start-ups rose from 107,000 in 1962 to 281,000 in 1979) there has been a very marked decline in single-family house building since 1980, with only 192,000 start-ups in 1985, though the decline here came later and less sharply in this sector than in apartment-block construction.

The recession changed relations of force in favour of the small firms. 'Small and medium-sized builders have taken advantage of the situation to turn the tables on the big companies which had moved into their territory. The SMEs [small and medium-size enterprises], closer to their client base and with a better knowledge of its wants

and tastes, have beefed up their sales forces in recent years and, for
the most part, they performed creditably in the depths of the
recession. In 1984, for example, Vercelletto at Mamers had 350
house start-ups (by comparison with 250 in 1983), Cleverte at Lyon
226 (as against 158); Maison Chapel at Brignoles 107 (as against 60)
and Maisons Archambault at Tours 50 (as against 22). It seems,
however, that this respite was short-lived, since figures for 1985
show that stagnation has spread to small and medium-sized builders
too. Many of them have even experienced an appreciable fall-off in
their levels of business. Moreover, the big players, who have learnt
from their setbacks, have changed tack since the beginning of the
year and are now imitating the strategies of the SMEs.'[53] To
maintain the fight against the small and medium-sized builders, the
big companies reorganized and, by the creation of regional
subsidiaries, or through original forms of subcontracting, set up
structures akin to the SMEs in an attempt to get closer to the
consumers and their desires. For example, Bruno-Petit subdivided its
Bruno-Petit and Châlet Idéal brands into more independent SMEs,
ceding a minority share in the companies to their new directors.
Similarly, Maison Phénix established smaller structures in the
regions. This internal diversification of large firms was accompanied
by a marked trend towards concentration: in 1982, the market share
of builders erecting more than 250 houses per year (who represented
5 per cent of all builders) was 50 per cent of total house building,
while that of the national companies, who accounted for only 1 per
cent of builders, was 33 per cent.

Some of the biggest companies attempted to reconcile the standardization of production with the personalization of the product by technical and
commercial strategies aimed at providing individual combinations of more
or less standardized elements and offering a whole range of building
methods (the most effective innovation being the mass organization,
through subcontracting, of a traditionally built product, the 'mason-built
house') and of sales packages (the house completed and ready for
immediate occupation; the house only requiring finishings to be added;
the house in 'kit' form or extendable, etc.). Claude Pux, then chairman of
the Union Nationale des Constructeurs de Maisons Individuelles (UNCMI),
cited a survey which listed 985 models for 34 building companies in 1984
and declared that this number would continue to grow. Some builders now
offered only personalized houses and dropped their catalogues. *Le
Moniteur des travaux publics et du bâtiment* of 2 May 1986 carried the
headline: 'The single-family house is becoming personalized. The national
building firms have a new hobby-horse: "personalized projects". A
counter-offensive against small and medium-sized builders, accompanied

by their regionalization.' And the director in charge of the advertising budget at Maisons Phénix laid out the new marketing strategy in an interview (in 1987): 'A few years ago all builders sold houses from a catalogue. Since then, sales techniques have developed right across the board. We don't want to sell like that any longer. People today want a personalized house. If you confine them to a catalogue, they feel they're just choosing from among houses on offer. We won't have that now. We want them to feel they're really building their houses and fully choosing what they want. As a first change, here at Phénix we don't give names to our houses any longer. We started this a year ago. Each salesman will have visuals of houses (photos) he can show to the client – houses we've built or could build. There won't be a catalogue any more, but a construction project file. We'll give the client cards with visuals of unnamed houses on them – the house with a convertible loft, for example – perhaps with a ground plan, which can be modified. We'll draw up a construction project file for each client. We won't force anything on them at the outset. This is more or less the way an architect operates. You have to respond to people's motivations, and they want to choose. All the building companies are in a battle over the personalized house. They're aware that demand has moved on.' The fact that the language of 'personalization', which had long prevailed in the banking world in the area of credit, also came to apply, under the impact of the recession, to the product itself, merely contributed, then, to reinforcing considerably the coherence and symbolic effectiveness of the commercial strategy implemented by the building firms.

This diversification does not exclude a clear standardization of products within the same firm and a homogenization of the products of firms occupying neighbouring positions in the field. A saleswoman from Kaufman and Broad states this quite plainly: 'When it comes to the competition, there's little to choose between us ... We have the same kinds of firm, we use the same materials and then we try to give something extra.' If the standardization effect is a direct product of the technical need to reduce costs, the homogenization of products between companies seems, in part at least, to arise out of the competition that leads the largest of these firms to offer their clients products that can rival the most successful houses built by their most direct competitors (in the circulation of information, the clients themselves no doubt play a major role; by using what they have learnt from one builder to test out the others, they provide the sales staff with information on the line being taken by their competitors). The fact that competing firms keep a close eye on each other, even going so far as to spy on one another or steal each other's ideas,[54] or that they resort to poaching managers and sales staff (which represents a transfer of embodied technical capital) doubtless plays some role in the almost simultaneous appearance of similar

models in companies occupying neighbouring positions, such as
Phénix (declining) and Bouygues (in the ascendant).[55] For example,
the 'Grand Volume' house, which proved a great success for Maison
Bouygues when it was launched in 1984, appeared a very short time
before the 'Spacio' house, which failed dismally for Phénix.

But, in fact, in the short-term struggles which lead them to take
ideas, procedures and staff, etc. from each other, competitors
commit the 'strengths' they can throw into the battle, *the entire past
of the structural relation being present in each moment of that
relation* – notably, in the case of the Bouygues–Phénix rivalry,
through the very structure of employment within the company and
all the forms of inertia and hysteresis ensuing from that structure.
Broadly speaking, we can say that the recession ensured the triumph
of the most traditional demand at the technical and aesthetic levels:
breeze blocks for the walls, industrially produced false gable trusses
for the frame, wood for the external door and window fittings (with
the very expensive and not very robust 'Île-de-France' style small-
paned windows). The shrinkage of the market was reflected in a
narrower social spread among the clientele. Now, we know that the
largest industrial companies, particularly Phénix, the market leader,
had pursued a policy of mass production aimed at reducing costs by
standardizing the product and increasing sales by capturing the
lower end of the market (the big national producers, who had
between them a large share of the production of single-family
houses, mainly built villa homes of 4–6 rooms with a habitable
surface of 50–120 square metres on a single level and without a
cellar, whereas the regional builders offered larger houses, with 5–8
rooms and between 110 and 120 square metres at a higher price per
square metre). It follows from this that the fall-off in the demand
from the least well-off affected the largest firms first and restored the
advantage of the regional builders, who had always targeted a better-
off client base.[56] The builders specializing in building for the lower
end of the market (Maison Phénix, Maisons Mondial Pratic) reacted
by attempting to gain business among the more prosperous.
Conversely, however, some large companies producing mainly for
a better-off clientele managed to maintain their position only by
diversifying their activities: this was the case, for example, with
Kaufman and Broad who, though initially specializing in building
'village developments' for the executive market, had to move into
building apartment and office blocks and retirement homes. La
Société des Constructions Modernes Laguarrigue is another example. Whereas in 1982 it was building for a relatively well-off clientele,
it began to offer less expensive houses for a clientele with more

modest finances in an attempt to offset the effects of the recession and the fall-off in its operations (these were the Record range, which in 1986 had a starting price of 221,000 francs for a surface area of 73 square metres).

The strategies of the firm as a field

However, to account more completely and precisely for the relations of force between firms and the development over time of those relations, that is to say, for the strategies firms implement to transform or maintain those relations, particularly in response to the asset redistribution occasioned by the recession, we have to change the scale of our approach and shift our focus from the field of firms overall to each of the firms taken individually, which, at least in the case of the large firms, are relatively autonomous units functioning also as fields. It is clear that the firm is not a homogeneous entity that can be treated as a rational subject – the 'entrepreneur' or the 'management' – oriented towards a single, unified objective. It is determined (or guided) in its 'choices' not only by its position in the structure of the field of production, but also by its internal structure which, as a product of all its earlier history, still orients its present. Being divided into organizations mainly directed towards production, research, marketing, finance, etc., it is made up of agents whose specific interests are bound up with each of these organizations and functions, which can come into conflict for many reasons, in particular over the power to decide the directions the firm will take. Its strategies are determined through innumerable decisions, small and large, ordinary and extraordinary, which are, in every case, the product of the relationship between, on the one hand, interests and dispositions associated with positions in relations of force within the firm and, on the other, capacities to make those interests or dispositions count, capacities which also depend on the weight of the different agents concerned in the structure, and hence on the volume and structure of their capital. This means that the 'subject' of what is sometimes called 'company policy' is quite simply the field of the firm or, to put it more precisely, the structure of the relation of force between the different agents that belong to the firm or, at least, of those among them who have the greatest weight in the structure and who play a part in decision-making proportionate to their individual weight. Case studies aimed at investigating how decisions come to be taken remain more or less meaningless so long as they confine themselves to the merely phenomenal manifestations of the exercise of power, that is to say, to discourse and interactions, ignoring the structure of relations of force between the institutions and the agents (often formed into bodies) contending for decision-making power or, in other words, the dispositions and interests of the various directors [*dirigeants*] and the 'strengths' at their disposal for realizing those dispositions and interests.

The strategies of the directors engaged in the competitive struggle within the field of power of a company, and the visions of the future, forecasts, projects or plans they strive to impose depend, among other things, on the volume and structure of their capital – whether it is economic (shares etc.) rather than educational, or vice versa – and, more especially at this level, on the kind of educational capital they possess and also on the position – itself linked to the foregoing properties – which they occupy within the firm (finance director, commercial director, personnel director, production engineer, etc.). If we know that, in the largest and most highly bureaucratized companies, the orientation towards one or other of the major functions – financial, commercial or technical – is closely linked to the species of educational capital possessed, and, at the same time, to social and educational trajectories generative of specific dispositions (and also of social capital, linked to membership of professional bodies), we can understand that the struggles that take place among the company's directors over decisions, both ordinary and extra-ordinary – and, most particularly, when crises of succession occur – owe a great deal to the concern the various directors may have, and, through them, the various professional *corps* (*ingénieurs des Mines*, *ingénieurs des Ponts*, *inspecteurs des Finances*, alumni of the École des Hautes Études Commerciales (HEC), etc.), to promote the activities they are involved with, and thus to maintain or improve their position by perpetuating or changing the balance between the functions to which their interests are attached.

We cannot, then, understand the strategies of the various companies contending to dominate the market in single-family houses and, in particular, the battle between the largest firms, Maison Bouygues and Maison Phénix, unless we take into account the whole of their social history and, in particular, the evolution within each of them of the relations of force between the different categories of directors who, when they have power, can sacrifice *the firm's interests* to the satisfaction of their *interests within the firm*. For example, to grasp the reasons or causes why Maison Phénix persevered for so long, in spite of the crisis besetting it, on the course mapped out by its founder, which it followed like a boat drifting on rudderless, we would have to reconstruct the evolution of the structure of the relations between those among the directors who saw themselves as struggling to maintain that course and those who, by contrast, wanted to set the firm moving in another direction.

Maison Phénix, a small engineering company, which initially worked mainly for the French state electricity company (EDF), grew rapidly and by the late 1960s found itself in a quasi-monopolistic situation in the industrially built single-family house market. Though its decline does not become visible until the 1980s, there are signs of it much earlier, from the mid-1970s onwards, when Maison Phénix faced a succession crisis. On the retirement of André Pux, who possessed the legitimacy and authority of a founder ('When he said, "Go on building houses as before, don't change anything", people didn't dare say anything'; '"Start by earning money. After that you'll have a right to speak", and he had the authority to say that'), it was not long before the financial groups took a controlling interest. The new managing director, Roger Pagezy, an *ingénieur des Mines*, was the representative of the large Pont-à-Mousson group of companies. Claude Pux, the founder's son, who set up the company's commercial sector, but who had neither prestigious educational qualifications nor, apparently, his father's backing, attempted to use the regional subsidiaries to assert his own position with the new managing director. But these subsidiaries, whose autonomy had initially been encouraged (49 per cent of their capital had been sold to their managing directors, whereas 49 per cent was retained by the parent company and 2 per cent held by Claude Pux), were subsequently reined in (the chairmen of the regional subsidiaries were replaced and in 1982 the group bought out their capital). The effects of the crisis of succession were all the more serious for the fact that it occurred at a moment when competitors were developing, making substantial investments in advertising and expanding their geographical areas of operation.

The founder's departure, the succession crisis, conflicts between the head office and regional subsidiaries, an increase in competition and the general decline of activity in the sector after 1980 were all factors that led, among other things, to a loss of *confidence in the firm* and in the value of its products. The failure of Phénix's 'Spacio' model, at the point when Bouygues's 'Grand Volume' house, though very similar both technically and financially, was enjoying very great success, cannot be understood in isolation from the whole universe of relations within the firm (where trade unions came on the scene in the mid-1980s). While 'company spirit' had declined very markedly at Phénix, where 'demoralized' salespeople seemed no longer to *believe in their product*, over at Bouygues the sales force, who were subject to very close supervision ('They're on your back more here,' said one defector from Phénix), were more committed to the firm and more 'aggressive' and effective. Through their commercial strategies (the traditional option – the 'mason-built house' at Bouygues, as opposed to the shamefaced modernity of Phénix) and the dispositions of those whose responsibility it was to implement them (in particular the sales force), the whole social policy of the firm, the relations between the commercial departments and the departments responsible for advertising and research etc., went, as it were, into their practices, with the consequences we have already seen. This is proof that it is indeed the whole of the firm, with its structure and history (and, through it, the whole structure and history of the field) that are present, at every moment, in each of its strategies, and that these cannot be reduced to the instantaneous decree of a rational calculating agent.

The crisis of succession was to be followed by many more. And Phénix continued to lurch from one reorganization to another, and on into successive difficulties. In 1979, Saint-Gobain-Pont-à-Mousson sold 45 per cent of its share in the company to a number of investors, the largest of which was the Compagnie Générale des Eaux. This brought a number of changes among the team of directors. 1984–5 saw a further reorganization. Maison Phénix experienced many failures, particularly in its various development initiatives or its attempts to purchase foreign companies (an ambition it would be forced to relinquish). All the 'strengths' that had enabled it to occupy a dominant position in the field, its technical capital (the relatively economical construction method, on which its success had been based, being now discredited by its competitors), but also the symbolic capital which the authority and legitimacy of its founder represented both inside and outside the firm, the highly developed spirit of enterprise and the belief in the product, were gradually diminished without anyone being able to find – and, most importantly, impose – the new 'strengths' which a transformation of the mode of production might have afforded. This was no doubt because every one of the technical or commercial innovations required would have meant disrupting the hierarchy of the various functions and sectors of the company, in particular of the technical and commercial sectors, and hence would have necessitated a revolutionary redefinition of the systems of interest attaching to the different positions.

Thus the differentiated and structured space of *supply* or, in other words, the space of the house-producing firms (or their agents, from the directors down to the sales force) which, in order to maintain or improve their position in the structure, have to deploy production strategies – and hence products, houses – and marketing strategies – principally in the form of advertisements – that are themselves dependent on the position their 'strengths' afford them, stands in a relation of *homology* to the differentiated, structured space of *demand* or, in other words, to the space of the house purchasers. The match between supply and demand is not the product of the miraculous aggregation of countless miracles achieved by rationally calculating agents capable of making choices best suited to their interests. Contrary to appearances, there is nothing natural or obvious in the fact that the least well-off purchasers find themselves directed towards those companies offering the most basic products, particularly from the aesthetic point of view, while the others gravitate 'spontaneously' towards the firms occupying positions within the house producers' space homologous to their own position in social space, that is to say, the producers and products best suited to satisfy their taste for comfort, tradition and originality – in a word, their sense of distinction. If this match occurs, it is because the correspondence between the social characteristics of the buyers and that of the companies, and hence of their products and staff, particularly their sales staff (the companies which offer houses at the bottom of the range to the least well-off clientele, i.e. to blue- and white-collar workers, have the least qualified sales forces, often consisting of former blue-collar workers) or of their advertisements (closely linked to the social status of the clientele, itself often linked to the position of the company within the field), underpins a whole series of strategic effects which are in the main involuntary and semi-unconscious. In the light of this, for the myth of the 'invisible hand', that cornerstone of liberal mythology, we have properly to substitute the logic of the spontaneous orchestration of practices, based on a whole network of homologies (between products, vendors, buyers, etc.). This sort of 'leaderless orchestration' underlies countless strategies which we may term 'subject-less', because they are more unconscious than properly willed and calculated, such as, for example, the salesman's strategy of identifying his interests with those of his customers or himself standing surety for the transaction ('I've got the same one myself'), which is conceivable and, above all, symbolically effective, only on the basis of an affinity, guaranteed by homology of positions, between the habitus of the buyers and that of the sales staff.

APPENDIX I

INTERVIEWS

1 TWO SETS OF 'FIRST-TIME BUYERS'

Monsieur and Madame P., who have lived in a Phénix house on a 134-house estate at Le Perray-en-Yvelines in the Paris region since 1977, are among those 'new entrants' to the property market who, having very little economic, but a relatively high level of cultural or educational capital, acquired land and a house by obtaining various forms of credit. Monsieur P. was born in Tarbes. His father, who was first a house painter, then a storeman/deliveryman, came to the Paris region because he could not find work in his own area. His wife was born in Brittany where her parents were caretakers. For the first three years of their marriage they rented a flat, but they 'had always intended to buy a house, a detached house'. Monsieur P. was 35 at the time of the interview (in 1985). He has a CAP qualification as an electrician and as a diesel engine mechanic and has had various jobs in the automobile industry, first at Citroën, then at UNIT, IVECO and finally with Renault Véhicules Industriels, where he works as an electrician. Madame P., who is 32 years old and went through secondary education without obtaining a baccalaureate, was a secretary in a property company for 11 years. On the birth of their daughter, now aged two, she gave up work. She is thinking of going back to work when her child reaches school age.

At the time of buying their house, they had only a limited choice on account of their resources. They 'ended up' at Phénix at Coignières. The other homeowners on the estate are mostly quite close to them socially and would have had only a slight chance of becoming owner-occupiers in another economic situation and at another phase of the market. They are 'relatively well-off' workers, white-collar workers, post-office workers, bank clerks, insurance office staff, a few middle managers and technical staff, a primary school teacher. Two of Monsieur P.'s colleagues also live on the estate. The houses were sold very quickly, over a two-week period, in 1977. The sales people 'did not need to pressure' the customers.

Monsieur and Madame P. shopped around for their house. They 'looked everywhere', visiting show houses and the Paris trade fair. They took all the specialist magazines, sent in the coupons and got all the information. 'Mostly, it was really just descriptive catalogues. They didn't give locations, didn't show where the houses were.' Having very little to put into the purchase (around 40,000 francs in 1976), they had to find both land and a house which were not too expensive. If they had looked for the plot first, then the house a few years later, that would have been 'difficult, because it would have meant two lots of loans': 'We said to ourselves, "If they lend us money to buy the land, we won't have any to buy the house." And as you have to build within three or four years, we couldn't be doing with that. So it was as well to find something where it's all done together, the land and the house.'

They were offered a plot at Gallardon: 'We didn't want to be there. It's right out in the sticks. There's a train in the morning and another in the evening, even though it's got a bit more built-up since then. So we ended up at the Phénix office in Coignières. There, they told us: "We don't have a plot around here. There isn't anything. But, if you like, we're building a village development at Le Perray-en-Yvelines." Right for us. It was 15 kilometres further out [than Trappes, where they wanted to live], but all right.' Six or seven months later, they got 'a letter from Phénix at Coignières', asking them to come in and see the show house. So they went to Phénix, but did not buy on the first day. Monsieur P. tells the story: 'They offered us a two-bedroom house beside the new motorway route. We'd been before and seen the whole thing, the plot, and we'd said "we don't want to be there by the motorway", it hadn't been built yet, there was just the embankment ... You couldn't see it on the plans – well, hardly. There was just a line there, on the plan, and no one said it was the new route for the Nationale 10, where there's quite a bit of traffic. The only plot they offered us was that one by the new route. "Aren't there any others?" we said. There were some others, with rather oddly shaped plots, and we didn't want those either ... So that day there was nothing. We came back later and they offered us a three-bedroom house. But we wanted two bedrooms in the beginning, and we ended up with three, since we didn't want ... [trails off].' And he adds: 'The location was good, it was perfect. But there was one room too many. That made it a bit dearer at the beginning.' The house, together with the land, cost 270,000 francs in 1977: 'The starting price wasn't at all expensive,' notes Madame P. And her husband agrees: 'It was relatively cheap compared with the others.' However, the price they would eventually pay would in fact be much higher: 'With the loan, what you end up paying is twice that!'

Yet every effort was made to suggest that the house was 'cheap'. When they reserved it in 1976, they had to pay only 2,500 francs. 'You could pull out and you'd only lose 500 francs administrative costs. So, there wasn't any great risk,' explains Monsieur P. Since the amount they had to put down as a deposit was 40,000 francs, they had to look for loans. Crédit Foncier offered them a loan of 'around 126,000 francs'.[57] They also had 50,000 francs in a building society account. And then, 'because that wasn't enough', they also applied for a loan of 50,000 francs from the company Madame P. worked for. A former colleague of Monsieur P.'s, who had bought a Phénix house, said he was 'happy' with it. So Monsieur P. had no bad feelings about it. They had 'been told' that Phénix houses were 'not well soundproofed, not solid, because it was slabs of concrete, prefabricated stuff. That put me off a bit,' relates Madame P., who says a little later: 'But for us at the beginning it wasn't dear and in a place that suited us.' And Monsieur P. adds: 'We'd have liked something different, but we couldn't afford it.' Making a virtue of necessity, they thought: 'All right. It isn't any worse than the alternatives.' Both have worked very hard to improve their house, building a terrace, putting in insulation, installing double glazing, planting a kitchen garden and laying a lawn on a previously uncultivated plot. Obviously, 'the houses are a bit too close together'; and they are critical of the poor soundproofing of the walls, the size of the garage, the lack of a cellar or workshop area, the noise from the boiler, etc. The station is a long way away. The salesman had assured them a new one would be built opposite the estate, but it was actually rebuilt on the site of the previous station. The land around the house is of poor quality. When the house was built, 'the builders sold off the soil they dug up, and afterwards brought in tar and lots of rubbish they'd recovered' and put in just 10 centimetres of topsoil. It is much harder for them to list what they like about the house. They are at least satisfied in one respect: their house was not a 'catalogue home'. It does not figure in the Phénix catalogue, since an architect designed the houses specially for this programme.

They know they may stay in this house for their whole lives, but they have hopes of moving on in five or six years' time, getting 'something better'. 'Our aim', says Madame P., 'is still to have a house of our own, particularly on our own.' 'A hundred square metres of floor space would be enough for us,' adds her husband, who would very much like to have a cellar: 'To me, that's freedom.' They don't want another Phénix house or an industrially built construction. 'The ideal would be to have it built by a master-builder and to tell him, "I want it done this way."' And if they are forced to use a builder, they will be more 'demanding' than they were the first time.

Monsieur and Madame B., who in 1980 bought a Bâti Service house on a 40-house estate at Essarts-le-Roi, near Rambouillet, not far from the forest, are also among those 'new entrants' to the property market who, though located in the left-hand sector of the social space, have more economic capital, and certainly more cultural and educational capital, than Monsieur and Madame P. Monsieur B., who was 30 years old at the time of the interview (1985), was born in Algeria, where his father was a career soldier – 'the equivalent of senior supervisor level'. He arrived in France in 1962. After secondary schooling and higher education at ENSAE (the École Nationale de la Statistique et de l'Administration Économique), he joined EDF [the French national electricity company] in Paris as an engineer. His parents (his mother is a secretary) 'had pulled out all the stops to give their children a good education'. His brother is a doctor, his sister a nurse. Madame B., who was born in Tunisia, is the same age as her husband. The daughter of the owner of a small firm, she took a master's degree in computer studies, then attended the Institut d'Administration des Enterprises and is a software engineer in a large private company. They have been married for two years. They have two daughters and hope to have another child 'within the next two years'.

After initially renting a flat in the Paris suburbs, they made up their minds, as soon as they had 'a bit of money put aside', to 'go for it and buy something'. Since they could not come to terms with the small spaces of Paris apartments, but did not want to live in a block of flats ('I wouldn't feel at home in a block. The fact of sharing, of having shared areas such as the lift ... I wouldn't like that much,' explains Monsieur B.), and having 'made up their minds to commute', they started looking for 'something around 400,000 or 450,000 francs' in Saint-Quentin-en-Yvelines or the surrounding area. They almost bought a Ricardo Bofill development,[58] but they pulled out at the last minute, as there were a number of things they didn't like: the shape of the rooms, the lack of a cellar, etc. 'One day, in one of the local property papers, we saw Les Essarts-le-Roi. We knew Les Essarts and liked it. At first we thought, "we would be a bit further from Maurepas for getting in to Paris, and we don't like that much." Then we came and had a look ... Well, unfortunately, there wasn't anything to see! It was all at the planning stage. There was a big Bâti Service billboard up, and a kind of little caravan with a woman in it, bored to death. She had a nice mock-up of the estate.' After going to see a house equivalent to theirs nearby, they made up their minds within a few days. 'As regards price, it was a bit dearer than we'd bargained for (520,000 francs), but we felt we could manage if we were a bit careful.' They obtained the necessary loans without difficulty, signed a contract in 1980 and moved in in 1981. They liked the 'area' and they had 'friends' there. 'Above all, we were very happy to be truly alone ... and you could put up a little fence or hedge. We didn't have any illusions, because we knew it was still an estate, that there were problems about shared areas and the like, but really nothing like there would be in a tower block.'

Their social trajectory, their successive moves and their occupations no doubt inclined them to a somewhat disenchanted, functionalist view of their housing. What they were looking for, and what they liked in the Bâti Service house they bought was 'something functional with orderly rooms with plenty of storage ... we wanted something simple, with clean lines. When we went to see the Bâti Services houses, then frankly we didn't say: 'that's brilliant!' 'We said, "it's a good, straightforward, regulation kind of house."' But they wouldn't have had a Phénix house: 'It's a bit Merlin-Plage,[59] you know. It looks like a lifesize Meccano house and I don't think it ages well.'

Monsieur and Madame B. monitored the building of their house closely, and this enabled them to avoid some difficulties at the handover. They noticed, for example, that the kitchen window had been forgotten and put in the garage. When they told the site foreman they thought he had made a mistake, he got angry. However, two days later, everything had been put right. They have had a lot fewer problems due to bad workmanship than most of the other homeowners on the estate. For example, one neighbour had a downpipe blocked and they had to go through his kitchen floor with a pneumatic drill. But there had still been a lot of incidents: general

restrictions on the use of electricity in the first two months, garages flooded
by storms, parking areas so small and poorly designed that there are a great
many disputes, entire walls coming away, not to mention the dogs problem
– 'what with the dogs that bark and the ones that pee everywhere
(laughter), there are dogs all over.' The difficulties at the time of moving in
and the conflicts with the builder helped to foster a kind of neighbourliness
and mutual aid, but relations slowly went downhill and tensions developed.
Monsieur and Madame B. took care to remain aloof from the 'neighbourly
thing', the round of invitations, while being 'on good terms with everyone,
but superficially'. The other occupants of the estate are, in the main,
slightly older couples (aged 35–40), most of them with two children ('a
majority of public sector workers and civil servants. A lot of people
working at Renault, some at the EDF, the post office or in the civil service,
such as the Inland Revenue and the police ... middle managers and
supervisory staff, a lot of them work together').

Monsieur and Madame B. know they won't spend their whole lives on
this estate. They expect to move on in about four years' time, and they
would like their next home not to be on an estate. 'I want a fully detached
house with walls all round. That's all there is to it. I would prefer
something standing entirely alone,' declares Monsieur B., while his wife
hopes the next house will not be too isolated, not too far from the schools
or a town centre. They would like to stay in the same 'area'. From the
aesthetic point of view, they would prefer 'an old stone house', but
modern houses 'are more functional. You're sure it works because there
are no surprises. And then, it might even be quite an interesting
experience, if you can draw up the plans yourself. But, then, I don't know.
I'm a bit hesitant ...'

2 TECHNICAL CAPITAL AND ASCETIC DISPOSITIONS

Monsieur and Madame R. and their three sons live in a house that
Monsieur R. built himself, to his own specifications, on a plot his father
and grandfather had bought on the hills overlooking a mining town in the
Aix-en-Provence region. Monsieur R., who comes from a mining family
and was brought up by his grandparents, both of whom worked in the mine
– his grandmother worked grading and washing coal – is 35 years old and a
foreman in the mine. 'I work down the pit, at the coal face. I cut coal,
though we use today's modern methods, but mining will always be mining.'
His father also worked in the mine for five years before settling, after his
return from prisoner-of-war camp, in a nearby city, where he first worked
as a clerk in a tax office, before opening a chemist's shop.

Monsieur R. has built up a varied technical capital over several years.
Between the ages of 16 and 30, he studied for, and obtained, no fewer than
five vocational qualifications (CAPs) in the mine's accelerated learning
centres. 'If we start at the beginning, I was a coachbuilder (in garages).
Afterwards, I took a qualification in painting, followed by one in draughts-

manship, then qualifications as a miner, a blaster and, lastly, an electromechanical engineer. This enabled me to do the electricity, the plumbing and the heating ... and I can also turn my hand to a bit of roofing.' 'It's incredible. With all the qualifications he's got you'd think we should be millionaires (laughter), because I've got nothing! Nothing. I haven't a single vocational qualification,' exclaims Madame R., who comes from a rather humble family repatriated from Algeria, has never had a job and looks after their three sons aged fourteen, six and five.

After living in a council flat in an urban redevelopment zone (ZAC) in a nearby city for the first six years of their marriage, then in a tied company house near the mine where they lived rent-free, Monsieur R. began to build his house. Thanks to a high level of technical capital, combined with ascetic dispositions he shares with his wife ('we're both busy bees, me and him,' says Madame R.), he managed to achieve his plan with a very low amount of initial capital – around 40,000 francs – without resorting to credit. 'You can do quite a bit with 40,000 francs, you know. At the time, breeze blocks were 1 franc 75, so you could buy five or six thousand breeze blocks – enough to build two houses. So we bought the essentials for starting the house ... We can say that, with those 40,000 francs, I'd completely done the *vide sanitaire*,[60] the first screed, I'd put up the ground floor walls and I was beginning to put in the upper storey. Let's say, more or less, that I'd managed to do all the breeze blocks and the outer shell with that money, not counting the carpentry and all that.' For five or six years they made all the savings they could to be able to buy the necessary building materials. 'As he worked, the money came in, we saved up and we bought what we needed,' explains Madame R. Having decided to 'do everything for the house', they did not buy anything which was not essential. 'We didn't even buy a plate nothing, absolutely nothing. We bought food, two pairs of jeans and two pullovers a year. We can say that for five years we put everything into the house – the interior, because my husband's doing the exterior work now and we go without a lot less than we used to.' Monsieur R. has done practically everything on the house himself, with the exception of the plastering of the ceiling, the staircase and the central heating installation, for the 'good reason' that it would have taken four or five months to do these things and that would have delayed their moving in.

The building of the house, which cost 220,000 francs in total, meant that the couple had to economize severely. Perhaps even more, however, it involved a considerable investment in time. 'When I was building my house here, I was working 18 or 19 hours a day. Sometimes I got up at half past three in the morning, then worked till half past nine at night without a break, with just a sandwich between midday and two o'clock. It was like that for three years. And I never let up, Saturday and Sunday included, Christmas Day and New Year's Day too.' Monsieur R. sees himself as 'no exception. If you work down the pit, you've got to be a good worker, no doubt about it. If you weren't, you wouldn't go down the mine.' A great deal of time had to be invested in doing the work. And also in choosing the tradesmen to do the work which Monsieur R. didn't do himself or to find the best quality materials as cheaply as possible. 'Before we went out and got someone to come and work on the house, we did two months' work ourselves, asking around about particular people; the main thing was to get lots of information, to find out if the tradesman was reliable, to check that we wouldn't have to redo the work three times, because there's nothing gained by that. The point isn't really the money, but the fact we'd be wasting time,' explains Monsieur R., who a little later adds: 'We always haggle over prices with the various traders. She does it because that's how she is, being born in Algeria. For me, that's how things have always been done. You try to come to an arrangement.' But, when it comes to floor-laying, 'You can't save much. Perhaps 10 per cent all told. And you can only do that by working out what's cheapest, looking all over, searching through all the catalogues. It takes a long time and, in the end, often you don't save very much. But we've always tried to have good materials not too dear. As cheap as possible, in fact.'

It is clear the house now gives them a lot of satisfaction: 'Certainly, our house has a history. Each part of our house has a history, whereas people who buy their house signed, sealed and delivered, as they say . . .' Madame R. does not finish her sentence, pregnant with unspoken implications. A little later, she will, however, explain that taking out a 20-year loan to buy a house is too long, and, above all, 'it's not fair' because 'you pay something like three times the cost of the house.' 'And then what you also find is that the father and mother often work to cope with their debts and, unfortunately, the children . . . You see, my eldest son there, he's just home from school. It's twenty past three. He knows his mother's here and he comes home.' As for the house, they are 'proud of it. We could talk about it for hours.'

The history of their house is inseparable from their family history. They planned over many years to build it. They had 'always talked about doing it'. And, since he was 'a little boy', Monsieur R. had known he would build a house to live in here. They wanted to 'have their children' before Madame R. reached 30, so that they would avoid having the burden of housing costs and the costs of raising their children – which are particularly high during adolescence – at the same time. For them, the period of greatest deprivation is past. They go out to eat sometimes: 'not very often, but we do. We go out with our children because we're so used to having our children with us that, even if we go somewhere, we always take them with us. One of the things about us is that in spirit we're a family and we intend to remain that way. This is very important to us. Our children are part of us, and we're part of our children and our house. It all hangs together,' explains Madame R. When, after six whole years spent building the house, they went to Corsica for a holiday, they went as a family to a holiday village. They went off fishing at nine in the morning and the other families saw nothing of them. 'It's silly really. We didn't join in with the life of the camp at all. Apart from the eldest boy who went dancing one or two evenings. The fact is we can make our own entertainment.'

The internal organization of the house has been planned with the future – and old age – in mind. The bedroom and bathroom will be on the ground floor when they are no longer able to climb the stairs. They hope to be able to take advantage of Monsieur R.'s retirement, which he will take at 53, to travel and have the 'life of a couple' which they have not hitherto enjoyed, since, when they met, Madame R. already had a son by a previous marriage. They are always thinking 'forward'. They are already considering splitting their plot into three so they can build a house for each of their sons, or so their sons can build there themselves. Of course, 'nowadays you have to travel for work' and their sons will not perhaps be able to live there, but 'we'd certainly like our kids to have a house all the same, so that they have a roof over their heads.'

APPENDIX II

STATISTICAL TABLES

OWNERS AND TENANTS OF HOUSES AND FLATS

Distribution by socio-professional category

	Owners						Tenants						
	House			Flat			House			Flat			
	Île-de-France	Provinces	France	Île-de-France	Provinces	France	Île-de-France	Provinces	France	Île-de-France	Provinces	France	Total
Agric. workers	0.6	0.7	0.7	0.2	0.0*	0.1	3.5	1.9	2.0	0.3	0.5	0.4	0.6
Farmers, small	–	1.1	1.0	–	0.4	0.2	–	0.2	0.2	–	0.0*	0.0*	0.5
Farmers, medium	0.0*	1.2	1.1	–	0.1	0.1	–	0.4	0.4	–	0.0*	0.0*	0.5
Farmers, large	0.1	0.6	0.5		0.2	0.1	–	0.2	0.2		0.0*	0.0*	0.3
Retired farmers	0.3	3.9	3.5	0.2	1.4	0.9		2.5	2.3	0.1	0.8	0.6	2.0
Unskilled craftsmen	0.5	0.9	0.9	0.8	0.6	0.7	0.4	3.1	2.9	2.0	2.8	2.6	1.6
Unskilled industrial workers	1.5	3.9	3.7	1.4	1.5	1.5	5.6	9.3	9.1	3.8	7.8	6.6	4.9
Drivers	1.6	2.8	2.7	1.1	1.3	1.2	1.6	3.1	3.0	3.1	2.7	2.8	2.6
Skilled materials-handling workers	1.2	1.5	1.5	0.6	0.6	0.6	3.0	2.5	2.6	1.6	2.1	1.9	1.6
Skilled craftsmen	3.8	4.8	4.7	2.9	4.3	3.8	6.5	8.4	8.2	5.8	7.9	7.2	5.8
Skilled industrial workers	4.8	8.7	8.3	3.4	5.2	4.5	6.5	9.7	9.5	6.6	9.5	8.6	8.0
Foremen	5.9	3.7	3.9	2.6	2.2	2.4	4.6	3.1	3.2	2.3	1.4	1.7	2.8

Domestic and maintenance	0.6	0.8	0.8	1.4	0.7	1.0	0.5	1.0	0.9	2.1	2.0	2.0	1.2
Retired blue-collar workers	9.4	12.5	12.2	4.5	8.9	7.3	8.4	11.6	11.4	6.2	8.5	7.8	9.9
Craftsmen	3.0	4.0	3.9	2.0	11.5	3.0	4.6	2.3	2.4	2.1	1.8	1.9	2.9
Shopkeepers	2.6	1.8	1.9	1.9	2.3	2.2	2.1	2.0	2.0	1.2	1.4	1.4	1.7
Retired craftsmen, shopkeepers	2.6	3.9	3.8	3.4	6.4	5.3	0.4	1.3	1.2	1.1	2.0	1.7	3.0
Police	1.6	1.0	1.1	0.5	0.8	0.7	2.3	1.8	1.8	2.0	1.8	1.9	1.4
Commercial employees	0.4	0.6	0.6	0.5	0.7	0.6	2.5	0.7	0.8	1.7	2.1	2.0	1.1
Clerical, private sector, civil service	3.4	2.1	2.3	4.9	4.3	4.5	2.6	2.7	2.7	8.3	4.6	5.8	3.8
Clerical, public sector	1.8	2.6	2.6	2.1	3.0	2.7	2.4	2.3	2.3	6.3	5.3	5.6	3.6
Retired white-collar workers	6.1	5.5	5.5	6.6	6.7	6.7	3.5	3.4	3.4	6.1	5.7	5.8	5.6
Intermediate occups, civil service, commerce	5.8	3.0	3.3	7.2	3.8	5.1	6.0	2.9	3.1	5.6	3.2	3.9	3.7
Intermediate occups. public sector	1.1	1.1	1.1	0.9	1.0	1.0	1.5	1.2	1.2	1.2	1.0	1.0	1.0
Intermediate health workers	0.9	1.2	1.2	1.5	1.5	1.5	1.1	1.0	1.0	1.8	1.9	1.9	1.4
Technician	6.5	3.6	3.9	6.0	3.5	4.4	7.7	2.4	2.8	4.7	2.9	3.5	3.7
Teacher, primary	1.2	1.7	1.7	1.6	2.3	2.1	1.8	1.1	1.1	1.4	1.6	1.5	1.6
Retired intermediate occups	7.2	5.3	5.5	6.1	7.4	6.9	–	2.3	2.1	2.9	2.6	2.7	4.4
Entrepreneurs, corporate managers	0.4	0.6	0.5	0.8	1.2	1.0	–	0.1	0.1	0.2	0.2	0.2	0.5
Executive private sector, civil service senior manager	5.3	1.9	2.2	7.3	3.7	5.0	4.2	2.7	2.8	3.9	1.3	2.1	2.6

continued

Table continued

	Owners						Tenants						
	House			Flat			House			Flat			
	Île-de-France	Provinces	France	Île-de-France	Provinces	France	Île-de-France	Provinces	France	Île-de-France	Provinces	France	Total
Engineers	7.1	1.9	2.5	8.2	1.4	3.9	8.2	2.6	3.0	3.0	1.3	1.8	2.5
Executives, public sector	1.3	0.8	0.9	2.7	1.1	1.7	1.8	1.4	1.4	1.3	0.8	1.0	1.1
Teachers, sec. and higher ed.	1.7	1.2	1.2	2.1	2.0	2.0	1.0	1.2	1.2	2.0	1.2	1.4	1.4
Professionals	1.6	0.9	1.0	1.9	2.0	2.0	1.0	1.2	1.2	2.0	1.2	1.4	1.0
Artistic	0.5	0.2	0.2	1.4	0.3	0.7	1.3	0.5	0.5	1.2	0.3	0.6	0.5
Retired executives	4.1	2.6	2.8	6.6	6.7	6.7	1.3	1.0	1.0	1.9	0.8	1.2	2.5
Other	3.6	4.9	4.8	4.5	6.9	5.9	1.6	5.4	5.1	5.0	9.6	8.1	6.2
Total	100	100	100	100	100	100	100	100	100	100	100	100	100

– Nil category.
* Negligible.

Distribution by educational qualifications

| | Owners | | | | | | Tenants | | | | | | |
| | House | | | Flat | | | House | | | Flat | | | Total |
	Île-de-France	Provinces	France	Île-de-France	Provinces	France	Île-de-France	Provinces	France	Île-de-France	Provinces	France	
No qualifications	17.7	28.5	27.3	11.4	20.4	17.0	23.6	34.0	33.3	22.1	31.5	28.5	27.0
CEP[a]	46.5	48.1	47.9	32.9	42.2	38.8	37.8	40.4	40.2	35.6	39.3	38.1	42.6
BEPC[b]	14.3	9.5	10.0	15.6	14.5	14.9	11.4	10.9	10.9	14.7	12.2	13.0	11.7
Baccalaureate	7.2	5.8	5.9	12.4	9.2	10.4	10.8	5.8	6.2	10.9	7.9	8.9	7.6
DUT[c]	4.0	3.5	3.5	5.0	4.3	4.5	4.5	3.1	3.2	4.2	3.9	4.0	3.8
Degree	8.0	3.1	3.7	16.9	6.4	10.3	7.8	4.7	4.9	8.8	3.6	5.3	5.2
Other	2.2	1.5	1.6	5.8	3.0	4.0	4.0	1.0	1.2	3.6	1.5	2.1	2.1
Total	100	100	100	100	100	100	100	100	100	100	100	100	100

[a] Certificat d'Études Primaires: primary school leaving certificate.
[b] Brevet d'Études du Premier Cycle: equivalent to General Certificate of Secondary Education in the UK.
[c] Diplôme Universitaire de Technologie: two-year technical diploma, post-baccalaureate.

Distribution by income

	Owners						Tenants						Total
	House			Flat			House			Flat			
	Île-de-France	Provinces	France	Île-de-France	Provinces	France	Île-de-France	Provinces	France	Île-de-France	Provinces	France	
< 29,999 F	3.5	5.6	5.4	3.5	5.1	4.5	4.2	7.3	7.1	4.3	9.1	7.6	6.2
30–49,999 F	7.3	10.8	10.4	4.9	10.3	8.3	7.3	14.4	13.9	7.7	16.5	13.7	11.7
50–64,999 F	5.3	9.8	9.3	6.2	9.3	8.2	9.3	12.9	12.7	10.9	15.9	14.3	11.3
65–79,999 F	4.6	9.6	9.1	6.9	10.6	9.2	5.9	12.2	11.8	12.0	13.5	13.0	10.8
80–99,999 F	8.2	12.7	12.2	10.5	12.8	11.9	12.3	16.3	16.0	13.8	14.9	14.5	13.4
100–119,999 F	7.8	12.6	12.1	8.4	9.4	9.1	10.4	11.9	11.8	11.0	11.0	11.0	11.3
120–149,999 F	15.2	16.1	16.0	14.8	14.8	14.8	17.6	10.6	11.1	16.1	10.8	12.5	14.1
150–199,999 F	22.0	13.6	14.5	18.0	16.6	17.1	17.0	8.2	8.8	13.3	5.7	8.1	12.0
200,000 F+	26.1	9.1	10.9	26.7	11.0	16.8	15.9	6.0	6.7	10.8	2.5	5.1	9.2
Total	100	100	100	100	100	100	100	100	100	100	100	100	100

Source: INSEE survey, 1984; tables produced at our request.

APPENDIX III

Le Salon de la Maison Individuelle (Paris Trade Fair)

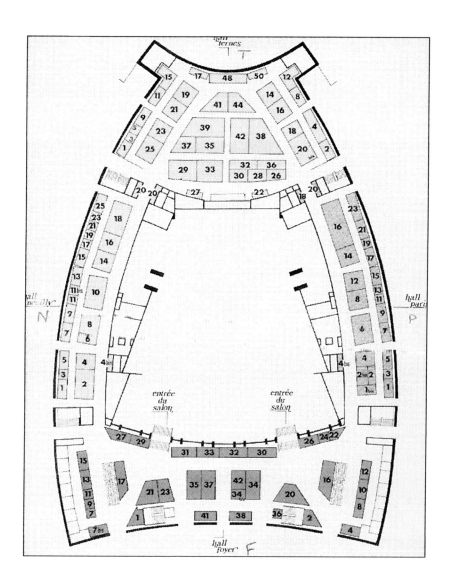

This diagram and the extract from its key overleaf are taken from the guide to the fair (*Guide de visite du Salon*, 1985, pp. 6–7).

The Salon de la Maison Individuelle, where the companies, groups or firms that want to have a presence in the market are represented (in most cases taking up space proportional to their weight in the field) provides a kind of directly legible concrete representation of the field of production (with the small, craft-based enterprises missing, of course) and of the structure of supply. So, in 1985, the largest house-building companies – Phénix, Maison Bouygues, GMF and Bruno-Petit – had large stands near to each other in a central location. Medium-sized companies were also strongly represented, the smallest most often being relegated to the smallest stands and the edges of the hall. There were, however, some exceptions. Sergeco, a medium-sized company operating only in the Île-de-France region, had a substantial stand, not far from Phénix and Maison Bouygues (the company was in an expansion phase at the time and was seeking to improve its visibility; it had, for example, recently put a show house in an unusual location – the Gare de l'Est rail station in Paris – and put up displays on several RER lines serving the Paris suburbs, etc.). There were few property developers present, doubtless because they prefer to be at other kinds of event. At the back of the hall came the representatives of government and nationalized bodies (Ministry of Urbanism, Housing and Transport, Électricité de France), the professional bodies (Union Nationale des Syndicats Français d'Architecture, Union des Constructeurs de Maisons Individuelles, Avocats Services). The banks and finance companies were relatively scattered, with some at the back of the hall and others in more central positions. As for the specialized magazines, they mostly occupied small stands (except for one, the *Indicateur Bertrand*, which had a rather more substantial one).

CONSTRUCTEURS

T 36	A.J.M. Constructions
P 5	ALRIC Société
T 26	ARVI S.A.
P 2	BATCO Société
N 19	BATISSEURS D'ARMOR
T 26	BATIVOLUME
T 14	BEAUCE PERCHE CONSTRUCTION
P 4	BERVAL
P 21	BIZZOZZERO CONSTRUCTION
P 8	BREGUET CONSTRUCTION
F 41	CARD S.A.
N 13	CARON ET CHAMBON
T 5	CASTEL CONSTRUCTIONS
N 9	CLEVERTE
N 16	CONSTRUCTEURS DES RÉGIONS DE FRANCE
N 17	CO RELA
P 20	C.T.R.
N 15	C.T.V.L. CONSTRUCTIONS TRADITIONNELLES DU VAL DE LOIRE
T 35	DONA CONSTRUCTIONS
T 34a	ENTREPRISE CURNIER (S.E.S. DUMEZ)
T 4	MAISONS BRUNO-PETIT
T 28	MAISONS CANDET
P 19	MAISON CÉVÉNOLE
N 7	MAISONS CHALET IDEAL
P 34	MAISONS COPRECO
T 37	MAISONS COSMOS-SEMIBAT
T 18	MAISONS DE L'AVENIR
T 42	MAISON DU G.S.C.I.C.
T 38	MAISONS ESTELLE
T 3	MAISON ÉVOLUTIVE – COFRA
F 18	MAISON FAMILIALE
T 25	MAISONS FRANCE CONFORT
P 13	MAISONS GOELAND S.A.
P 17	MAISON ISOLA
N 10	MAISONS KITECO
T 33	MAISONS LARA (SOCAREL)
P 6	MAISONS LELIÈVRE
P 1	MAISONS LEON GROSSE
N 14	MAISONS METAUT
N 20	MAISONS PASCAL MANTA
T 36	MAISONS PHÉNIX
N 11	MAISONS PRESTO-CONFORT
T 42	MAISONS PUMA
N 16	MAISONS ROUSILLON
P 7	MAISON SIC

LOTISSEURS

S 11bis	CENTRALE TERRAINS COGIM
T 11	IMOBEL S.A.

MATÉRIAUX

F 9	ATLANTIC
F 13	PLACOPLATRE
F 11	SURCHISTE Société
F 16	TUILES ET BRIQUES DE FRANCE

ORGANISMES DE FINANCEMENT

T 50	CIRCI
F 23	COMPTOIR DES ENTREPRENEURS
T 20	CRÉDIT AGRICOLE
T 29	CRÉDIT FONCIER DE FRANCE
T 17	FICOFRANCE
N 2	G.R.E.P. CAISSE EPARGNE ECUREUIL
Pbis10	MINISTÈRE DES P.T.T
F 27	S.A.C.I.A.C
P 1bis	SACIEP
T 21	U.C.B. Union de crédit pour le bâtiment

ORGANISMES PUBLICS,

2

The State and the Construction of the Market

The demand with which producers must reckon is itself a social product. The principle underlying it is to be found in socially constituted schemas of perception and appreciation that are socially maintained and reactivated by the actions of advertisers and of all those who, through women's magazines and magazines in the homes and gardens sector, specify, reinforce and shape expectations in the area of housing, laying their own styles of living before the public, and also by the actions of state bodies which contribute very directly to orienting needs by imposing quality standards (mainly through the action of locally based authorities, such as the departmental architects, the Direction Départementale de l'Équipement (DDE), consultant architects, etc.). However, what specifically characterizes that demand is that it is, in large part, produced by the state. The building companies, particularly the largest of them, and the banks with which they are associated, have means far more powerful than mere advertising for shaping that demand; in particular, they can influence the political decisions that are likely to orient agents' preferences by encouraging, or to varying degrees countering, the initial dispositions of potential clients through administrative measures which function to prevent or promote those dispositions being put into effect. There are, no doubt, few markets that are not only so controlled as the housing market is by the state, but indeed so *truly constructed by the state*, particularly through the financial assistance given to private individuals, which varies in quantity and in the forms in which it is granted, favouring particular social categories and, consequently, particular fractions of builders to differing degrees.

'Housing policy': from large housing estates to the single-family house

In the 1960s a neoliberal policy gained ascendancy that was ideally suited to reconcile those who, in keeping with an old traditional view, saw access to the ownership of a single-family house as a way of attaching new homeowners to the established order by ensuring that each had 'the individual right to acquire a minimum patrimony', as Valéry Giscard d'Estaing wrote in his *Démocratie française*, with those who, while at times denouncing the policy and mythology of the private house, had no measures to propose for moving beyond the usual alternative between individual housing and collective housing subsidized by the national or local community, and associated confusedly with collectivism.

The establishment in September 1966 of the mortgage market, which enabled the banks to offer long-term credit and reduce the level of deposit payable, at the very point when new forms of intervention were being offered to the financial institutions in both the banking and non-banking sectors (creation of the *compte d'épargne-logement* [homebuyers' savings scheme]; special deferred loans from the Crédit Foncier, which were replaced in 1972 by so-called 'covenanted loans' [*prêts immobiliers conventionnés*] for property purchase; extension of medium-term CCF[1] bank credit; property development loans, etc.), promoted a massive funding by the banks of construction activity, which particularly benefited the largest builders: whereas in 1962 the banks were responsible for only 21.7 per cent of housing finance, by 1972 their share of the market had risen to 65.1 per cent, while in the same period the involvement of the public sector fell from 59.7 per cent to 29.7 per cent and the share of non-financial lenders from 18.5 per cent to 5.2 per cent.

Phénix, the oldest of the construction companies, which was created in 1945, did not achieve a sizeable level of annual production (200 houses) until 1960; most of the building firms appeared in the 1960s and began early in that decade to organize in an attempt to convince the public authorities to return to a policy favourable to single-family housing. In 1961, for example, the managing director of the Phénix company founded the Syndicat des Constructeurs de

Maisons Individuelles (SMI),[2] which later became the Union Nationale des Constructeurs de Maisons Individuelles or UNCMI),[3] bringing together a small number of entrepreneurs who 'believe[d] in the development of single-family housing'. In 1962, with the support of the SMI, the Comité Interprofessionnel de la Maison Individuelle (CIMINDI)[4] was formed, with the aim of providing support for all professional initiatives furthering the building of single-family houses. The SMI played a part in developing legal provisions governing the profession (such as the law of 16 July 1971) and operated as a pressure group, particularly on mayors, arguing for the current policy of building large housing estates to be replaced by a policy of developing single-family houses. In 1968, these builders found an ally (or spokesman) in the person of Albin Chalandon, the Minister of Infrastructures and Facilities (*ministre de l'Équipment*), who made it his objective to accelerate the state's withdrawal from this field of activity (a withdrawal begun in 1966 with the creation of the mortgage market) and bring housing within the logic of the market, to promote home ownership (by developing property loans, extending housing allowance to new categories of beneficiary, and making building plots available to builders), to limit the construction of tall buildings (circular of 30 November 1972) and to encourage the building of single-family houses (among other things, by launching an international single-family house competition on 31 March 1969).

'Catalogue' building firms developed rapidly in the 1970s, encouraged by the facilities offered to clients through public channels of credit and a reduction of the levels of deposit demanded: whereas a house built to order (from a small builder, an architect, etc.) required a high capacity for saving, 'catalogue' building benefited from the highest level of loan funding and required the lowest initial down payment. The law of 16 July 1971 reorganizing all the occupations in the property industry established the single-family house construction contract, providing potential homeowners with a set of guarantees in respect of building companies and, at the same time, offering new capacities of intervention to the banking establishments, which now gave builders their backing and established close relations with the largest of them. We can see, then, that the relations of force between the large industrial enterprises and the small and medium-sized companies coexisting in the same market are dependent on 'housing policy' and, in particular, on the regulations governing public assistance to construction and the granting of loans for that purpose, introducing a whole range of acts of arbitrage between the occupants of the various positions in the field of production.

Chronicle of the genesis of a policy

The housing market is sustained and controlled, directly and indirectly, by the public authorities. The state lays down its rules of operation through a whole *set of specific regulations* over and above the normal legal infrastructure (property law, commercial law, labour law, contract law, etc.) and general regulations (price freezes or controls, credit controls, etc.). To understand the logic of this bureaucratically constructed and controlled market, we have to describe the genesis of the rules and regulations that define its operation; in other words, we have to write the social history of the closed field in which, with different purposes in view and different weapons to hand, members of the higher civil service with responsibility for housing, construction and finance matters, and representatives of private interests in the area of housing and finance confront each other. It is in the relations of force and the struggle between, on the one hand, bureaucratic agents or institutions invested with different (and in many cases competing) powers and having at times antagonistic corporate interests, and, on the other, institutions or agents (pressure groups, lobbies, etc.) which intervene to enforce their interests, or the interests of the people who elect or appoint them, that the regulations which govern the property world are defined, on the basis of antagonisms or alliances of interests and affinities of habitus. The struggles to transform or conserve legitimate representations which, once invested with the symbolic and practical efficacy of official regulations, are capable of genuinely commanding practices provide one of the basic dimensions of the political struggles for power over the instruments of state power, that is to say, generalizing Max Weber's formula, for the monopoly of legitimate physical and *symbolic* violence.

To understand 'state policy' in each of the areas that fall within the ambit of the state, one would have to know how the various positions adopted on the problems under consideration are presented, and the relations of force between the persons defending those positions; it would also be necessary to know the state of opinion of the *mobilized, organized fraction of the 'opinion-makers'* (politicians, specialist journalists, publicists, etc.) and of pressure groups (professional or employers' organizations, trade unions or consumer groups, etc.), while at the same time bearing in mind that sociological enquiry merely registers the result at a particular moment of a political labour to which the members of the higher civil service have themselves contributed, the effects of which may also be exerted on them in their turn.

The field of the higher civil service is the site of a permanent debate on the very function of the state. The civil servants closely associated with bureaucratic organizations oriented towards one or other of the great state functions (ministries, directorates, services, etc.) tend to assert and defend their existence by defending the existence of those bodies and working towards the fulfilment of those functions. But this is merely one of the underlying causes of the antagonisms that divide the field of the civil service and orient the great political 'choices', particularly, here, in the field of housing. To explain why the 'public authorities' have 'chosen', in the case of housing, to coordinate production and distribution through administrative regulation rather than to leave matters to market forces, we must further take into consideration, first, the state of social representations, whether implicit or objectified in law or regulations, which lay down that certain non-substitutable services are to be provided for all; and, second, the imperfections or shortcomings of competition and of the logic of the market which, in a determinate state of the social awareness of what is tolerable and intolerable, makes necessary an intervention aimed at protecting the interests of users of the services against unacceptable discrimination through the price mechanism. We may thus venture that the production of a good or service is the more likely to be controlled by the state the more indispensable that good or service is to what may be called *mobilized or active opinion* (as opposed to the ordinary idea of 'public opinion') and the less able the market is to deliver it.

If the field of the higher civil service has an unquestionable autonomy, rooted in its objective structures, its traditions and rules and the dispositions of its agents, the fact remains that the competitive struggles that occur within it owe their logic in part to external pressures, injunctions or influences. Each of the agents or groups of agents tends, in fact, to derive support, in order to impose its political vision (and advance its specific interests), from external forces and their spokespersons within the representative bodies (parliamentary assemblies, commissions, etc.) and to draw, more or less consciously, on the representations social agents produce individually and collectively. Genuinely to understand the state of these representations, one would have to describe the action of agents and institutions which, both within the civil service and outside it, contributed to having the right to housing included in basic French rights (by the law of 22 June 1982, paragraph 1, article 1): social reformers, family associations, trade unions, parties, social science researchers, etc. It is, in effect, the long history of all these reforming undertakings that finds its culmination in 'housing policy', as realized, at a particular moment, in a certain number of institutions (regulations, specialist bodies, procedures for financial assistance, etc.), as the provisional objectivization of a particular state of the structural relation of force between the different agents or institutions concerned that are acting to maintain or transform the status quo in this regard.

If we have chosen to focus on the period 1974–6, during which 'housing policy' was the theme of much debate and reform (the White Paper on *habitations à loyer modéré* (HLMs),[5] the Barre Commission, the Nora–Eveno Commission, and, to a lesser extent, the 'Housing Committee' of the Seventh Plan), this is because that period represents a critical moment when antagonisms came out into the open and the regulatory order that remained in force until the late 1980s was put in place. The idea of a reform of housing policy had been in the air since the early 1970s. The system of building subsidy then in force was dominated by so-called *aide à la pierre*, public financial assistance, given to match investment by a contractor, in the form of a loan at a highly advantageous rate.[6] This system of allocation, which was established by the law of 3 September 1947, was supplemented in 1948 by some limited measures (known as '*allocation logement*'[7]) of personal aid (*aide à la personne*), public financial assistance assessed on the basis of the resources and family situation, given to individuals to provide relief of part of the cost of monthly repayments on loans contracted for the purpose of purchasing a dwelling.[8] Numerous criticisms have been levelled at this system, even though it was diversified and supplemented over the years by a whole series of complementary measures. It has been criticized for producing various negative effects, such as social inequality in housing, inadequate quality of new building and the deterioration of the existing housing stock. In the late 1960s, the need for reform seemed particularly pressing in 'governing circles', as can be seen from the individual or collective thinking that informed the work of the commissions for the fifth and sixth French Plans.

The year 1965 saw the appearance of Claude Alphandéry's *Pour une politique du logement*; in 1969, the Rapport Consigny appeared, the report of a commission formed at the request of Albin Chalandon; and in 1969 too, the Commission de l'Habitation of the Sixth Plan, chaired by Claude Alphandéry, delivered its report. (Unlike Pierre Consigny, who was by then ensconced in administrative functions, Claude Alphandéry was still playing an important role as an innovator in 1975: he was head of the Building Directorate of the Ministry of Infrastructures and Facilities.) However, none of this work really challenged the principle of *aide à la pierre*. The main contribution to the thinking of the reformers was provided by two young civil servants in the Planning Directorate of the Finance Ministry (a ministry headed, at the time, by Valéry Giscard d'Estaing): Yves Carselade, *ingénieur du Génie Maritime*, and Hubert Lévy-Lambert, *ingénieur des Mines*.[9] These two young men based their work on a mathematical simulation known as Polo – a model developed to forecast the consequences of decisions in the housing field in order to criticize the aid regime then in force (the rules for allotting HLMs favoured the most creditworthy households to the detriment of the poor; personal assistance would be less expensive for the state than *aide à la pierre*) and to defend a return to market logic combined with personal (or, more precisely, personalized) assistance, varying according to the incomes and family situations of the beneficiaries. All the indications are that these two civil servants (who are included in the statistical analysis below) were mainly prompted by the entirely theoretical intention of developing a model, applied here to housing as a particular field of application, for the simulation of economic phenomena, rather than a political project for change.

It was not until the 1971–4 period that the authorities began to implement all these theoretical proposals as part of a series of reforms: the law of July 1971 creating social housing allowance, housing finance reform in 1972, the targeting of Crédit Foncier loans towards middle-income households and the creation of covenanted property loans. However, as these measures left the foundations of the system intact – that is, *aide à la pierre*, 'modulated' according to the category of housing – their only effect was to render the system considerably more complex without making it more efficient. If the evidence of Pierre Richard, a young *ingénieur des Ponts et Chaussées*, is to be believed, the idea increasingly began to spread that *aide à la pierre* had to be abandoned.

The spearhead of the reformers, formed out of the conjunctural alliance between young graduates of Polytechnique who, like their predecessors Yves Carsalade and Hubert Lévy-Lambert some years before, were striving to invent more efficient and economical ways of allocating state aid, and of young graduates of the École Nationale d'Administration (ENA) who, while being concerned, like them, to reduce the costs to the state, wanted to advance a free market vision, had to reckon with a bureaucracy of managers who, being concerned to defend their specific positions and corporate interests, proceeded with much greater caution. Antoine Jeancourt-Galignani, a young Inspector of Finances (born 1937; his father was a barrister in the Appeal Court), who would later occupy the post of *rapporteur général* to the Barre Commission, was very close to the young innovators of GRECOH, the Groupe de Recherche et d'Étude pour la

Construction et l'Habitation. This body, which functioned virtually as an economic and financial *cabinet*[10] to the Construction Directorate, had within it, alongside an *énarque*[11] like Jacques Lebhar (born 1946; his father a financier), a majority of *polytechniciens*,[12] such as Georges Crepey (born 1943), who graduated from the École des Ponts et Chaussées in 1967 and was, successively, head of the Economic Research Office of GRECOH (until 1971), head of the Statistics and Economic Research Service at the Direction du Bâtiment, des Travaux Publics et de la Construction (DBTPC)[13] and, finally, in 1974, director of GRECOH in the Construction Directorate – a man who was to play the crucial role of deputy *rapporteur* (deputy to Antoine Jeancourt-Galignani) to the Barre Commission, and who also had connections with Pierre Durif, the head of the Housing Research Division of INSEE and creator of the Allo model for dealing with housing allowance (whose work on the single-family house market, cited above, was regarded as authoritative). This network of researchers and research services, which aimed to continue the work of Yves Carsalade and Hubert Lévy-Lambert by giving it more concrete form, played a crucial role in conferring the authority of the coherence and rigour of formal models on that reforming intent. (We see, in passing, against the charge of 'holism' which one attracts as soon as one pays the slightest attention to the social properties of agents, that the approach chosen here restores the interest in individuals, and in individuals restored to their full dignity as agents acting by virtue of their embodied social properties – their habitus – and hence different and unequal.)

The debates conducted within the bureaucratic field are clearly not unrelated to external discussions and conflicts, to which higher civil servants refer, and which they call on to support or justify their positions and projects. This is particularly the case in respect of the HLM movement. The 1972 reforms (modification of the assisted loans regime; expansion of housing allowance and provisions for the renovation of old housing stock) were not sufficient to eliminate the disadvantages of *aide à la pierre*. In spite of a further breakdown of the categories of housing and the creation of housing allowance, the least well-off families could not gain access to social housing, which provided certain beneficiaries with something akin to a guaranteed, permanent benefit in kind. Increasing the number of categories of housing, instead of having the opposite effect as intended, merely produced greater social and spatial segregation. At the 35th HLM Congress (10–13 June 1974), the Union des HLM and its president, Albert Denvers, expressed alarm at the deterioration of social housing and elaborated a series of measures for immediate application. But these arrangements were upset three months later by the appointment of Robert Lion, the head of the Construction Directorate, as president of the Union.

'It was already quite bizarre for an *inspecteur des Finances* to be in the Construction Directorate; but to go and take over responsibility for the HLM movement! ... I wasn't going down the usual career path ... I liked the HLMs ... It was to some degree a suicide mission ... There was a general deadlock, a great state of tension. I went to HLMs in the summer of 1974. I realized it would take a serious shake-up to get things moving. I took an oppositional stand on housing policy in a way that was regarded as shameful by many. At that point the idea formed of creating a broad movement of reflection around the HLMs – and a broad movement of opinion, as I would put it. The HLMs didn't know where they were going. A project was needed. And that's how, in 1974 we launched the working groups, with a great hullabaloo, which were to lead to the White Paper and which preceded the Barre Commission. The Barre Commission was a riposte mounted by the Élysée,[14] particularly by Pierre Richard, who was in charge of housing matters at the Élysée (interview, Paris, Jan. 1988).

So, between November 1974 and March 1975, when the HLM Congress was held at Grenoble, 450 people – trade unionists, elected local politicians, financiers, private builders and representatives of the HLM movement – organized in four commissions, chaired by Jean Turc, Claude Alphandéry, Hubert Dubedout and Claude Gruson, carried on a lively debate on the problems posed by social housing. In May 1974, the election to the presidency of Valéry Giscard d'Estaing, whose ministry had provided a home for the first econometric studies of housing and who had made a certain number of commitments in that area, brought decisive backing for the liberally inclined reformers. Jean-Pierre Fourcade became Minister of the Economy and Finances; Robert Galley was made Minister of Infrastructures and Facilities; Jacques Barrot was appointed Secretary of State for Housing and Pierre Richard, an *ingénieur des Ponts et Chaussées*, born in 1941, who had been a technical adviser to Christian Bonnet when he was Secretary of State for Housing, became technical adviser to Valéry Giscard d'Estaing, where his work would be framed within the context of the policy of 'advanced liberalism' that the new president was to implement during the first part of his seven-year term. Richard, who was now responsible for problems of town planning and housing at the Élysée, was at the hub of the thinking on housing between 1974 and 1976. He it was who suggested to the President that he set up a 'British-style' commission to tackle housing reform, on the lines of the Sudreau Commission; he, too, was to provide the link between the HLM movement and the commission. Given the stirrings within the HLM movement, things developed rapidly: 'We prodded them into action,' Robert Lion was to say later. Knowing that innovations could not begin in the Infrastructures Ministry and that the Infrastructures and Finance ministries would 'always be at daggers drawn', Pierre Richard proposed doing 'something consensual'. His idea was to start a great national debate on housing around a totally independent commission, which, without committing the state, could hear all the parties concerned, while avoiding any open conflict with the HLM movement. In autumn 1974 countless discussions on the make-up of the commission took place between Valéry Giscard d'Estaing, his adviser Pierre Richard and the Secretary of State for Housing, Jacques Barrot.

The National Commission on Housing Reform was officially created by the Council of Ministers on 22 January 1975, at almost the same time as the publication of a White Paper on the HLMs was announced. The list of the ten members of the commission, which was published at the end of that same Council of Ministers, was criticized for the high proportion of so-called 'financiers' on it. The two key appointments, that of *rapporteur général* and deputy *rapporteur général*, went to Antoine Jeancourt-Galignani, the former director of Construction Funding at the Treasury Directorate – an appointment made out of consideration for the Finance Ministry – and Georges Crepey, an *ingénieur des Ponts* and director of GRECOH – an appointment made to reassure the Ministry of Infrastructures and Facilities, but the latter individual, breaking with the most widely held Infrastructures doctrine, was to question the system of *aide à la pierre*. The commission's first session took place on 28 February 1975 (at a point when the White Paper on the HLMs was being drafted). The commission worked very quickly, because Raymond Barre was able to submit his report on 23 December 1975.

From the interviews we have been able to carry out with the various members of this commission, it seems that the 'dominant personalities' were Pierre Richard, who, although he was not a member of the commission, followed its work very closely, reported back to the Élysée and attempted to form a bridge to the HLM movement; Pierre Durif, who helped the *rapporteurs* with the building of forecasting models; Michel Mauer, a property developer with Cogedim, who represented private property development; while Michel Saillard, the director general of SCIC (Société Centrale Immobilière de la Caisse des Dépôts) and spokesperson for the major subsidized programmes, defended *aide à la pierre* and Henri Charrière, the director of planning and research at the Compagnie Bancaire, expressed the positions of his bank in a plea for market operation in all its purity. Raymond Barre, who tacitly supported the young reformers without openly declaring his own position, left great latitude to the two *rapporteurs*, who, after a few months, presented him with a draft report that he was able to approve since it was in keeping with his convictions as a liberal economist.

The structure of the bureaucratic field

Having outlined the history of the innovative initiatives that prepared the ground for the reform of housing subsidy, we may attempt to determine what in 1975, on the eve of that reform, was the structure of the distribution of forces (or 'strengths') between the *effective agents*, that is to say, between the individuals who had sufficient influence effectively to orient housing policy because they possessed one or other of the active properties in the field. Once we have established this structure, we can go on to examine whether, as we might suppose, the positions they take up in the struggles to preserve or transform the regulations in force correspond to the positions the agents (or bodies of agents) occupy within that structure: whether, in other words, objective differences in the distribution of interests and 'strengths' can explain the strategies adopted in the struggles and, more precisely, the alliances formed within those struggles or the divisions into separate camps.[15]

To determine the list of effective individuals, we have proceeded by trial and error, bringing in, alongside criteria 'of reputation', derived from the analysis of published accounts and interviews, institutional criteria, such as acknowledged positions of power. Using a procedure which has inevitably to be followed in similar cases, we were able to exit from this 'hermeneutic circle' only by a constant back-and-forth movement between identifying the agents socially designated as 'important' and making explicit the principles practically deployed in this identification process; this made it possible gradually to furnish this process with a precision and rigour it did not necessarily have in practice: the delimitation of the population of effective individuals – heads of the major directorates of the ministries concerned, directors of banks, property developers, heads of professional bodies, directors of HLM offices, etc. – enabled us to make explicit the 'strengths' which conferred that effectiveness on them, while the determination of active properties forced us, in turn, to specify the population of agents which, because they are endowed with these properties, are most likely to be effective.

Among higher civil servants we thus selected a set of people occupying strategic positions in the space of powers relating to housing. At the

Finance Ministry, where the civil servants with responsibility for housing concerns are very few in number, we selected the representatives of the departments concerned with the reforms: the Treasury Directorate, bureau A3 responsible for construction funding, the Budget Directorate, in particular, bureau 5D with responsibility for housing and town planning, and the Forecasting Directorate.

At the Ministry of Infrastructures and Facilities, created in 1966 and consisting of very complex central and local structures, we selected the Construction Directorate, responsible for the management of *aide à la pierre* (and hence responsible for 400,000 dwellings in 1974), for the supervision of contractors (HLMs and mixed economy companies) and for the drafting of the legal framework for construction. Attached to this directorate are the Groupe Permanent pour la Résorption de l'Habitat Insalubre (GIP), the Agence Nationale pour l'Amélioration de l'Habitat (ANAH), which between them are responsible for rehabilitating old housing stock, 'le plan Construction', an innovation of Robert Lion's, which was intended to stimulate research into, and innovation in, housing conditions, the Groupe Habitat et Vie Sociale[16] (for large housing schemes), the Service des Affaires Économiques et Internationales (SAEI)[17] and GRECOH. This latter body, created around 1968–9 and given the task of researching a new housing policy, was an economic and financial *cabinet* within the Construction Directorate; it had connections to the state financial bodies, such as the Family Allowance Fund etc.

Another department of the Infrastructures Ministry, the Direction de l'Aménagement Foncier et de l'Urbanisme (DAFU)[18] which regulates construction (plans, outline plans, planning permission), was responsible for new towns, urban development zones (ZACs), and projects for urban renovation and property restoration, while also overseeing land use policy ('future development zones', reserved areas); we also included the Directions Départementales de l'Équipement (DDE), the external services of the Infrastructures Ministry, which are almost totally dominated by *ingénieurs des Ponts et Chaussées*. Of the departments attached directly to the Prime Minister's office, we selected the Commissariat Général du Plan et de la Productivité, the Groupe Central des Villes Nouvelles and the Commission Nationale des Opérations Immobilières et de l'Architecture.[19]

In the Ministry of the Interior, the General Directorate for Local Authorities was the parent organization for local authorities and for those HLM offices attached to them; the Délégation à l'Aménagement du Territoire et à l'Action Régionale (DATAR),[20] which was restored to the Interior Ministry after the election of Valéry Giscard d'Estaing, played a role in decentralization, rural renewal (with the so-called 'contrats de pays') and the promotion of small towns.

The Architecture Directorate, which previously came under the Ministry of Cultural Affairs, where it played a very important role (it oversaw the application of the Malraux law on conservation areas), was moved to the Infrastructures Ministry in the early 1970s, then merged with the Town

Planning Directorate, with the result that the architects came under the control of the *ingénieurs des Ponts et Chaussées*. At the Ministry of Health, the Social Security Directorate was responsible for overseeing the family allowance funds, which managed housing allowance.

In the para-public and semi-public sectors, we identified the following as worthy of inclusion: the Caisse des Dépôts et Consignations,[21] the SCIC and a certain number of public capital works establishments or mixed economy companies, the Crédit Foncier de France, the Comptoir des Entrepreneurs and the HLM movement, which in 1975 comprised more than a hundred separate organizations, grouped in five categories: the public offices of the HLM, created on the initiative of a local authority and providing rented accommodation; the public offices of capital works and construction; the HLM limited companies providing rented accommodation and starter homes; the HLM cooperatives, providing services and managing loans to new homeowners; and the Société de Crédit Immobilier de France, offering property or housing improvement loans. The public housing authority was very close to the Construction Directorate and, though not greatly present in the struggles over housing policy, except on specific demands, it reacted sharply, through its president Albert Denvers, a socialist MP from the Nord département, against the suggestions of certain groups involved in the Sixth Plan who wanted social housing returned to the market economy. Robert Lion became *délégué general* in late 1974, breathing new life into the movement.

In the private sector, we selected the Union Nationale des Constructeurs de Maisons Individuelles, a body founded in 1961 by Claude Pux, the managing director of the family building company Phénix, which was originally known as the Syndicat des Constructeurs de Maisons Individuelles and whose stated aim was to convince the public authorities to return to a policy favourable to single-family housing, to which end it participated in drawing up regulations governing the profession and was represented on all the consultative bodies, administrative groups, parliamentary commissions and professional federations in the building trade, both centrally and at regional and local level, where it advocated the reorganization of channels of funding and argued for local authorities to have control of urban development (against '*dirigiste*' town planning and the large 'housing schemes'); the developer-builders most active in struggles over construction policy (there are 550 of these in all, grouped in the National Federation of Developer-Builders, producing 100,000 homes a year, two-thirds of them with state aid); the most involved of the banking establishments, which were beginning to play an increasing part in housing finance (29 per cent in 1965, 54 per cent in 1972): the Crédit Agricole and the Crédit Mutuel, four of whose local funds gave preferential financial treatment to households, distributed covenanted property loans and provided support to the HLM societies. We also selected three specialist banking establishments, the Union de Crédit pour le Bâtiment, the Banque pour la Construction et l'Équipement and the Banque de la Construction et des Travaux Publics.

We also chose the landlords' national body, the Union Nationale de la Propriété Immobilière (UNPI), which campaigned against the 1948 law on rent control and called for a return to a free market in the rented sector; the main tenants' movement, the Confédération Nationale du Logement (CNL), whose president was Claude Massu, the author of a work entitled *Le Droit au logement* (The right to housing), published by Éditions Sociales,[22] which recommended the maintenance of regulation and the extension of housing allowance; and users' movements, such as the Union Nationale des Allocations Familiales (UNAF) and the Union Départementale des Associations Familiales (UDAF), very closely linked to the local family allowance funds.

Lastly, we selected those local elected politicians involved in the HLM movement (in 1976, 128 deputies and senators, 700 regional councillors or members of the regional economic and social committees were involved in the management or direction of HLM bodies) or belonging to boards of other organizations in the construction sector (mixed economy companies, for example) who, in one respect or another (involvement in commissions, specialization in housing issues, etc.) contributed to influencing housing policy.

To characterize each of the personalities, we have taken into account their age, sex, birthplace, social origins, marital status (and number of children), secondary and higher education, honours received, the *corps* and sector to which they belong, participation in various specialist commissions, all of this information being derived from interviews with the persons concerned or with various informants and also from various works of analysis or testimony (see bibliography in appendix II, p. 125).

In an attempt to get beyond mere description, to which the most useful of the analyses of the operation of bureaucratic organizations have confined themselves, we would like to propose here a genuine *explanatory model* of individual and collective strategies. Having taken into account the full range of effective agents (individuals and, through them, institutions) and the full range of properties – or 'strengths' – underlying the effectiveness of their action, we may confidently call on correspondence analysis,[23] which, *when used in this way, is in no sense the purely descriptive method which those who contrast it with regression analysis contend*, to bring to light the structure of positions or – and this amounts to the same thing – the structure of the distribution of specific interests and powers that determines and *explains* the strategies of the agents and, as a consequence, the history of the main interventions which led to the elaboration and implementation of the law on building subsidies.

In fact, correspondence analysis brings out a first predictable opposition (the first factor represents 6.4 per cent of the total inertia) between the members of the highest reaches of the public service, that is to say the bureaucratic field properly so called, and the external social forces with which that field has to reckon, the representatives of private interests, such as the property developers (and in particular the spokespeople of the UNCMI and the Comité Interprofessionnel de la Maison Individuelle), the bankers, and also the local or national elected representatives specializing in housing questions, the regional housing officers (such as the directors of public establishments for the development of new towns etc.) or, lastly, the directors of bodies oriented towards the social management of housing (such as the directors of housing offices or of family allowance funds).

Being in many cases themselves the products of families already active in the higher reaches of the public service, and having been educated at the most prestigious secondary schools (Janson-de-Sailly) and the foremost *grandes écoles*, the top-ranking civil servants, with a mandate from bureaucratic institutions (such as the Treasury Directorate, the Construction Directorate, etc.) whose interest they espouse, among other things through a sense of professional solidarity, are endowed with a specific capital of competence linked to their educational background and also, most importantly, to the bureaucratic experience they have accumulated over their careers within the higher civil service. The agents situated at the opposite pole share a lack of experience of the higher reaches of the civil service and also generally lack the scarce educational qualifications held by higher civil servants (though they have in most cases received a higher education).

In the intermediate positions, we find, among others, the directors of public or private banks, who are often united by old-school-tie connections and professional solidarities, some of whom have successively occupied – thanks to the 'revolving doors' phenomenon – positions on either side of the centre of the space. This is the case, for example, with Antoine Jeancourt-Galignani who, after having played, as we have seen, a determining role in the preparation of the new measures, first as director of the Construction Finance Office, then as *rapporteur général* of the Barre Commission, was to participate in the discussion of the implementation of these measures as a representative of the Crédit Agricole; with the *inspecteur des Finances* Claude Aphandéry, who, after chairing the Housing Commission of the Sixth Plan, found himself head of the Banque de Construction et des Travaux Publics and managing director of the Immobilière building consortium; with Jean-Pierre Fourcade, the Minister of the Economy and Finance in Jacques Chirac's government, who was formerly managing director of the CIC banking group (affiliated to the Compagnie Bancaire de Suez); or, again, with Marcel Diebolt, the former Prefect of Paris, who subsequently became chairman of the Société Auxiliaire de la Construction Immobilière (SACI) and of the Banque pour la Construction et l'Équipement, etc. There is a particularly high level of interpenetration between the higher reaches of the public service and the semi-public or private sector in banking. In that sector, the same institution – the Compagnie Bancaire, for example – is represented by directors situated in different positions in the first dimension.

This first factor brings out the fundamental structure of the social space within which that *typically bureaucratic form of consultation that is the 'commission'* carries out its work: the bureaucratic field can fulfil the function of legislator only if, following procedures that remain under its control, it confronts official representatives of the officially recognized interests who, even when regional or public authorities, local or national elected representatives and accredited representatives of professional organizations or associations are concerned, are relegated to the camp of individual, private interests and condemned, as a result, to occupy a position subordinate to those who, by statute, have a monopoly of the legitimate definition of the general interest. Having control over the composition of the group of participants, into which, alongside the inevitable representatives of the professional organizations, they can bring isolated personalities prepared to support their initiatives, and being able to lay down the rules by which the discussion is conducted and the conclusions are recorded (among other things, by appointing the chairs and *rapporteurs*), the agents of the state are able to present an image, both to others and to themselves, of confronting the outside world in an open manner, while retaining monopoly control over the preparation of collective decisions, the implementation of those decisions and the assessment of their outcomes.

If the various commissions each have their specific history, there are, nonetheless, some invariant features and these can be seen particularly clearly in the case of the Barre Commission. First, a certain number of ideas which are in the (bureaucratic) air, such as 'the withdrawal of the state', 'debudgetization of the aided sector', etc., bring together a number of reforming civil servants around the conviction that the Plan is not the appropriate place to develop a reform of housing policy, because the widely differing and irreconcilable interest groups represented on that body cancel each other out. Second, the composition of the commission, carefully worked out at the highest level of the state, in a sense predetermines

The field of effective agents with regard to housing finance in 1975

Individuals
Horizontal axis 1, vertical axis 2 (n = 97)

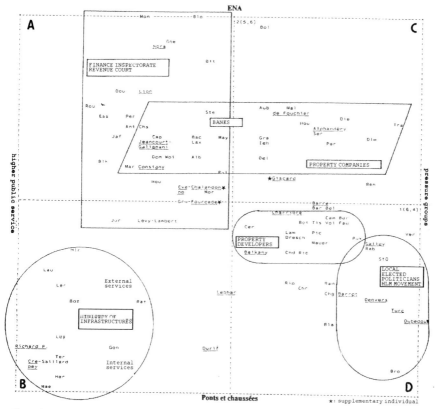

For the results and sources of the analysis, see appendices, pp. 123–5.

the outcomes it will be able to achieve: the three dominant personalities, Raymond Barre, who, despite his familiarity with the traditions of ministerial *cabinets*, knew little of the mechanisms of housing funding and had little involvement in that world, and who, as an economist, was known for his liberal ideas, and Antoine Jeancourt-Galignani and Georges Crepey, both of them specialists in the problems of housing finance, represented *a whole programme* in themselves. The two *rapporteurs*, who, with cover provided by a prestigious chairman, were to do the main part of the work of conceiving and drafting the report, had, together with Pierre Durif, presented a set of coherent proposals for a reform of housing finance policy shortly before the commission was created; through their

The field of effective agents with regard to housing finance in 1975

Active and supplementary variables
Horizontal axis 1, vertical axis 2

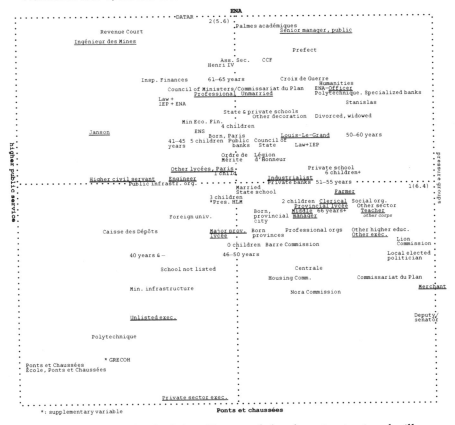

positions, they embodied the alliance of the three institutional pillars of innovative action: the Treasury (and the Finance Inspectorate), the Infrastructures Ministry (and the Ponts et Chaussées) and the research services (with INSEE). As a kind of *bureaucratically appointed and recognized active minority*, they were the ideal candidates for inspiring and guiding the *work of universalization* of which the commission, though it was not actually very diverse, was to make great show. The logic by which the commission was formed was an (unconscious) practical exemplification of the law that one contributes to producing discourse (here the final report) by producing the social space, materially embodied in a group, within which that discourse is produced. (We can see, in passing, how pointless it would be, at least in this case and doubtless more generally, to seek in discourse alone,

The field of effective agents with regard to housing finance in 1975

Individuals
Horizontal axis 1, vertical axis 3 (n = 97)

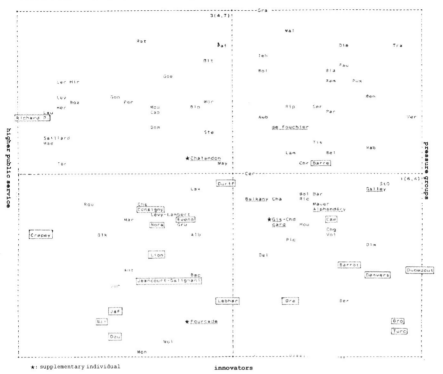

★: supplementary individual   **innovators**

as some advocates of 'discourse analysis' do, the laws of construction of discourse, which in fact reside in the laws of construction of the space of production of the discourse.)

However, neither the representatives of the public authorities, nor the spokespeople for private interests (or at least those who appear as such from the viewpoint of the bureaucratic claimants to monopoly control over the definition of the general interest) form homogeneous groupings. There are objective divisions within them and these find expression in their confrontations. The second factor (which represents 5.6 per cent of the total inertia) shows up another opposition, which relates particularly to the bureaucratic field, between, on the one hand, the 'financiers', who are in many cases products of the École Nationale d'Administration and the Inspection des Finances, people closely linked to the government (and in particular to the *cabinet* of the Prime Minister or of ministers

The field of effective agents with regard to housing finance in 1975

Individuals
Horizontal axis 2, vertical axis 3

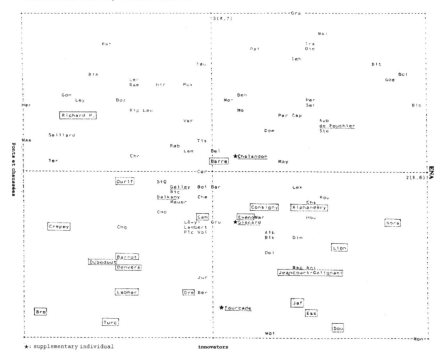

★: supplementary individual   **innovators**

concerned with housing) or to para-administrative bodies such as DATAR (the Delegation for Regional Development and Regional Action) and belonging to the Ministry of Finance or to private or public banks (and having public recognition in the form of various honours, particularly the Croix de Guerre), and, on the other, the 'technicians', who in many cases are sons of executives in the private sector, with a background in the École Polytechnique and the *corps des Ponts et Chaussées*, linked to the Infrastructures and Facilities Ministry and to GRECOH and members of the Nora Commission (and also, at the other end of the first axis, local elected representatives).

In the first of the sectors, sector A, determined by the first two axes, are grouped members of the higher civil service and the public banking sector, most of them from the *grands corps* (Inspectorate of Finance, Revenue Court, Council of State) and often heads of directorates of the Finance Ministry or members of ministerial *cabinets* or so-called delegations, such as DATAR. Closer to the centre we find executives from the public and private banking sector, the Crédit Foncier de France, Crédit Agricole and Paribas.

Sector B brings together *ingénieurs des Ponts et Chaussées* who are graduates of the École Polytechnique and are, in many cases, sons of senior private sector managers or industrialists. These 'engineers' are employed by the Infrastructures Ministry, an example being Georges Crepey (the son of a very high-ranking civil servant), who was to be at the centre of debates, or by public and mixed economy property development bodies.

In sector C we find almost exclusively directors of companies (often mixed economy companies) or bankers – belonging to public banking establishments specializing in construction, such as the Crédit Foncier or to popular or mutualist banks or, alternatively, to private banks. A number of these are former higher civil servants (particularly Inspectors of Finance) benefiting from their private sector contacts. They are older than the members of the other sectors and are mostly of more lowly social origins and generally more provincial.

In sector D we find mostly representatives of institutions specializing in social housing (HLM offices) and of professional groupings and also elected representatives at local and national level. This is also where INSEE, the General Planning Authority and the commissions responsible for preparing reforms are to be found. We see here some of the 'innovators': Pierre Durif, Jacques Lebhar, Michel Dresch, all of them young modernizing technocrats, and Jacques Barrot, Hubert Dubedout and Jean Turc, elected politicians who supported reform.

As for axis 3, this very clearly isolates the group of innovators. Though highly dispersed along the first two axes (there are among them Inspectors of Finance who graduated from the École Nationale d'Administration, and *ingénieurs des Ponts* from the École Polytechnique, but also higher civil servants and local government politicians – city mayors in particular), they share a certain number of secondary properties that distinguish them from their first category of membership, such as, for the higher civil servants, their relative youth, their high-born social origins (they are very often the sons of very senior public sector managers), their membership of research bodies and, in the case of elected politicians at national or regional level, their translocal notoriety and receptiveness to central problems.

On the one side we find young innovative higher civil servants occupying positions at DATAR, in the very active research departments of the Ministry of Infrastructures and Facilities – SAEI (International Economic Affairs Department), GRECOH (Research Group on Construction and Housing) – or at the Division for Housing Research of the national statistical office, INSEE: Jacques Lebhar, a graduate of ENA and an *administrateur civil*, head of GRECOH's Office of Financial and Fiscal Studies and a very active member of the Nora–Eveno Commission; Georges Crepey, an alumnus of Polytechnique and *ingénieur des Ponts et Chaussées*, but also a graduate of Sciences Politiques,[24] who was deputy *rapporteur* of the Barre Commission and a member of the Nora Commission; Antoine Jeancourt-Galignani, the Inspector of Finances who in 1969 was *chargé de mission* with Valéry Giscard d'Estaing, and then was head of the Office of Construction Funding at the Treasury Directorate and who, since 1973, had been deputy general director of the Caisse de Crédit Agricole; Michel Dresch, a close associate of Robert Lion's, *rapporteur* of the two working groups of the Lion Commission, who had also been head in 1972 of GRECOH's Office of Financial and Fiscal Studies. Close to these modernizing higher civil servants, we find local or national politicians who played an important role in the commissions, such as Jean Turc and Hubert Dubedout, members of the Barre and Lion Commissions, or Eugène Berest, a member of the Housing Committee of the Seventh Plan.

At the opposite pole come civil servants who are often older and less highly qualified, occupying positions in the public establishments linked to the Ministry of Infrastructures or in administrative departments. These people have often received the highest state honours (Croix de Guerre, Légion d'Honneur), many of them being Prefects or bankers in the public or private sector occupying multiple positions; only very seldom are they members of the various different commissions and they are, in general, not particularly favourable to their conclusions.

The space of positions and the space of position-taking

This analysis of the field of forces is not an end in itself and its implications are revealed in full only if we compare the various positions within the field to the positions adopted by their occupants in the debates leading up to the 1976 reform. In other words, it maps out a set of differential, and at times antagonistic positions, the occupants of which will organize into separate *camps* as the crisis caused by the reform projects unfolds. The positions taken both by individuals and by *corps* (though these are never entirely unanimous) tend, in fact, to be distributed between two poles: on the one hand, the position that the regime of building subsidies (*aide à la pierre*) should be maintained, either without modification – a position which was doubtless very uncommon – or combined with some form of personal assistance (*aide à la personne*); on the other hand, the complete abandonment (proposed by the Barre Commission) of building subsidies in favour of personal assistance.

The *explanatory effectiveness* of the correspondence analysis can be seen from the fact that the correspondence between the space of positions in the field and the space of position-taking by the protagonists is almost perfect. The Treasury civil servants subscribe to the pure form of the liberal vision, as proposed by the Barre Report, and reject the mixed solution combining building subsidies with personal assistance: in their concern to promote the 'withdrawal of the state', they wish to see forms of personal assistance that can compensate for the suppression (or reduction) of building subsidies (which would be reserved, if need be, for the most deprived) extended to all categories of household; taking the view that the private housing 'stock' is no concern of the state, they reject the idea of public assistance for the maintenance and improvement of the social housing 'stock' (the HLMs). As for the Budget Directorate, though the director himself favoured personal assistance and was, more generally, quite close to the Treasury positions, the Budget departments were inclined to retain building subsidies and feared the consequences of personal assistance partly financed from the Budget. Having a primary responsibility for construction, the Ministry of Infrastructures could not view with equanimity any interruption or slow-down of building, in which it had an interest (in one sense, a very direct interest through the percentages paid to the *ingénieurs des Ponts et Chaussées*). At that ministry, then, the desire was to see the current system maintained, albeit with some modifications. And that desire was particularly strong in the departments concerned with the management of building subsidies and oversight of the HLM bodies.

It was in the research departments, foremost among them GRECOH, the Forecasting Directorate, the Housing Division of INSEE and the Statistics and Economic Research Service of the DBTPC (the Directorate of Building, Public Works and Construction), that the clearest wish was expressed either for the personalization of building subsidies (the preferred option of GRECOH) or for their suppression and the introduction of personal assistance partly financed from the Budget. Outside the ranks of the higher civil service, the public or private contractors in industry and construction were close to the positions of the most advanced thinkers in the Infrastructure Ministry: they supported the continuation of building subsidies, but in a personalized form and, at any event, at reduced levels.

In this debate, then, the Finance and Infrastructures ministries (very much opposed on the second axis) deployed antagonistic, if not indeed irreconcilable, arguments, with the Finance Ministry campaigning for the pure and simple substitution of personal housing assistance for building subsidies, which they regarded as too expensive, while the Infrastructures Ministry, linked to the HLM movement and to social builders, wanted personal assistance to remain merely supplementary. Ranged in the camp of the 'liberal' reformers, then, were the following personalities: the President of the Republic and his *cabinet* (among others, Pierre Richard, closely linked to GRECOH; during the summer of 1976 he was to take on the main part of the preparatory work for the new parliamentary bill), Jean-Pierre Fourcade, who merely had reservations over the date at which the proposed new legislation was to come into force, Robert Galley, who after initial reticence came to favour personalized housing assistance (APL), provided that it was arranged in such a way as to enable 'humble households' to accede to home ownership, and Jacques Barrot, the Minister of Infrastructures, who would become a very vigorous advocate of the new policy. Against the project, on the Infrastructures side, were the HLM movement, which, through Robert Lion, had organized an extraordinary congress intended to control and head off radical liberalism (as advanced by the Barre Commission), by sacrificing what could not be saved and proposing a policy of moderate liberalism, combining personal assistance and building subsidies, and which criticized the reduction of the activity of the building societies (*sociétés de crédit immobilier*); the Crédit Foncier (responsible for special payments to builders of new houses and for special loans) and the Crédit Mutuel, which was henceforth to be excluded from the management and distribution of new loans, most of which would be taken over by the Crédit Agricole; the Caisse des Dépôts et Consignations; the family allowance funds, which found it difficult to adapt to the new regime, but which would be responsible for distributing personal housing assistance; the parties of the left, particularly the Communist Party; and, more generally, the local or national politicians of all persuasions involved with HLM bodies. The resistance mounted by these organizations and individuals, which could be seen in the preparatory stages of the reform, was to be manifested even more clearly in the phases of its elaboration and implementation, particularly on the part of the Directions Départementales de l'Équipement (DDEs), who were most unhappy to see their traditional relationships with the social builders, the HLMs, overturned, and who often formed alliances with local builders and with elected representatives of all political persuasions. (The National Liaison Committee for a Social Housing Policy, formed in July 1976 and representative of the entire 'social' housing sector – Association pour le Logement Familial, Association des Maires de

France, Caisse Nationale des Allocations Familiales, Confédération du Logement, Fédération Nationale du Bâtiment, Union des Caisses d'Épargne, Union Nationale des Associations Familiales, Union Nationale des Fédérations d'Organismes HLM, Union Nationale Interprofessionnelle du Logement, etc.[25] – condemned the withdrawal of the state and the encouragement, to the exclusion of all else, of the acquisition of ownership of single-family houses.)

The 'reasons' for the adoption of these various positions are different in each case. However, where administrative bodies are concerned, the main underlying factor is the tendency of bureaucratic institutions (and the corresponding civil servants) to 'persevere in being', that is to say, the concern to prevent a bureaucratic body losing all *raison d'être* by losing its function. This is particularly clear in the case of the Infrastructures Ministry which, being expressly mandated to promote construction, and, most particularly, the construction of social housing such as HLMs, saw in the complete abandonment of building subsidies the disappearance of one of its main reasons for existing: building subsidies, which needed managing, provided a purpose and justification for the activity of a body of civil servants who, with the return to market logic and individual laissez-faire, would see all their functions of promotion and control disappear. This tendency to self-perpetuation on the part of bureaucratic authorities, and of the persons who owe their bureaucratic existence and *raison d'être* to them, is the explanation for the oft-deplored inertia of these institutions, though it is also responsible, when these institutions are the products of social advances, for the perpetuation of structures and functions that are independent of the immediate constraints of the political and social balance of forces.

The underpinnings of the 'bureaucratic revolution'

We see, then, that correspondence analysis – by way of the distribution by the first two factors – reveals the distribution of the forces present and, through the sociological (and not logical) relation of implication that links position-taking to positions within the space, reveals the underlying principle of campaign strategies to maintain or transform that distribution: on the one side, we have the Ministry of Finance and also, without a doubt, the private banks, who had since the late 1960s been the main beneficiaries of the new forms of personalized, secured credit, to which the new measures of personal housing assistance were perfectly attuned; on the other side stand the Ministry of Infrastructures and all the agencies connected with the development of social housing, from the HLMs, of course, through to the public funding agencies, and also most of the elected local politicians, who had a direct interest in social housing, which can, among other things, serve as a political instrument by which to build up lasting clienteles. Privileged higher civil servants, such as those in the Infrastructures Ministry, may thus find themselves drawn, by the very logic of defending their *corps* and its privileges, into actions likely to contribute to defending the social advances linked to their bureaucratic interests. An analysis attentive to the complex logic of the bureaucratic field enables us, then, to ascertain and understand the *intrinsic ambiguity of the operation of the state*: though there can be no doubt that it tends, under cover of bureaucratic neutrality, to impose a policy corresponding to the interests of the banks and the large construction companies – which, acting through their social capital of connections in the higher civil service, force on that civil service a policy corresponding to their interests, namely, the creation of a market for banking credit for individuals and companies – it nonetheless contributes also, at least within certain limits, to protecting the interests of the dominated.

However, statistical analysis also shows (through the third factor) the forces capable of overcoming the antagonisms that organize and paralyse the bureaucratic world, that is to say, the set of innovators who, though highly dispersed on the first two axes, yet united by the third factor, were able to wrest that world from the status quo to which the balance of antagonistic forces seemed to condemn it. These agents, endowed with quite different properties and interests, share a set of *rare properties* that distinguish them from the rest of the population under examination here, and in particular from civil servants as a whole, who are cautious managers and more or less reticent towards the measures proposed for consideration. As graduates of the most prestigious higher education establishments (ENA, Polytechnique) and of the most prestigious *corps* (Inspector-ate of Finance, Ponts et Chaussées), they have reached extremely high and prestigious positions in the central administration at a very early stage in their careers (even if they are marginal from the standpoint of power), where they find themselves confronted, if not indeed in conflict, with older civil servants occupying more ordinary managerial posts at the end of that steady career that is the ordinary fate of civil servants who 'have come up through the ranks' and been promoted 'by seniority', often coming from so-called 'humble' backgrounds. The 'youth' of the innovators (Jacques Lebhar was 28 at the time, Philippe Jaffré 29, Michel Dresch 31) is in fact 'precocity' or, in other words, legitimate possession of attributes such that the properties attributed to the person, the academic or administrative 'gifts' and qualifications which sanction and underwrite them and which, being ordinarily accessible only at more advanced (biological) ages, seem extraordinary. This is a 'precocity' not unrelated, even if there is some resistance to accepting this finding, to the fact that they are from very high-ranking civil service families, indeed from a veritable bureaucratic aristocracy that is known and recognized as such (speaking of Georges Crepey, one informant states: 'the Crepeys ... a great civil service family ... his father was *président de chambre* of the Revenue Court.')[26]

They are, in this way, both *permitted* to indulge in bold 'strokes of brilliance', of the kind which 'young and talented civil servants' are expected to produce, and *encouraged* to engage in them. And the boost such strokes of brilliance give to their careers contributes to ensuring them a 'brilliant future': the fact of having participated in preparing the reform of building finance represents, if only by the 'contacts' it enables them to make – mainly on the commissions, where the 'young *rapporteurs*' get to work with established personalities – one of those typically bureaucratic feats that go down in the annals of the great state bodies, which, together with membership of ministerial *cabinets* – itself often not unrelated to contacts made while serving on commissions – contributes to furthering one's 'distinguished career' as a higher civil servant (the recruitment of the 'elite bodies' is always based on forms of co-optation that involve a *total* knowledge of the newcomers as persons – and, as far as possible, of their family circles and, particularly, their spouses). There can be no doubt that the presence at the head of the state of a president noted for his 'precocity' could not but give a circumstantial boost to all those also possessing that same property. This merely follows the law of institutions which states that those holding one of the properties favouring access to positions of power (such as an academic qualification) are immediately boosted in their competition with those possessing other properties (within a private or public firm) when the personality occupying the supreme position is also endowed with that property.

Among the distinctive properties of these 'innovators', one of the most remarkable, because it no doubt predisposes them to overcome the various kinds of corporatist boundary, if only by the extended range of contacts associated with it (for example, Robert Lion, a graduate of ENA, and Pierre Durif, a *polytechnicien*, met at Sciences Politiques), is the possession of very diverse academic qualifications, sometimes gained abroad, corresponding to positions normally very far apart within the bureaucratic space or, in the case of some of the chairmen of the commissions, most notably, Raymond Barre and Simon Nora, the membership of international bodies or ministerial *cabinets*. To cite only a few examples, Pierre Durif, the chief administrative officer of INSEE, was a graduate of Sciences Po as well as Polytechnique; Pierre Richard, adviser to Valéry Giscard d'Estaing, who provided the liaison with the innovators, was an *ingénieur des Ponts* who had studied at the universities of Paris and Pennsylvania; Georges Crepey, an *ingénieur des Ponts et Chaussées*, had also graduated from Sciences Po; Pierre Consigny, a former student of ENA, had a literature degree and had studied at Yale, etc. The fact that they occupied greatly dispersed positions along the first two axes doubtless contributed to the success of an undertaking which had to mobilize and reconcile divergent interests, most notably those of the civil servants of the Treasury and the Finance Inspectorate, who generally favoured the new forms of funding; those of the civil servants in the Infrastructure Ministry and of the *ingénieurs des Ponts*, whose corporate interests traditionally lay in maintaining building subsidies; and those of the mayors and local politicians, who, through their participation in the HLM movement, were most often associated with forms of construction threatened to varying degrees by the new measures.

Distance from ordinary bureaucracy and its routines, together with the dispositions normally associated with very elevated social origins and 'precocity' (such as 'audacity', 'ambition', 'enthusiasm', etc.) are doubtless what most clearly separates 'bureaucratic revolutionaries' from the great mass of the civil servants within the administrative structures: by contrast with these 'innovators', who for the most part have no experience of local appointments or of ordinary administration and who from the outset occupied positions in the research and planning agencies (such as GRECOH) – positions which were admittedly minor and marginal, but close, nonetheless to the centres of decision-making – the 'administrators', who most often had a legal background of no particular originality, had spent very long periods in local or purely administrative posts before arriving at central positions by the logic of *internal promotion*, without spending any time either in ministerial cabinets or abroad.

To these two categories of agent there correspond two modes of thought, two visions of the bureaucratic world and the action of the bureaucracy, and also two entirely opposed kinds of *bureaucratic capital* which we can immediately see as being sociologically linked to social properties of age, educational background and seniority within the civil service: on the one hand, the bureaucratic capital of *experience,* whether it be 'knowledge of people' of the kind acquired by a manager of staff or knowledge of regulations of the kind gained by an experienced office manager, can be acquired only *in the long term,* only over time, and is therefore linked to seniority within the service; on the other, there are forms of *technically-based* bureau-cratic capital, which can be acquired more quickly by more rationalized, formalized procedures – such as the statistical survey where knowledge of personnel is concerned, and mathematical modelling when it comes to assessing the costs and effects of a measure – and which are liable to pose a threat to the informational capital acquired by seniority. The force possessed by a particular civil servant or body of civil servants always relates in part to their ability to master, if not indeed *monopolize,* the rare resource that is information (we know that in internal struggles, 'information retention' is one of the weapons employed by those holding an informational capital based on experience and seniority). We may cite here the example, often cited by our informants, of Monsieur Latinus, the senior attaché to the Treasury in the years 1945–75, who, possessing a unique knowledge of all the regulations relating to the provision of building subsidies and the calculation of costs by category of dwelling, played a role not dissimilar to that known in some civilizations as a 'living library': these respected personages, indispensable to the smooth functioning of the bureaucracy because they alone are able to find their way through the tangle of regulations, circulars, supplements and corrigenda, are regularly consulted by their colleagues, particularly the youngest of them, and become arbiters and experts of a type whose actions are beyond the control of others. A part of what is ascribed to 'bureaucratic inertia' or the 'resistance' of civil servants, in what are effectively descriptions masquerading as explanations, can in reality be explained by the fact that certain measures threaten this capital linked to experience and seniority. More generally, all the forms of scientific or technical capital that make for accelerated use or accumulation of knowledge represent a danger to those possessing a practical competence based on experience alone.

It was an opposition of this kind (as brought out by the third factor of the analysis) that emerged between the administrators and the innovators on the occasion of housing finance reform. In the debates that set them against the civil servants of the Finance Ministry, particularly in relation to the assessment of the costs of the new measures and their effects, the innovators largely resorted to econometric techniques to gain acceptance for their position (and many of our informants note that, as early as the negotiations which led to the 1972 law on the calculation of housing allowance, the National Family Allowance Fund (CNAF) was placed in difficulty when it had to defend its draft law at the decisive stages, because it could range only unsophisticated methods of calculation against the models developed by INSEE for the Infrastructures Ministry).[27] Though we should avoid overestimating the effectiveness of formal models and the research departments that rely on them for justification, the fact remains that, when associated with other, no doubt more decisive powers, these instruments contributed greatly to the innovators' victory by introducing that very particular form of utopianism that is fostered by the routine use of formal tools such as mathematical models.

Commissions and the legitimation of an active minority

If we sum up the full range of properties possessed by the innovators, which are likely to unite them by bonds of sympathy associated with an affinity of habitus (in spite of the differences of position reproducing, in the subspace formed by the innovators, the differences constitutive of the overall field), we can see that these 'revolutionaries' are privileged individuals. And indeed, everything seems to suggest that in the bureaucratic field, as in many others, one needs to possess a great deal of capital to carry out a successful revolution. But this model of bureaucratic change would doubtless be incomplete if we did not introduce here another 'strength' possessed by almost all the protagonists: namely, the sense of the bureaucratic game which, in its most elaborate form, enables one, as a virtuoso of well-tempered transgression, to bend the rules. Thus we see Antoine Jeancourt-Galignani associating himself with Latinus, with whom he had apparently nothing in common, to produce the doubly informed article that was to be one of the launch pads for the movement of ideas that led to the reform of housing finance. Similarly, those who chose Raymond Barre to chair the decisive commission valued him both as a figure with no direct involvement in the stakes in play in the construction world and also as a man familiar with the workings and procedures of bureaucratic life; as someone informed about, and respectful of, the rules of propriety governing invitations and exchanges on commissions: and he did indeed conduct the whole undertaking with the greatest finesse, turning to best account that institutionalized instrument for transforming the bureaucratic institution that is the commission.

This typically bureaucratic organizational invention enables the bureaucracy to transcend its own limits and apparently enter into discussion with the outside world without ceasing to pursue its own ends and obey its own transformation rules. The active minority, being both concealed and legitimated by the partial universalization it derives from submersion in a collective subject, becomes a kind of legitimate pressure group, both publicly acknowledged and invested with a mission and a mandate. The subversive movement no longer comes under suspicion of serving the particular interests of a *corps* or clique (the 'young Turks'); it is the agent of a mobilization that is legitimate because it is effected in a formally correct manner. The bureaucracy recognizes this very special form of bureaucratic exploit, which elevates the participants into 'great servants of the state', snatched for a time from the anonymity of the public servant by virtue of their ability to conform to the norms of bureaucratic discretion, even in their rule-governed subversion of the bureaucratic rules.

Thus, after the lengthy endeavours that began with Albin Chalandon's first attempts, as Minister of Infrastructures, to extend the granting of housing allowance and promote the building of single-family houses (laws of 16 July 1971 and 31 January 1972), it was through a set of manoeuvres of which the HLM study days (*journées HLM*) for the White Paper and the Barre Commission were the high points, all of which presupposed a great, specifically bureaucratic, strategic capacity for mobilization and manipulation, that the new representations – from which the compromise that was able to ease the antagonisms between the various persons responsible for housing policy emerged – gained official acceptance in the higher reaches of the civil service. It is probably the case that Robert Lion's manoeuvre (he had had wind of Valéry Giscard d'Estaing's reform plans) by which, in a sense, the HLM movement seized the initiative, cutting the ground from beneath its opponents' feet, as it were, contributed, as much as the Barre Report (which, by its ultra-liberalism, would doubtless have prompted a contrary mobilization of opinion), to promoting the acceptance of a compromise solution combining building subsidies with personal housing assistance. Indeed, though the authors of the HLM movement's White Paper put forward many arguments for maintaining building subsidies that were not considered by the Barre and Nora reports, they showed a marked preference for personal assistance. And the enormous collective labour of awareness raising which took place with the national study days, particularly among local officials, contributed to gaining acceptance, within the HLM movement itself, for criticisms of the institution that had until then been addressed to it only from the outside; by aiming to set before the government authorities proposals they could not ignore (this explains the scope of the mobilization, which ran to 450 people), Robert Lion and his 'accomplices' (Michel Dresch, Claude Alphandéry, Claude Gruson, etc.), whose aim was to restrict the freedom of action of the central administration (which was indeed more or less absent from these '*journées*'), actually served its aims by preparing the sector of the field most distant from the liberal vision (sector D in the analysis) to accept reform.

Thus, perhaps because it was too clever, the strategy conceived by Robert Lion (a prestigious higher civil servant with a total knowledge of the political game, the stakes and his opponents) contributed to preparing the ground for the commission chaired by Raymond Barre, who, by his very intransigence, promoted the compromises Robert Lion wished to impose on him from the outset. The composition and operation of the two commissions confirm this relation of complementarity-in-antagonism that defines the relationship between collusive opponents. Just as the Barre Commission took little or no account of the family movements and the social bodies, so the HLM study days paid scant regard to civil servants.[28] In fact, the informants are not so very wrong in the end when they cite, in no particular order, as primarily responsible for the transformation of housing policy, figures who saw themselves, and were at times seen, as fierce opponents, yet whose endeavours turned out to be complementary and convergent (Georges Crepey, Pierre Durif, Jacques Lebhar, Pierre Richard, Robert Lion).

Invariants and variations

There is doubtless nothing 'conjunctural' about the logic that the structural history of the 1975 reforms has enabled us to tease out. 'Housing policy' was one of the first areas of conflict between the advocates of a 'social' policy – who cannot be identified with socialism, or even less with the socialists – and the defenders of a more or less radical liberalism. On the one side were those who wanted to extend or maintain the definition of 'social rights' then in force – the right to work, health, housing, education, etc., collectively and publicly recognized and provided, by way of various forms of insurance, unemployment benefit, housing benefit, family allowances, etc. – assessed according to the principle 'to each according to his or her needs' (the paradigmatic expression of which is the idea of a 'minimum subsistence income'). On the other side were those who wanted to redefine and reduce the interventions of the 'welfare state' by, among other things, implementing measures inspired by the principle 'to each according to his or her deserts' and tending towards making the assistance granted proportionate to monetary incomes, which would thereby be established as the ultimate measure of the social worth of agents.[29]

The 'philosophy' from which the technocratic avant-garde of the 1970s took its inspiration, which at the time met with fierce resistance even within the higher civil service, has since received a great deal of reinforcement – even from those socially mandated to defend social rights – a fact not unrelated, of course, to the arrival in power of a generation of leaders produced by Sciences Po and the École Nationale d'Administration.[30] In fact, as many of its defenders have declared on numerous occasions, the 'housing policy' that aimed to promote property ownership by measures tending to attune the available assistance and credit to the 'person' (as understood by the banks) was designed as a weapon against the 'collective' and the 'social' and, thereby, against 'collectivism' and 'socialism'. As with the *jardin ouvrier*[31] of an earlier age, the single-family house and the long-term credit that gave access to it were to tie in the 'beneficiaries' over the long term to an economic and social order that was itself the guarantee of all the guarantees which lastingly indebted property owners could give to the bank – and all this while offering the banking institutions an opportunity to mobilize dormant savings on a wider scale.

Under the impact of a whole set of factors extending far beyond the field of struggles over the definition of 'housing policy', the relations of force within this field have been increasingly modified in favour of the advocates of a more or less radical liberalism. And today the analysis would show that the same broad categories of agents divide up, more or less according to the same principles, with regard to the same problems, but with a general shift towards the liberal end of the scale in all the positions adopted, which has no doubt been determined, or made possible, at least in part, by the effects of 'liberal' policy with regard to subsidy and credit and, in particular, by the extension of home ownership first among managerial staff and, particularly in the 1980s, among the better-off sections of blue-collar workers and lower ranking white-collar workers. The debates sparked by the Quilliot Law of 22 June 1982 and by Pierre Méhaignerie's Housing Plan, which was intended to counteract some of the effects of that law, provide evidence that oppositions tend to be structured along largely the same lines between those who deplore the difficulties under which the HLM agencies have to operate and those who want to see the 'laws of the market' applied to housing, some of whom even advocate selling off HLMs to their owners. It is clearly the case that, through the Conseil National de la Construction,[32] which brings together architects, manufacturers of building materials and entrepreneurs (the Union Nationale des Constructeurs de Maisons Individuelles, the Fédération Nationale des Promoteurs-Constructeurs and, most importantly, the Fédération Nationale du Bâtiment), the professionals who in the past proved most attached to building subsidies (and determinedly hostile to the 1977 law) seem to have gone over to the free market liberal position, at least temporarily (this may perhaps be related to the sudden fall-off in building – from 500,000 dwellings built in 1974 to 295,000 in 1986); however, the banks, perhaps because they have exhausted the 'reserves' of potential purchasers of 'personalized credit' (as can be seen from the growth in the volume of repossession proceedings), still maintain a wait-and-see attitude, as does the Fédération Nationale des Agents Immobiliers (FNAIM)[33] and the Chambre Nationale des Administrateurs de Biens (CNAB)[34] or the private notaries and private landlords of the Union Nationale de la Propriété Immobilière (UNPI),[35] who fought fiercely against the Quilliot Law.

In fact, in spite of the boost the 'housing policy' implemented in the 1960s and 1970s gave to the 'liberal' camp, the forces favouring the defence of 'social rights' are still very powerful because they have been built into the institutions over a long period, that is to say, both into the objective (chiefly, administrative) structures and into the cognitive structures and dispositions these have contributed to producing.

APPENDIX I

MULTIPLE CORRESPONDENCE ANALYSIS

CONSTRUCTION OF THE DATA AND RESULTS

Table of 97 rows (individuals), 3 of which are illustrative and 47 columns (disjunctive variables), 2 of which are illustrative.

Variables. Age 7 [modalities]; occupation 16; marital status 3; number of children 7; place of birth 3; public/private secondary school 4, Jeanson-de-Sailly 2, Louis-le-Grand 2, Henri IV 2, Stanislas 2, other Paris or Paris-region lycée 2, provincial *grand lycée* 2, other provincial lycée 2; higher education: Humanities 2, Law + IEP + ENA 2, Law + ENA 2, Polytechnique + ENA 2, ENS 2, Polytechnique 2, Ponts et Chaussées 2, Centrale 2, other 2, studies abroad 2; légion d'honneur 2, ordre du mérite 2, croix de guerre 2, palmes académiques 2, other decoration 2; Barre Commission 2, Commission du Plan 2, Housing Commission 2, Lion Commission 2, Nora Commission 2; administrative connection 19, other *corps* 2; ministerial adviser 2, (ministerial) assistant secretary 2; local elected representative 2, national elected representative 2; Council of State 2, Audit Office 2, Finance Inspectorate 2, Ponts et Chaussées 2, Prefect 2, other *corps* 2; illustrative variables: director of HLM agency or authority 2, GRECOH 2.

Factors

		Eigenvalues	Percentages
1	–	0.11713	6.41*
2	–	0.10255	5.61
3	–	0.08659	4.74

* We know that the analysis of tables using disjunctive coding generally leads to low rates of inertia, 'which give much too pessimistic an idea of the amount of information extracted'. See L. Lebart, A. Morineau and N. Tabard, *Techniques de la description statistique* (Paris; Dunod, 1997), p. 130. The same observation is found in J.-P. Fénélon, *Qu'est-ce que l'analyse des données?* (Paris, 1981), pp. 164–5.

MAIN CONTRIBUTIONS

1st factor		2nd factor		3rd factor	
Individuals					
Richard	4.3	Bloch-L	4.6	Monod	4.6
Crepey	3.5	Mayet	4.5	Womanti	4.2
Dubedout	3.2	Hervio	3.9	Graeve	4.2
Laure	3.2	Brousse	3.6	Douffiagues	3.9
Mayet	3.2	Nora	3.3	Turc	3.7
Saillard	2.9	Ternier	3.1	Essig	3.3
Verger	2.9	Richard	2.8	Brousse	3.3
Traub	2.7	Gonon	2.8	Malecot	3.1
Lerebour	2.6		2.6	Rattier	2.8
Leroy	2.6			Jaffré	2.7
Hervio	2.6			Traub	2.6
Brousse	2.5			Diebolt	2.6
Ternier	2.5			Paira	2.5
Variables					
other corps	6.7	Polytechnique	6.2	ENA, IEP, Dr	6.2
not other corps	6.7	école des Ponts	5.8	no légion d'honneur	5.9
corps des P&C	6.1	corps des P&C	5.8	croix de guerre	4.5
école des Ponts	6.1	Finance Inspect.	3.6	local elected rep.	3.4
Polytechnique	3.6	croix de guerre	3	Revenue Court	3.4
local elected rep.	2.7	directeur de cabinet	3	aged 61–65	3
national elected rep.	2.7	other decoration	2.8	légion d'honneur	2.9
Janson-de-Sailly	2.7	palmes académiques	2.5	Prefect	2.7
public senior manag.	2.6	chargé de mission	2.5	Infrastructures	2.6
other studies	2.6			Stanislas	2.6
				professional	2.5

APPENDIX II

SOURCES

Alphandéry, Claude, *Pour une politique du logement*. Paris: Seuil, 1965.

Annuaire Desfossés-SEF. 2 vols, Paris: Cote Desfossés-Dafsa, 1975.

Barrot, Jacques, *Les Pierres de l'avenir*. Paris: France-Empire, 1975.

Bottin administratif et documentaire. Paris, 1975.

Cazeils, Jean, 'La Réforme de la politique du logement', thèse de troisième cycle. 2 vols, n.p., 1979.

Dresch, Michel, *Le Financement du logement*. Paris: Berger-Levrault, 1973.

Engel, Marc-Sylvain, *L'Aide personnalisée au logement*. Paris: PUF, 1981.

Heugas-Darraspen, Henri, *Le Logement en France et son financement*. Paris: La Documentation Française, 1985.

Lebhar, Jacques, 'Réflexions sur l'esprit d'une loi', *Les Cahiers du GRECOH*, 14: 4 (1976), pp. 5–8.

Lévy-Lambert, Hubert, *La Vérité des prix*. Paris: Seuil, 1967.

Lion, Robert, 'Édito', *Actualités HLM*, 142 (15 July 1977).

Massu, Claude, *Le Droit au logement. Mythe ou réalité*. Paris: Éditions Sociales, 1979.

Rapport de la Commission de l'habitation du 6e plan d'équipement et de la productivité. 2 vols, Paris: La Documentation Française, 1971.

Rapport sur l'amélioration de l'habitat ancien, ed. Simon Nora and Bertrand Eveno. 2 vols. Paris: La Documentation Française, 1975.

Rapport du Comité de l'habitat pour la préparation du 7e Plan. Paris: La Documentation Française, 1976.

Rapport de la Commission aménagement du territoire et cadre de vie pour la préparation du 7e Plan. Paris: La Documentation Française, 1976.

Rapport de la Commission d'étude d'une réforme du logement présidée par R. Barre. Paris: La Documentation Française, 1976.

Union Nationale des HLM, *Proposition pour l'habitat. Livre blanc*. Issued as a supplement to *HLM*, 244 (1975).

3

The Field of Local Powers

Just as, at the central level, 'housing policy' is the product of a long series of interactions performed under structural constraints, so the regulatory measures constitutive of that policy are themselves reinterpreted and redefined by a further series of interactions between agents who, as a function of their positions in objective structures of power defined on the scale of a territorial unit – a region or a département – pursue different or antagonistic strategies. This means one cannot conceive the relationship between the 'national' and the 'local', the 'centre' and the 'periphery' as a relationship between a universal rule and its particular application, between conception and execution. The view one gets from the 'centres' of power, the view that makes one tend to perceive (geographically or socially) 'peripheral' religions and forms of worship as magical rituals, regional languages as (provincial) dialects, etc., foists itself insidiously on social science and it would be easy to demonstrate that many uses of the opposition between 'centre' and 'periphery' (or between the *universal* and the *parochial*), apart from making effects of domination vanish beneath a semblance of descriptive neutrality, tend to establish a hierarchy between the two opposing terms: for example, peripheral actions are conceived as the mere mechanical application of central decisions, the local administration being there only to *carry out* orders or implement bureaucratic 'circulars'; or, without the two being mutually exclusive, these actions may be conceived as representing 'resistance' on the part of private interests or of local ('provincial') particularism to central measures.

Bending the rule

The apparently neutral and purely descriptive opposition between 'centre' and 'periphery' owes its symbolic force to the fact that it is obtained by superimposing two sets of oppositions. The first of these is built into both the bureaucratic structure itself, in the form of the whole series of divisions and subdivisions which match ever lower levels of hierarchy to ever smaller territorial units, and the cognitive structures of all civil servants, with the opposition between 'central' sites of 'command' and 'conception', on the one hand, and 'local', 'external' outposts, where decisions are 'carried out', on the other. The second is between the bureaucracy itself and everything external to it: 'subjects' or 'citizens', and also 'local communities' or, in other words, between the 'public services' and 'private interests', between the 'general interest' and the 'particular interest'. This gives us a whole set of parallel oppositions, partially substitutable one for another: 'central'/'local'; 'general' ('general interest', 'general ideas', etc.)/'particular' ('particular interests'); 'conception'/'execution'; 'theory'/'practice'; 'long term'/'short term', etc. The common matrix of these oppositions is the antithesis between two *viewpoints*: the viewpoint of civil servants, which is the generative principle underlying the bureaucratic world's discourse about itself – a discourse which the most presumptuous of the producers or reproducers of this occupational ideology sometimes term, a little pompously, 'administrative science' – the viewpoint of those who, being situated at the top of the bureaucratic hierarchy, are supposed to be 'above the fray' and hence, inclined, and able, to 'view matters dispassionately', to 'see things in the round', to 'take the broad view' or the 'long view', which stands opposed to the ordinary view of the mere executants or ordinary agents, who are inclined, by their 'short-term interests', to anarchic 'resistance' or 'pressure' contrary to the 'general interest'. This set of oppositions, rooted in a sense of superiority both technical and ethical (itself most often based on a socially and educationally guaranteed self-assurance), underlies the *technocratic worldview* which is that of all who, in so far as they share in the state monopoly of legitimate symbolic violence, have grounds socially, and are encouraged, to regard themselves as the functionaries and missionaries of the universal. This set of oppositions organizes the perception the *rapporteur* of a Commission on Housing Subsidies may have of participants external to the civil service or the image an engineer at the head of a Direction Départementale de l'Équipement (DDE) has of the mayors or councillors in his district. This is to say that the *prior objectification* of these principles of reality construction, which are built into reality itself and into the very minds of those undertaking the analysis of that reality (who may, for example, subscribe to the Husserlian vision of the philosopher as 'the functionary of humanity'), is essential if we are to avoid introducing into science, as instruments of the construction of its object, principles of division that belong there only as objects.

What is certain is that, in practice, for an entrepreneur and for most of the 'citizens', 'subjects' or 'those falling under its jurisdiction', the 'state' takes the form of regulations and the agents or agencies invoking those regulations, most often in order to say 'no', to prohibit something from happening (in the present case one is reminded of the existence of the state and of regulation at the point when a request for planning permission is made, when it makes itself felt in the form of land occupancy plans, of technical and aesthetic building regulations, etc.; at the point when loans are applied for; and when a contract of purchase or sale is signed, when the provisions on warranties and time limits etc. come into force). The perception oriented and governed by the regulations is a *selective* perception, which has the same limits as the statutory competence of the civil servant. It nonetheless asserts itself as *universal*, whether that universality is the universality of aesthetic standards or of the demands of rationality and technology, or both, and it is often formulated in propositions that have a collective, impersonal subject ('It is the view of the Ministry of Culture that ...'). And it takes this universal form even when it is not always easy to conceal the arbitrary nature of the point of view behind it, and to justify with aesthetic or technical arguments, for example, the legal or legitimate width of roof overhang or the full extent of the protected environment around a historical monument. However, when it is produced by the departmental architect this point of view, which cannot but appear particular to the user of the service (or, even more clearly, to another architect, situated in a neighbouring, but nonetheless very different point in social space), is able to gain acknowledgement as universal. The very status of the representative of authority, expressly mandated as a civil servant to enforce regulations which require that roofs overhang by no more than 12 centimetres or to specify that the area surrounding a historical building is protected for a radius of 400 metres, implies a '*monopoly situation*' in determining the good and the beautiful with regard to housing. This monopoly of legitimate symbolic violence asserts itself in the civil servant's claim, whether he or she be a departmental architect or DDE engineer, to occupy a standpoint that is no standpoint at all, that is to say, the absolute, universal, general, and hence delocalized, departicularized, deprivatized viewpoint of the neutral and accredited servant of the general interest. And it is not unusual for this claim to find in the dispositions inscribed in the habitus of the civil servant – for example, in the anti-capitalist hostility to the logic of profit and the aesthetic aversion to mass production which inspire in many departmental architects a marked prejudice against industrially built houses – the necessary psychological resources to assert itself with the full conviction of its necessity and universality.

In the battle for monopoly control, regulations are the civil servants' main weapons, alongside their technical and cultural competence, where this is relevant. And one might say, generalizing Weber's argument that 'one obeys the rule when the interest in obeying it predominates over the interest in disobeying it', that the civil servant applies or enforces the regulations to the extent, and only to the extent, that the interest in applying it or enforcing it predominates over the interest in 'turning a blind eye' or 'making an exception'. The rule which, as we have seen, was produced in the confrontation and transaction between antagonistic interests and visions of the social world, can be applied only through the action of agents given responsibility for enforcing it – agents who, possessing greater discretionary powers the further they are up the bureaucratic hierarchy, can work to execute the rule, or to transgress it, depending on whether they derive greater material or symbolic advantage from behaving in a strict or accommodating fashion. (It follows that one cannot establish a *mechanical* relation between positions and position-taking: position-taking always involves a greater or lesser element of free play, which agents can use to a greater or lesser extent depending on their dispositions, which themselves match their positions more or less closely.)

The authority of civil servants may assert itself in pure and simple identification with the regulations, in effacing themselves before the rule, abasing themselves before it so as fully to enjoy the power it affords – that is, most often, a power to prohibit. This strategy which consists in giving up the freedom always inherent in *even the humblest* post, and behaving as anonymous, interchangeable figures, entirely reduced to their functions, is doubtless more likely to be used, because it is encouraged more and is more *advantageous*, the further down the hierarchy one goes. However, it offers itself as a possible alternative at all levels – thus opening the door to strategic play – to the opposite course of conduct which consists in behaving in an 'understanding', 'humane' manner, in availing oneself of, and gaining advantage (albeit a purely moral advantage of ethical conformity) from, the free play which every post allows its occupant (if only because no description of a post and no set of regulations can ever foresee every eventuality).

This is the point at which we should recall that a field, as a flexibly structured and minimally formalized area of free play, or even a bureaucratic *organization* as an artificially structured game, constructed with explicit ends in mind, is not an *apparatus* obeying the quasi-mechanical logic of a *discipline*, capable of converting all action into mere *execution* – a limit that is never reached, even in so-called 'total institutions'.[1] The *disciplined* conduct that has all the appearance of *mechanical execution* (which makes it a source of comic effects) may itself be the product of strategies equally as subtle (we may think here of the good soldier Schweik) as the opposite option that consists in bending the rules, in distancing oneself from the regulations. The bureaucratic game, which is doubtless one of the most strictly regulated of all, nonetheless includes an element of indeterminacy and uncertainty (what is known, in a mechanism, as 'free play' or, simply, 'play').[2] Like any kind of field, it presents itself in the form of a certain structure of probabilities – rewards, gains, profits or penalties – but one which always involves a degree of indeterminacy: however narrowly their posts are defined, and however much they are constrained by the necessities of their position, agents always possess an objective element of freedom which they may or may not exploit, depending on their 'subjective' dispositions; unlike a mere cog in a machine, they can always choose, at least to the extent that their dispositions prompt them to do so, between obedience *perinde ac cadaver* and disobedience (or resistance and inertia), and this *room for manoeuvre* affords them a possibility of bargaining over – of negotiating the price of – their obedience or consent.

Having said this, and at the risk of disappointing those who will see in these analyses an unexpected (or unhoped for) resurgence of 'freedom', we must remind the reader that it is not a pure, and free, subject who steps up to occupy that margin for freedom that is always afforded to civil servants to varying degrees, depending on their position in the hierarchy. Here, as elsewhere, it is the habitus that steps in to fill the gaps in the regulations and, both in the ordinary situations of bureaucratic existence and in the extraordinary opportunities which total institutions (such as concentration camps) offer to social drives, agents can, for better or for worse, seize upon the discretion offered to them in their actions, and take advantage of the position of superiority afforded them by their function – even where that superiority is minimal and temporary, as in the case of the counter clerk – to express the socially constituted drives of their habitus.[3] Thus junior supervisory and monitoring posts in 'total institutions' (boarding schools, barracks, etc.) and, more generally, executive offices in large bureaucracies owe a number of their most characteristic features, which are never laid down in any bureaucratic regulations, to the dispositions imported into those offices, at a particular moment, by those who occupy them: functionaries 'fulfil their functions' with all the characteristics, desirable or undesirable, of their habitus. And a number of the 'virtues' and 'vices' of petty bureaucracy are imputable as much, if not more, to the fact that junior civil service posts were until recently very welcoming to the rising petite bourgeoisie and to their strict but narrow, rigorous but rigid, ordered but repressive dispositions.

Not everything in the bureaucratic contract is contractual: the regulations that define the duties of the subordinate party also define the limits of the arbitrary rule of the dominant. This is, in fact, the fundamental ambiguity of law: just as it is difficult to defend oneself against the practical regularities or tacit injunctions of a universe like the family, in which ethical constraints remain for the most part unstated, lying in the murky depths of shared assumptions, so it is possible to derive advantage from an explicit rule by reinterpreting the statement of duties ('the civil servant must deal with the case within eight days') in such a way as to transform it into a claim of rights (the civil servants has eight days to deal with the case). Though the rule restricts the executants' margin of freedom, by indicating what they must do and what they cannot do, in so far as it is subject to *interpretation* and *application* (in Gadamer's sense), it also circumscribes the power of the superior and, by defining what he can rightfully demand, sets a limit to his arbitrary power and to abuses of authority. It is this fundamental ambiguity of the bureaucratic order that is shown up in a 'work to rule', which demonstrates that one merely has to obey to the letter the rules which govern a system nominally based on conformity to rules to bring it to a standstill. And the scope for interpretation afforded to *all* agents, the extent of which is no doubt the most exact measure of their power, reminds us that the bureaucratic order could not function if it did not provide scope at all times for *an infinitely subtle casuistry of rights and exemptions*.

Properly bureaucratic power and the licit or illicit profits it can bring depend on the freedom to choose between the rigorist and strict application of the rule and transgression pure and simple. And, as if to complicate the task of those seeking 'incentives' by which to improve the productivity of bureaucratic work, it is by basing oneself on the same principle, that of the freedoms one acquires by granting freedoms – that is to say, by granting indulgences, by turning a blind eye to breaches of formal discipline and tolerating minor transgressions of formal and formalistic imperatives – that some holders of bureaucratic power can build up for themselves a symbolic capital that enables them at all levels of the bureaucratic hierarchy to mobilize energies, and even enthusiasms which the pure and simple imposition of the formal rule would leave untapped, and thereby to achieve a kind of surplus labour and self-exploitation. The option of opening up the possibility of an *exception* to the rule represents one of the most common and effective ways of acquiring that particular form of *bureaucratic charisma* that is acquired by distancing oneself from the bureaucratic definition of the civil service role.[4] The civil servant constitutes himself as a '*notable*', enjoying a certain *notoriety* within the limits of a territorial area and an *acquaintance group*, by building up a *social capital* of useful relations and a *symbolic capital* of gratitude thanks to that very particular form of *exchange* in which the 'currency' is nothing other than exceptions to rules or accommodations to regulations granted or offered, as a 'favour', to a user of the service or, more commonly, to another 'notable' acting in the name of one or other of his 'protégés'.

Hence the application of the rule, which may be a non-application, a *dispensation*, a legitimate privilege, depends very much, in each case, on the dispositions (habitus) and interests (of their position and that of the body to which they belong) of agents who, while deriving their power from the regulations, have virtual monopoly control of their *application* to particular cases, that is to say, of the interpretation and imposition of the regulations (such as the DDE official in respect of 'planning permission' or the departmental architect in respect of architects' plans or all those who, at some point in a process of *bureaucratic decision-making* have to register an 'opinion', assessment or appraisal on a form provided for that purpose). These 'agents of execution', who are never mere executants, always have available to them a range of possible 'choices' lying between two limits, though these are doubtless never actually reached: at one end of the scale is the strict, complete application of the regulations, with no consideration for the details of the case in question, which, as the phrase '*summum jus, summa injuria*' reminds us, may be an impeccable form of the abuse of power; or, by contrast, a legitimated transgression, an official or semi-official *dispensation*, in the sense of an exception to the rule made within the rules, and a legally sanctioned privilege. In fact, the second possibility assumes full meaning and value only in relation to the first; it is in so far as it suspends the possibility of the pure and simple application of the rule (which can be brandished as a threat in a sort of legal *blackmail*) that the exception granted becomes a *service rendered*, and hence a specific resource, capable of being exchanged and of entering into the circuit of symbolic exchange that forms the basis of the social and symbolic capital of the notable. In contrast to bureaucratic authority, this *credit* is essentially personal: it accrues to that person who, by authorizing an exception to the rule, registers his or her personal freedom instead of behaving as an impersonal figure identified purely and simply with the rule he or she subserves.

There is no law without privileges, dispensations, exemptions and 'derogations': in other words, without all the kinds of special authorization to transgress the regulations that can be granted, paradoxically, only by the authority responsible for enforcing the laws. Monopoly control of the implementation of regulations can thus procure for the person enjoying it the benefits and satisfactions attaching to observance and the material or symbolic profits associated with legitimate transgression, bribes and 'backhanders' being only the crudest forms of these: the bureaucratic suspension of prohibitions or obligations may be a source of advantages that are described in more euphemistic terms, such as credit for services rendered, which can be traded with other holders of bureaucratic power and, hence, of potential privileges (this is what bureaucratic jargon calls 'oiling the wheels') or with other notables and, in particular, with elected officials, members of parliament, councillors and mayors, who augment their symbolic capital by intervening and interceding with the bureaucracies or, alternatively, with ordinary members of the public who have sufficient social capital to enter into relations of exchange. By way of this mechanism, which is at the very heart of the bureaucratic monopoly, the arbitrariness associated with the temptation to accumulate 'personal power', to accumulate a symbolic capital associated with the *person* of the office-holder, introduces itself into the implementation of the regulations, threatening 'bureaucratic rationality' at its very foundations, that is, threatening the calculability and predictability which, according to Max Weber, define it.

Transgression within, or as authorized by, the regulations is not a mere failure of bureaucratic logic; it forms part of the very idea of regulations, *de facto* and *de jure*. *De facto* because, however precise the rules governing the application of the regulations (in particular, the circulars which the 'drafters in the central administration' produce for the executants in the 'external services'), they can never cover all possible cases and situations, and if they did so, they would make 'execution' impossible. Paradoxically, a rule is not really a principle of action; the part it plays is that of a weapon and a stake in the strategies that orientate action. And transgression forms part of the very idea of regulation *de jure*, because legitimate dispensation from the bureaucratic rule may be built into the very logic of the bureaucratic institution, in the form of official or semi-official *appeal authorities* which, through the division of the labour of domination they establish, enable the higher body, endowed by its position in the hierarchy with a higher degree of liberty, to *derive a symbolic profit* from the rule-bound rigidity of the lower one (the hierarchy between the two functions meaning that, in many cases, the 'repressive' dispositions of the petite bourgeoisie – legalism, austerity, earnestness, etc. – serve as a *foil* for bourgeois dispositions – detachment, humour, loftiness of attitudes, etc.).[5]

(We can see here how difficult it is to fulfil the functions of monitoring, supervision and evaluation which are necessarily the responsibility of the central authorities, and which in all traditions expand, sometimes to the point of hypertrophy, as bureaucracies develop – to such an extent that in many cases they come to constitute the major part, both quantitatively and qualitatively, of what is commonly called bureaucracy. The members of the monitoring bodies, who stand higher in the hierarchy, are most often endowed with greater cultural and symbolic capital than the functionaries lower down the scale; on the other hand, they are, both in principle and in actuality, further removed from the 'realities' (among other reasons, because they cannot get too close to them without forfeiting their superior position), and the technical competences through which they gained their positions, whether it be the literate culture of the Chinese mandarin or the mathematical or legal culture of the European senior civil servant, are not always directly useful or applicable, even for purposes of mere monitoring, in the round of ordinary bureaucratic life. The practices of junior civil servants thus oppose to the forms of rational monitoring, which are made possible by the bureaucratic instruments that have, little by little, been invented for the purpose (such as the statistical surveys of activities that are recorded in the department's files, or the deliberate inspections carried out regularly or exceptionally) a kind of constitutive opacity, linked to the logic of those practices, which is a logic of practical know-how, operating on a case-by-case, item-by-item basis, and which is highly likely, even where there is no direct intention of concealment, to confound the codified, rationalized exigencies of the monitoring authorities. In fact, the structural rift between the two logics, which is undoubtedly what makes bureaucracies able to adapt to particular cases in their unpredictable diversity, is also responsible for their tendency to escape rational control. Moreover, it is certain that the inevitable casuistry of the practitioner directly confronted with the practical problems quite naturally offers almost infinite scope for dissimulation to those who wish, and arc able, fully to exploit the ambiguities of the rules and, above all, the full range of resources for bending the rules. This is why legalism, which consists in seeing the rule as the principle of practices and, more precisely, in deducing practices from the rule that is supposed to govern them – though it is most particularly encouraged by the ordinary representation bureaucracies have of themselves and wish to present of themselves, as both productive of and products of, regulations – is doubtless the most formidable obstacle to a true knowledge and understanding of the real functioning of bureaucracies.)

The territorially based field

How are we to describe the social processes which lead to the practical implementation of regulations and give the state its real face, the one it wears when it embodies itself in the innumerable actions of countless agents mandated bureaucratically to act in its name, who, within territorially based fields, confront each other with various different powers and divergent interests? The 'choice' each of these holders of bureaucratic power can make between rigorism and laxism, or between the different forms of abuse of power, through hypercorrectness or through 'distancing from the role', reaches its limits at the point where competition with the other claimants to monopoly control of the implementation of bureaucratic rules begins. No official can, in fact, be unaware that each citizen can take advantage of the structural conflicts between contending authorities within the bounds of an administrative unit such as the département (for example, the Prefect and the head of the DDE) to have their undesirable decisions put into abeyance or postpone the effects of such decisions; or that the individual concerned, exploiting in this case not the horizontal relations within the territorially based field (such as the département), but vertical relations within the relevant authority, may even attempt to have the ministry intervene and possibly even have the civil servant who refuses to come to some accommodation with the rules transferred to another post. For example, the departmental architects and, particularly, the engineers of the DDE can play on the structural ambiguity of their position of *twofold dependence* – on the Prefect and the 'local communities', on the one hand, and on their own internal hierarchy and ministry, on the other – to afford themselves a kind of independence that enables them to strike compromises, make exceptions, do deals and hence achieve substantial material and symbolic advantages. However, the proconsular temptation, with all the abuse of power it implies, is limited by the control and censorship exerted by the territorial field of competition and, through it and its interventions, by the central authorities themselves; it is limited, too, by the logic of 'transfer' and 'advancement' which exerts a pull towards the 'centre', that is to say, towards more extensive, but also better controlled powers.

So, as all the informants remind us, particularly those whose careers have brought them into different local situations, and as our observations (in the Loiret and the Val d'Oise) have enabled us to confirm, the configuration of forces present within a territorial field varies from one département to another, and within each département, depending on the interests and dispositions of the agents occupying the key positions: the Prefect, the head of the DDE, the Président du Conseil Général, the city mayors. At the same time, however, it is clear that we find invariant elements in the complexity and multiplicity of configurations within which the interactions between the agents and institutions capable of intervening directly or indirectly in the housing question or in the 'decisions' that may be taken in these matters are determined. The most acute awareness of the infinite diversity of concrete combinations does not, in fact, prevent us from devising the basic principles of a model capable of rendering individual practices and strategies, if not predictable, then at least immediately intelligible: apart from the dispositions associated with their social trajectories, such a model should take into account for each of the agents the power (or capital) and interests linked to the current and potential position they occupy in a twofold relationship – the vertical one within the specific hierarchy of the *corps* to which they belong, and the horizontal one within the local field. In proceeding in this way, we should be equipped to grasp the overall configuration of the local field and the singular form of the interactions that may take place within it (positive interactions, such as cooperation, alliance, etc., or negative ones such as overt or covert conflict).

The fact that the implementation of regulations comes about within this context of multiple, competing powers that are pitted against each other within the territorial field while remaining integrated within national fields (the field of Prefects, of architects, of DDE engineers, etc.) and that constantly oscillate between the temptation towards 'local feudalism' and the ambition to rise within the central hierarchy (particularly that of the administrative *corps*), no doubt provides a certain protection against abuses of power, at least to those who have the necessary resources to enter into the cycle of exchange of services, a protection also against the total takeover of the entire game by one of the powers, or by a central authority. Thus each of the weak positions in the territorial field can find paths towards independence in the 'billiard game' (as one of the informants terms it) that consists in using one authority to evade the dictates of another (which latter authority may on some other occasion or in another territorial field be used to resist the former). Everyone can, up to a point, evade the clutches of one or other of its competitors by setting it in competition with others. As witness this entirely typical comment from an official in the disputed claims department of a DDE in a prefecture in the Paris region: 'We [in the DDE] are agents of the state. A mayor can't order me to support a proposal. But as we wish to retain the trust of the mayors, we accept, so as not to lose our credibility. If we refuse, the mayor will call in a private consultant and they'll always agree to what he wants. Private consultants, private architects can do Land Occupancy Plans; and they'll act on a commercial basis; for example, they'll do a Land Occupancy Plan in a fortnight. There isn't the quality in something like that. On the other hand, we in the civil service know the ground. We work with the mayors on a daily basis. The subdivisional officer is always on the spot. With us, it's the Groupe d'Étude et de Planification [Planning and Studies Group] that does the Land Occupancy Plans.' Moreover, though the DDE can reject the mayor's orders or turn down his requests, it needs to retain the custom of the local authority, and it has to avoid the kind of complaints and protests that might tarnish its image with the central administration. For their part, the mayors may free themselves from the clutches of the DDE (the larger the commune, the easier this is to do) by pitting them against a private architect, but it is in their interests to ensure the specific competence of the DDE, and even its active complicity, to carry out works which might contribute to their re-election. For this reason, a mayor, in common with many other local office-holders, finds it easier and safer to entrust the design and execution of his or her projects to DDE officials, calculating that, since they are associated in this way with his own business, they will be able to provide him with the means to realize his policies in return for the advantages they derive from the situation.

As another example of these intersecting constraints, which lead to negotiation as a way of avoiding the repercussions of direct confrontations: 'Let's take a concrete example – planning permission. Ninety-nine per cent of communes use the DDE for examining planning applications (Plan of Land Occupancy approved or not). The mayor, who isn't necessarily a specialist in town planning is going to follow the DDE's opinion. But if the planning application doesn't conform to the Plan of Land Occupancy, the DDE can refuse to examine it and call on the Prefect to have it annulled. Only, the mayor will be unhappy. So the DDE will negotiate with the mayor behind the scenes to have him change his mind without the Prefect knowing about it.' In other cases, the applicant who is unhappy with DDE decisions can complain to the mayor of the commune or appeal to his or her councillor to intervene. That elected representative, concerned to accommodate a voter, may intervene with the DDE or, worse, bring in the Prefect. These are all unpleasant, and possibly even dangerous, situations in so far as they can threaten either the authority of the technical services and the – always very delicate – balance of their relations with the Prefect, or the relationship between the DDE and the mayor, an actual or potential client, or even, in cases of serious conflict, the very position of the civil servant, who is always at risk of being transferred. Here again, this web of constraints leads the technical services to hedge their decisions about with consultation and discussion.

Weak organizations, and also the central power, may, like the users of the services, draw on these webs of relations of competitive interdependence to play different agents or bodies off against each other and create a degree of freedom for themselves out of conflicts between them. For example, organizations that exist to provide information, such as ADIL (Association Départementale Information Logement)[6] and CAUE (Conseil en Architecture, Urbanisme et Environnement),[7] which find it very hard to be recognized as possible interlocutors by the dominant agencies within the territorial field, have a source of potential support in political office-holders, who were at the outset at least apparently favourable to them (indeed, they contributed to creating them). However, since they pride themselves on 'not being drawn into politics', they present an image of neutrality that inclines them to forego that particular form of leverage. They might also derive support from the various branches of the civil service, and particularly from those in the DDE, but as these latter are inclined to look unkindly on their interventions, which disrupt the privileged relationships they have with 'their' politicians, these two bodies often end up fulfilling an educative role, which sometimes takes the form of a kind of agit-prop for the users.

This being said, above and beyond all the forms of equilibrium that may be achieved in each département and with regard to each of the issues which may divide the various bodies that have responsibility for housing – the Prefecture, the DDE, CAUE, ADIL, local politicians, mayors, councillors, deputies, associations, family allowance authorities, HLM agencies, lending bodies, etc. – the fact remains that, particularly where important matters such as planning permission, Land Occupancy Plans and Urban Development Zones (ZACs) are concerned, the greatest structural weight invariably lies with the DDE, the Prefecture and the mayors; and the central position is monopolized by the DDE, around which everything revolves and which asserts its influence the more completely when the communes it is dealing with are small and relatively divided and hence forced, for lack of economic and technical resources, to rely on it for the execution and even the design of their urban development projects.[8] The structural antagonism between the DDE and the Prefect, which is the equivalent, at this level, of the opposition between the Finance Ministry, with its ENA graduates and the Ministry of Infrastructure, with its *ingénieurs des Ponts,* is a balancing factor that offers a possible recourse for the citizenry and their representatives. Having said this, only a whole series of individual monographs could grasp the invariant elements and the variations in the confrontation between two bodies that are equally inclined to regard themselves as the elite of the elite, but who are separated by their language, ways of thinking and their entire worldviews; and it would take several volumes to describe the different variants of the strategies used by the Director of the DDE – an *ingénieur des Ponts* and a graduate of Polytechnique, with the full weight of his esoteric technical knowledge behind him, not to mention the privileged relationship which unites him with his civil service *corps* and his parent ministry and the economic and political weight with local communities he derives from his triple role as overseer, planner and director of works – to contest in actuality the official pre-eminence of the *énarque*[9] at the département level.

Builders and property developers are, for their part, very unequally equipped to enter the bureaucratic 'billiard game'. Though departmental architects are sometimes prejudiced against them, the large national builders no doubt have a structural advantage, at least in this field, over small and medium-sized regional building firms (who can draw on more support from deputies and senators): they are doubtless better equipped to influence decisions where housing policy is concerned, or to get around the regulatory obstacles the lower tiers of the civil administration are not reluctant to put in their way by intervening with the central authorities, ministers or ministerial cabinets. Here again, however, though the model we propose enables us to lay down at the outset what, in each case, will be the relevant parameters of the field of possible forces, it is only in a particular *conjuncture* that it will be possible to determine what exactly will be the system of bureaucratic constraints specific to any particular configuration of the structure of the locally based single-family house market that will have a very precise influence on an individual transaction.

One temptation might be to conclude from these analyses, as the best observers often do, that the 'bureaucratic system', a colossus with feet of clay, would be doomed to impotence by the rigidity of its hierarchical structures were it not for the permanent intervention of those 'spontaneous' regulations, corrections, adjustments and accommodations effected in the relationship between the 'local' agencies of the state bureaucracy – mainly the DDE – and the representatives of 'local communities', invested in this way with an extraordinary power ('the little local mayor is the yardstick by which the whole of administrative action operates').[10] This 'bottom-up' view is accompanied, most often, by a vaguely functionalist representation which presents the impossibility of controlling the field of territorial authorities and the scope which rivalry between competing institutions offers to local notables and their electors as the basis of a constant dialectic between the 'bureaucratic system' and the environing reality, and hence as the underlying principle of an equilibrium between the *anomie* of a society bereft of rules or incapable of imposing their application and the *hypernomie* of a rigid social order, incapable of affording accommodations with its own prescriptions.

This somewhat optimistic representation has the merit of taking into account the complexity of interactions concealed beneath the apparent monotony of bureaucratic routine. Reality is, however, doubtless even more complex, and we cannot forget that each of these interactions is the site of power games and important stakes, and hence a site of violence and suffering. In fact, not just anyone can enter the circuit of fruitful exchange by which norms are adjusted to realities: notables enjoy the benefit both of the rule and of its transgression; by contrast, for the common run of 'subjects' and 'citizens', lacking the resources essential to obtain those waivings of the rules that the privileged enjoy, 'rules are rules' and, in many a case, 'supreme justice is supreme injustice.' Both at the level of the conception and elaboration of laws and regulations and at the level of their implementation, in the obscure transactions between civil servants and users of the public service, only dialogue with the notable is really tolerated, that is to say, the civil service will speak only with another, slightly cut-down, version of itself: in this way there is established that *adjustment without negotiation* (the total opposite of the *negotiated compromise* with an organized grassroots movement) which is provided at the collective, national level by the *commission* and at the individual, local level by *intervention* – two forms of exchange, generative of symbolic profits, between agents who are sufficiently *au fait* with the real rules-for-bending-the-rules to take advantage (for themselves and their protégés) of a rational management of laws and exemptions, of rights and privileges.

However, we would also have to examine the incalculable costs of all the effects of bureaucratic *hypernomie* and, in particular, the costs in time, work, administrative procedures and sometimes in money that ordinary citizens often have to pay to win acceptance (against the abuse of position, against the arbitrary power exerted in hyperlogical application of the rule, against the rigidity authorized by bureaucratic monopoly) for the often tiny departure from the brute, and brutally applied, norm that brings bureaucratic behaviour a little nearer to the ideal of a really (rather than formally) rational administration or, more simply, a little closer to the expectations or legitimate demands of the users of the services.

APPENDIX

THREE POINTS OF VIEW ON THE LOCAL FIELD

A SMALL BUILDER

In the following extracts, the manager of a small regional building firm (in the Île-de-France) speaks (in 1985) of his troubles with the various officials at département level, particularly the architects of the DDE and the Bâtiments de France.[11]

MONSIEUR D.: Those people [the architects] have no training at all at the technical level ... they don't have a technician's intellectual approach. They're artists. So they do things *they* think look good. And that means, look good as they see it. I tell you, I won't argue with them on that score, but what counts for me is making things look good for my clients. The main thing for me is what my clients want. And seeing that it's within the realms of possibility for them in financial terms. In other words, I take a down-to-earth view of these things ... Anyway, it's quite simple: it's the market that determines what you do. So we're in the right because we're the ones who've got the market. If they'd been in the right, we wouldn't exist and they'd be doing our job. Obvious, isn't it?

INTERVIEWER: It seems you have quite difficult relations with architects generally ... it's not that you have a grudge against them, but ...

MONSIEUR D.: Oh yes, I do, because I have good reason to. I resent them because it seems to me quite simply that they're people in a monopoly situation and I think that's unacceptable ... You see some scandalous abuses from what are called the Bâtiments-de-France or DDE architects. There are no kinds of standards they have to work to. None. So they do as they please ... For example, when they tell you roofs mustn't overhang by more than 12 centimetres ... I can't see what damage it can do to the environment to have a roof overhanging by 30 centimetres instead of 12. It's completely bloody stupid. Pardon my language. ... But then they change architects and everything changes. What was nice before is nasty now ... There's a whole profession howling about this, but it carries on just the same. Though things have got a bit better. But at the beginning – until about five years ago I'd say – it was mad, totally mad.

INTERVIEWER: How do you mean?

MONSIEUR D.: Well, you turned up with a house, I mean with the plans, and they covered them in red ink. They messed the whole thing around and what you were left with didn't work at all ... Then we got into endless battles. It was actually through those battles that we managed to bring them round a little bit to our way of thinking. There's been something of a coming together over ... the last few years. But in the beginning, I have to tell you, what a battle!

INTERVIEWER: How was it?

MONSIEUR D.: Relations were dreadful. We really were the enemy as far as they were concerned. Some of my colleagues at the national level were accused of defacing the landscape. Which is completely stupid. You don't deface anything when you build houses. And anyway, after five years or so, with all the greenery and everything the people put round it, you can't see it any more ... And then there were people whose planning permissions were being systematically turned down. That was terrible, because there were people like us who were investing to sell and then these other people came along and put loads of red ink all over their plans and said, 'Do it again.' There were two or three years of extreme tension, I don't mind telling you. Then things calmed down under pressure from the ministry ...

Monsieur D. went on to speak of the difficulties he had encountered in his efforts to gain permission to exhibit one of his houses in the forecourt of the Gare de l'Est in Paris for four months.

MONSIEUR D.: I can tell you about the house we put on show at the Gare de l'Est, for instance. The Ministry of Culture takes the view that putting that house there is damaging the environment. I don't think they've been seeing all that clearly, eh? They should come and have another look. I don't mind taking them and showing them round the area, because there are some rather dubious things down there. Take all the advertising hoardings, for example, with the regulations and so on. So for them to come and say to me ... I can understand they might find it shocking. I can understand it can't stay there forever. But it wasn't meant to be on show forever, just for four months. So, to say it damages the environment ... that's ridiculous talk in my view.

INTERVIEWER: Hold on, you got a letter from the Ministry of Culture?

MONSIEUR D.: I even had a rejection from the city hall.

INTERVIEWER: How is it that the house is there all the same?

MONSIEUR D.: I had a battle with the Prefecture and the Prefecture gave the go-ahead ... Er ... whereas the Paris city hall had turned it down. And the Ministry of Culture also rejected the application, against the advice of the Prefect. Er ... they were even prepared to take out a demolition order. So you see how high the feelings run!

INTERVIEWER: That's incredible. But how did it all end? Was it because you knew people personally?

MONSIEUR D.: Not at all, not at all. It was by ... By ... how can I put it? ... approaching the authorities and going to talk to people to convince them. Because if we'd said we were going to put an aeroplane on show, or ... tanks from the last war, no one would have objected at all. And quite simply because there were no architects involved ... I have to tell you, this is how I got through – because, when they rejected my house, it was finished, oh yes – between the point where I asked for permission to put it up and the point when they said no, the house was finished right there. It had taken them two months to draw up a document. Over the same period, I'd built a house, and in temperatures below 18 degrees C. You can see we don't work to the same timescales. We're not the same breed at all.

INTERVIEWER: So when their document came, how did you react? Did you panic?

MONSIEUR D.: No, not too much ... Well, I was a bit worried, as you can imagine (*he laughs*) ... but I was expecting something like that and there was always the possibility of an appeal to the Prefect. In fact, that's what I did. And then, most importantly, I had the SNCF with me, since I was building on railway-owned land. So I said to the SNCF, 'It's your problem. You sort it out. I rented that space from you and you knew what I was intending to do with it.' From that point on, it was one branch of the public services against another. It was a game of chess from then on, and not a very easy one I can tell you.

INTERVIEWER: And the Prefect?

MONSIEUR D.: I had approval from the Prefecture which I got ... er, I don't know, but a month after the house was finished. So, I had the Paris city hall, the Ministry of Culture, and an association in the tenth arrondissement called Mieux Vivre dans le 10e Arrondissement ranged against me ... And then the funniest part is that this house is one that was designed by us and put to the architects of Bâtiments de France for the whole Île-de-France region for approval. They said it fitted in perfectly with all the sites, since it's a kind of authorized design, even if it's not officially authorized, since such a thing doesn't exist. But in this case, they said, 'Given that at the Gare de l'Est you're on a listed site, since there's the what's-its-name church less then 400 metres from your house, you can't do that' ... Really, it would be nice to know where the environment starts. When you see the SERNAM lorries, which are wrecks on wheels, outside the Gare de l'Est, I don't mind telling you my house is a lot prettier than they are. We put flowers in the courtyard, it does no harm ...

A CIVIL SERVANT IN THE DDE

'Relations between the town planning department – that's to say, the DDE – and all its partners vary a great deal from one département to another. I can start with the relations between the DDE and the departments of the Prefecture. You know it's the Prefect who has overall responsibility for the DDE and all the state services come under him. The way the DDE and the other services in general operate depends on the sensitivities of each Prefect or Secretary General with regard to problems. In the Loiret, we're lucky to have a Secretary General who's very sensitive to housing problems, which means that relations are excellent between the Prefecture and the DDE. We're in touch on a quite regular basis. The Prefect has the decision-making power, but we play a large part in the preliminary deliberations. We're never just presented with a *fait accompli*. In some départements, the housing service [of the DDE] is treated by the Prefecture as a body simply for carrying out orders. There are others where the Prefecture isn't too

concerned with housing matters. In that case, everything's delegated to the
DDE and it's given plenty of latitude: the DDE does all the work and it 'gets
through' anything it wants. There's the whole range of different situations.
In the Loiret département, we're in more or less the average situation. The
Prefect makes the decisions, but in fact he makes precise orders for certain
things to be done. He asks us to carry out assessments, which we do: we
discuss them, come to an agreement and, in my view, things operate pretty
normally. The sad thing is that, where housing is concerned (in the Loiret
département), we have a Council that is very, very unconcerned with
housing problems ... In some départements, the département plays a part
in the operations, provides assistance to the bodies concerned, the
communes, and undertakes work to upgrade run-down areas. Here they
don't. The view at the département level is: 'Housing isn't within our remit.
We don't play any role.' We've tried to make them understand that there
are social problems related to problems of housing and that social problems
do come within their remit. Their answer is that they do enough on social
work in the département ... This comes from the leader of the Council.
And you find the same problem with the main city, which is Orléans ... It's
the same. The city authorities of Orléans aren't involved in housing
questions. Not up to now at any rate.' (Extract from an interview carried
out in December 1988 with a civil servant from the DDE of Orléans,
Director of the Urbanisme Opérationnel et Construction [operational town
planning and building] group.)

A CONSULTANT ARCHITECT

Monsieur R., an architect, is the director of a CAUE in the Île-de-France
(the CAUEs, which were created on the basis of the law of 1977 on the
initiative of the Minister of Infrastructures, are responsible for providing
advice to individuals and local authorities in the field of architecture and
town planning). He tells how the body that he heads was set up.

MONSIEUR R.: I have to say, first of all, that the Prefects had a very
important role in setting up the CAUEs. That is to say, they chaired the
commissions that were the working groups for establishing the CAUEs.
This is a very important point, because the Prefect wasn't always the
strongest force in his département in those days, unlike the present
situation.
INTERVIEWER: Meaning?
MONSIEUR R.: Meaning that in some cases the DDE was stronger than he
was.
INTERVIEWER: And here?
MONSIEUR R.: Here, at the time, the Prefect of the département was a
political Prefect, a Gaullist ... and the more technically complicated things
were, the more he tended to be wary of them. And the DDE found it
difficult to ... I'd say, difficult to assimilate a very political, proactive
language to an ... Er ... monopolistic technical language. In a word, there

was a bit of a problem between them. And then, the Prefect had a Secretary General who had links ... Well, in short, you had the context of a normal département, a normal province. Well, the Prefect wanted to control the initial trials ... So we came to an agreement, in double-quick time, between the Prefect, on the one side, and two architects – the Bâtiments de France architect and myself, as the person the Prefect had appointed to present and carry out trials ... In the meantime, the DDE set up another structure, trying to get a firm foothold in the CAUE, and wanted – how can I put it? – to ... quibble about how the thing was set up. They said, 'You have to do this particular thing.' You know ... they insisted on all the formalities! The DDE said, 'We need something extra, so we're going to cast our planning permissions in architectural terms.' They didn't call this 'pedagogical' at the time. They talked about education: 'We're going to teach people to ...' And gradually that approach took over entirely. The DDE developed a structure of that type. And in the last meetings [to set up the CAUE] – because time was getting on and in September 1978 we were still at the working group stage – the Prefect brought everyone together, knowing that I'd prepared a report (he was the only one who knew anything about this) that laid down some objectives ... At this meeting the DDE, the Agriculture Directorate, Health and Social Services and the school inspectors were all represented. Well, the DDE were there quoting the 1977 law which said they were in overall charge! And one of their concerns was: 'There shouldn't be a director of the CAUE.'

INTERVIEWER: Why was that?

MONSIEUR R.: That would allow them to second people on *their* contracts to work as a technical team. And they'd use town planning study funds for that. The only problem was that there were professional representatives of the architects there, and they started to come out with some high-flown stuff. The DDA tried to corner them by saying, 'You haven't read section 3, paragraph 2 and so on', and in reply they went on about architecture. To cut a long story short, the Prefect very soon got tired of the whole thing. He looked over at me – I was sitting just about opposite – and said, 'Is your thing ready? Are you sure?' And I said, 'In fact, it's going very well. We've got six months' work behind us. It can be extended to the whole area. And it isn't set in stone, it's an open system ...' He cut me off and called for the adoption of my report. It went through. The others said nothing, not knowing what it was about. And after adopting it, he read it out. Well, then, they pulled some very long faces indeed ... So, next, the approach was: 'Right, now we've created the CAUE. We inform the Conseil Général that there's the inaugural general meeting.' The general meeting took place and that's where the first real political problems appeared. Some of the councillors were very poorly informed about how the CAUE had been set up and how it was to operate, because it had been the DDE that supplied the information. So you can imagine what that was like! Any number of wild notions were flying around ... The DDE tried to start putting people in as a technical team, while the work continued elsewhere. And when the blokes who wanted the key jobs in the CAUE started to scream and shout about it all, the elected people backed off. Well, the chairman of the CAUE, who had been elected, did. He was a rather 'Third Republic' kind of man, very calm, a *conseiller général*, mayor of a commune of more than 10,000 inhabitants. There were people around the Bâtiments de France, attached to the Prefect, who also tried all they knew to get their way ... All that went on for a year.

[In the end the CAUE was created]

INTERVIEWER: So, how did the DDE react?

MONSIEUR R.: Very, very badly. The Bâtiments de France reacted well. But as soon as the chairman of the CAUE decided it was becoming operational and appointed me director (with the approval of the Prefect, because he had to give in too), the DDE ...

INTERVIEWER: The Prefect wasn't in agreement either?

MONSIEUR R.: My appointment was linked to two signatures – the CAUE chairman's and the Prefect's. And the Prefect wanted something different. But, he had to give in because there was no way round it. And there had been 18 months' work on all this, too, so he was pretty much painted into a corner.

INTERVIEWER: And the DDE reacted very badly, you say?

MONSIEUR R.: Very, very badly. It was open warfare. That's to say, they withdrew more or less right away from the steering committee and never came back. They started spreading false information about the CAUE. And they created a CAUE within some of their own departments, which they saw as *their* CAUE. By that, I mean they had architects working in the DDE and they said, 'what's needed is architectural assistance.' So they opened offices doing more or less what we were doing. And the two carried on in parallel.

INTERVIEWER: And whose side did the Conseil Général take?

MONSIEUR R.: Like very often with a Conseil Général, it didn't take anyone's.

4

A Contract under Duress

After this long detour through the analysis of the structures and the objective relations of force between agents and institutions, we can thus come to what, in good empirical or empiricist method, appears to be the first stage of the research, and often the last: the direct interaction between purchaser and vendor, which can be observed and recorded, and sometimes concluded by a contract. Now, there is no interaction that so well conceals its structural truth as the relation between buyer and seller in the property transaction. And nothing would be more dangerous than merely to take that exchange at face value, as is done, in fact, by some proponents of 'discourse analysis' or ethnomethodology, on the pretext of faithfulness to reality and attention to the data, finding support and sustenance for their hyper-empiricist vision (though it hides behind justifications from phenomenology, this is what it must be called) in the latest technological developments – in particular in the tape-recorder and, above all, the video camera; and who, believing they have found in this filmed and recorded behaviour or speech the sacrosanct 'data' they can oppose to the statistical tables of the adherents of the 'quantitative tradition' that is still dominant today, in fact share with these latter a positivist epistemology of submission to the 'given' as it presents itself.

There could be no better time to recall that the truth of the interaction is not to be found in the interaction itself (a two-way relation that is always in fact a three-way relation, between the two agents and the social space within which they are located). Hardly anything of what defines the economics of housing, from the administrative regulations or legislative measures that orient property loans policy to the competition between the builders or banks which underpin these measures and regulations, including, along the way, the objective relations between the regional or municipal authorities and the various administrative authorities responsible for applying the regulations relating to building, is not in play in the exchanges between house sales staff and their clients, but it is invariably expressed (or betrayed) in unrecognizable form. The singular, personalized interactions, precisely located in time and space, between Monsieur S., a visitor to the 1985 Salon de la Maison Individuelle, and a salesman, or between another salesman and a couple (Monsieur and Madame F.) who went along to the Florélites show village one Sunday afternoon with two of their children to choose a house, are merely actualizations at a single point in time of the objective relationship between the financial power of the banks, embodied in an agent entrusted with the task of exerting that power tactfully (to avoid frightening clients, whose only means of expressing their freedom is to leave), and a client defined, in each case, by a certain purchasing power and, secondarily, by a certain power to exploit it, which is linked to his or her cultural capital, itself statistically linked to his or her purchasing power.

Having several times observed the stereotyped scenario acted out in the interchange (that is to say, the process by which a relation of force that apparently first favoured the potential buyer was gradually reversed and came little by little to be turned into an interrogation), we proceeded to carry out systematic observations of how the sales staff were installed and presented themselves and how they 'hooked' the client; these observations were carried out for the most part at the Phénix, Sergeco, Bouygues, Manor, GMF, Cosmos, Espace, Kiteco and Clair Logis stands at the Salon de la Maison Individuelle at the Palais des Congrès in Paris and at the 'show village' of Florélites Nord. We also recorded dialogues between sales staff and buyers, and meetings with sales staff in which we presented ourselves as potential buyers (endowed with a certain number of demographic and social characteristics established in advance on the basis of a kind of experimental plan). We further carried out a series of in-depth interviews with salespeople, commercial secretaries and sales training officers with large national construction companies. We were also able to obtain information from a building firm on the level of education of the salespeople.

In this way we were able to establish that the exploratory investigation of the comparative merits of the different house models, by means of which the clients seek to have the salespeople, and through them the builders, compete for their custom, is more or less quickly transformed, under technical – and, most importantly, financial – constraints, into an investigation on the part of the salesperson (who is also selling the credit) of the guarantees offered by the purchaser. The interview, which is initially intended to test out the salesperson, almost always ends in a kind of lesson in economic realism, during which the client, assisted and encouraged by the salesperson, works to adjust the level of his aspirations to the level of his possibilities in order to prepare himself to accept the verdict of the tribunal of the economy, that is, to accept the real house, often very far removed from the one of his dreams, to which strict economic logic entitles him.

The exchange is organized in a three-phase structure, which, with a few variations, was found in all the cases studied. What varies is the speed – and bluntness – with which the salesperson takes over the transaction and, more broadly, *the tempo of the exchange*: sometimes the salesperson takes the exchange in hand from the outset; at other times, the process is more gradual and the client's efforts to retake the initiative have some degree of success and consequently last for some time. The salesperson is the agent of economic necessity. But he or she can impose that necessity gently and gradually or, on the other hand, quickly and bluntly. As happens in all cases where a sequence of actions is determined in advance, either by the principles of a tradition, as in the case of the ritual exchange of gifts or words etc., or by the constraints of an external necessity, the only free play, the only margin of freedom, exists in the sphere of time and tempo. Here the salesperson, operating strategically, has to impose the necessary outcome without making this felt too harshly, which means going through the motions of observing the ordinary courtesies. This accounts for the considerable amount of time the salesperson takes to clinch the deal – time needed to enable the client gradually to close the gap between his or her expectations and what is actually possible.

The description of the behaviour of the sales staff offered by a Maison Bouygues sales representative corroborates our observations, at the same time as it offers some elements of the job description which contribute to explaining that behaviour: 'There were people who were prepared to be given a rough ride, to have an interview just sitting down quickly at a table. We sorted out the good ones from the others, the ones who had the money from those who hadn't. Then those who hadn't were moved along. It was actually like that. This isn't really a caricature. So we went on working like that. There are still people doing this now. Try it and see. Go to the show houses in the village developments. You'll see that you come along with questions to ask, wanting information. The salesman reverses the whole situation. He says, "Sit down, how much do you earn, how many children do you have?" So he can see straight off, in two and half minutes flat, if you can afford it or not.'

Generally, after a preamble of variable duration, the salesman takes over the direction of operations and, through the process of questioning the buyer as to financial guarantees, establishes himself as a quasi-bureaucratic authority, acting as judge of the client's financial capacity, entitlements and possibilities, and in certain cases even goes so far as to substitute himself purely and simply for the client and take over decision-making power from him or her; this he does through rhetorical strategies of 'ambiguization', the aim of which is to present a wholesale takeover of the situation as the implementation of a total care package: being skilled in presenting himself as an expert with the capability to make the clients happier than they even know how to themselves, the salesman also knows how to present himself as an *alter ego* capable of putting himself in the clients' place and taking their affairs in hand, 'as they would do for themselves'. He is thus able to settle matters with a: 'That means a PAP [first-time buyer] loan over 20 years and a complementary loan.' This use of impersonal verb forms, which renders the proposition in question anonymous and universal, while merging the salesman and the potential buyer in a collective subject (though doing so less ostentatiously than by using the pronoun 'we'), appears very frequently with the same functions in the language of the salespeople.

The bluntness of the salespeople is explained when one realizes that, since most of them began their careers in the period of expansion when clients were falling over each other to buy houses, they tend to see the first contact as a kind of filtering, intended to sort out the 'serious customers' in order to avoid wasting effort in failed attempts (success rates vary between 1 in 10 and 1 in 20). Consequently, so as not to waste time on the people they describe as 'sightseers' or 'afternoon strollers', they get straight to the point, quizzing those identified as possible clients (couples, particularly those with children) on their income, in order to eliminate as quickly as possible those who cannot afford the house of their dreams. These salespeople, who are often trained by hard-bitten old salesmen, tend to regard all those clients 'whose eyes are bigger than their stomachs', or 'who are full of fanciful notions', with a mixture of cynicism and resignation, spotting them from the outset and dealing with them in more or less the same way each time, being in a hurry to know whether they are 'serious' and, if they are, to inject a dose of reality as quickly as possible.

> 153

Monsieur S.

At the Salon de la Maison Individuelle, Monsieur S., who is clearly looking at houses, goes up and down the aisles, asking questions at one stand, taking catalogues and leaflets from another, then approaches Stand C. As soon as he arrives on the stand, a man of youthful appearance in a sharp suit approaches him and asks if he would like some information. When he replies in the affirmative, the man invites Monsieur S. to follow him, offers him a seat in a booth set a little apart and sits down facing him.

SALESMAN: Do you know more or less what you're *entitled to?* Before we start, let's get to know each other a bit, let's see what you want. Right, I'm going to give you some information about this.

There then begins a session of close questioning on where he lives, how many children he has and their ages, whether he rents or owns his present home, how much rent he pays ('For a little bit more than that, you can own your home'), the place of work and occupation of the couple, their means of transport, the amount they can advance as a deposit, the number of rooms desired, the surface area they want and the desired location. In each case, the visitor tries to reply as best he can.

SALESMAN: Listen, there are going to be five of you living in this house, aren't there? For five people, you need 80 ... er, I don't want to get this wrong, 88 or 99 square metres, something like that ... (he consults his file and reads) 'Five persons = 88 square metres minimum to qualify for a loan.' (He picks up his calculator, asks the couple's income and arrives at a result.) So, 13,000 francs a month, on that you can repay up to 33 per cent; that's what the banks allow. That is (he uses his calculator) ... you can repay 4,290 francs. What do you think of that as a repayment?
VISITOR: Mmm, well ... I've decided to buy my own house, so that means I'm ready to make some sacrifices.
SALESMAN: Right, I'll write all this out for you neatly.

He takes a form, repeats all the questions he has already asked, this time noting down the answers, then explains to the visitor that there are two types of loan available, the *Prêt pour l'accession à la propriété* [PAP or first-time buyer loan] or the *prêt conventionné* [covenanted loan]. These he explains in a manner at once obscure, confused and full of authority.

SALESMAN: Now I'll explain. The PAP loan is, if you like, a loan assisted by the state at a rate that's advantageous in the early years, but never finances the whole operation. That means that with this PAP loan you'll have to add an extra bank loan that will complement the PAP. Now, you have another option, which is a covenanted loan, which is a bit dearer at the beginning but which, over 20 years, works out about the same as a PAP with a

> 154

Strategies of ambiguization, aimed at abolishing the distance, and mistrust, between the seller and the buyer, find natural support in the 'personalization of credit', an innovation in banking techniques that establishes a *new kind of guarantee*, chiefly in the form of the notion of *permanent income*, the total income likely to be received over a working life (or over a long period). Against these guarantees (typical of the age of calculability and predictability), which can be provided only by agents with *careers*, and hence with regular incomes regularly distributed over time, the bank can now lend money without asking for 'real' guarantees (in the form of property) and offer a loan proportionate in size, duration and cost to a set of characteristics of *the person defined bureaucratically*, such as expected earnings, family size, etc. It is this technique (often described as a 'democratization of credit') that has enabled banks to gain a new clientele, the *middle-class wage earners* (upper and middle managerial staff). Being assured of a bureaucratically guaranteed career, these are the people best placed to provide the 'personal' guarantees represented by a perfectly secure, calculable permanent income and, thanks to the possibilities of credit offered in this way, they can, in a period of high urbanization, achieve their ambition, which was in the past largely the preserve of those with economic capital, of owning their own dwelling, be it a flat or a single-family house.

The bank identifies the value of the person with their overall earnings expectations, that is to say, with their annual income expectation multiplied by their life expectancy or even, particularly when venturing to deal with social categories offering fewer guarantees of all kinds than managerial staff in the public sector, their overall expectancy of creditworthiness, which also depends on ethical dispositions and, in particular, on all the ascetic virtues that govern control of consumption and respect for commitments. In most cases, the builder and the salesperson who represents him in the transaction act as extensions of the bank, to which, in exchange for financial advances or preferential rates, they provide a kind of right of pre-emption over a fraction of the clientele in the property market and hence control of a growing proportion of the credit market; it follows that, in so far as most transactions boil down essentially to drawing up a *credit plan*, with discussion of the technical characteristics of the house being most often a mere adjunct to this, the negotiation that leads to the signing of a property contract is a mere variant of the transactions made directly at the bank itself.

The establishment of a personal or 'personalized' credit contract thus presupposes the prior collection of a set of data about the

> 155

complementary loan. So, the PAP you get from the Crédit Foncier, the complementary loan to the PAP is from your bank or a finance company – or even the Crédit Foncier too, they can do it ... Er ... You get the covenanted loan from a finance company or your bank.

VISITOR: And who takes care of that? You, don't you take care of anything? Do I have to make all these applications myself?

The salesman then goes into the *We-take-care-of-you-from-A-to-Z* sequence, which forms part of the strategic arsenal of all sales staff and is explicitly taught on the sales training courses.

SALESMAN: We, if you like, take care of everything. You just have to read the documents and sign. That's all ... We take care of you from A to Z. (Here, without allowing the visitor time to catch his breath, he moves straight on to the presentation of the building company, going into a second obligatory sequence: the *We're-the-top-company-in-France-for ...*') Let me fill you in a bit ... We were the first company to be awarded the 'high insulation' charter mark ... We're the top company for civil engineering construction and for building flats and tower blocks ... In detached houses, we build around 3,500 a year throughout the whole of France. We're not the first in the field, because the first is a company that just builds detached houses. We do lots of other things. So we can't be first. But we are second. (And he concludes, anticipating the client's expected question.) So, how are our houses made? Our walls are made of concrete panels, which are 1 metre 40 by 70 cm and 8 cm thick. Why? Because we don't want to build in breeze blocks. We take the view that breeze blocks aren't a solid building material. You'll never see any big building, *not one*, built with breeze blocks. They're all built in reinforced concrete. Why's that? There's a reason for it. It's *sturdier*.

The visitor is content just to listen.

Second phase. The visitor very gradually takes the initiative when the technical side of the product is presented. The salesman, who wants to go into more technical detail on the houses for which he is the representative, finds himself obliged to reply one by one to the more practical questions the visitor is beginning to put to him on this subject. 'Is it well insulated internally?'; 'How many windows are there per room?'; 'What about electric heating?'; 'Is there a *vide sanitaire*?'; 'On the floor, is it lino?'; 'Does that cost extra? You haven't given me a price for ...'; 'And is the kitchen equipped or not?'; 'Can you put cupboards up in the bathroom?'

Thrown a little by the visitor's questions, the salesman gives his replies, which he intersperses with attempts to regain control of the exchanges ('So that's how our houses are built') and to launch into a highly technical account, to which the visitor, visibly out of his depth, lends hardly any

> 156

borrower. And this bureaucratic interest for the bureaucratically defined person, that is to say, the person as an entirely impersonal and interchangeable entity, and for the generic properties the bureaucratic forms mechanically register, which can serve as a basis for a rigorous calculation of earnings expectations, may, because all these characteristics are attached to his or her singular person, seem to the client like a personal interest in his or her person in its uniqueness. The purely technical enquiry thus constitutes a propitious basis for symbolic strategies aimed at exploiting the ambiguities of the situation more or less consciously to satisfy the client's expectations: the client is all the more inclined to seek to establish a personal relationship of trust given that he or she cannot but be anxious about the immense disproportion between the size of the stakes and the extreme paucity of information available, which makes the decision appear a veritable gamble. (Do we really need to add that the problem of whether these strategies are conscious or unconscious, and hence of the good faith or cynicism of the agents, is virtually devoid of meaning? Like those cinema or stage actors who are sometimes called 'instinctive', and who, since they simply inhabit the various 'roles' with their own habitus, always play more or less the same character, the salespeople, in any deal they are trying to clinch, engage all the resources of a system of dispositions that turns out to be the more effective the closer it is to the clients' own: we know, for example, that the sales force of Maison Phénix, who are often former blue-collar workers and generally have little formal education, were remarkably successful so long as they were required to sell a 'bottom-of-the-range' product to a working-class clientele, a product which matched their positions and dispositions, and was adapted to their resources and tastes.)

Being intended to provide the bank with essential information with which to establish a precise assessment of the guarantees on offer, the questions the clients must answer, if they want answers to the questions they themselves have put, may also be perceived as personal questions in the ordinary sense of the term. And the technical operations the establishment of a personal credit contract requires may also, given a certain practice of 'ambiguization' such as to make them seem more palatable, provide an opportunity to establish a person-to-person relationship of a kind likely to induce clients to lower their defences, suspend their critical faculties and put themselves in the other's hands. The logic of economic rationality, which leads to more or less money being granted at a higher or lower rate for a longer or shorter period, depending on the guarantees the client can offer, coincides with the commercial logic which states

> 157

attention. 'Insulation? But our external insulation is good enough.' 'Yes, we don't put in a *vide sanitaire?* This is because a *vide sanitaire* is an extra'; 'I'll give you that piece of information, sir. *Don't you worry.*' 'The kitchen isn't equipped, but there are all the sockets supplied for the refrigerator, the freezer, the washing machine, everything. It's all taken care of. That means you just have to move in your furniture and the house is ready to live in.' 'The bathroom? That's to say, in practice you walk into the house, hang up your jacket, lay down your toothbrush and live in the house. That's all there is to it.'

VISITOR: And which model would suit me?
SALESMAN: We could work that out on the basis of the *financial package.*

He picks up his calculator, redoes all the calculations, adds in Personalized Housing Allowance (APL), starts again, makes a mistake, corrects himself, then concludes:

SALESMAN: Right, with that *we*'re in good shape to build what *we* want. Right, you want a plot ...
VISITOR: Well, it's the house that's important to me. Do you take care of plots? Is the plot additional to the house?
SALEMAN: Yes, but *we*'re all right. I mean when you have this kind of finance ... If I had this every day I'd be happy. Sometimes we have to ...

The salesman then shows the visitor a catalogue that includes all the various different house models. They all have a garage ('but the garage is an extra'). To the visitor, who would like to have a house with an upper storey for 'independence', he replies: 'It's easier without. If you have an upper floor, everything changes.' The catalogue only includes houses built on one level, but 'you can always add a cellar if you like.'

VISITOR (coming back to the question of the plot): What would the surface area be?
SALESMAN: What would you like?
VISITOR: Enough to build the house and then have a little garden, that's all.

The salesman suggests a surface area of 700–800 square metres, for 'the budget we have'.

VISITOR: Is that a decent size?
SALESMAN: Oh, well, when you have all that, when you have that area to mow ... Of course ... no, 700 or 800 square metres is quite all right ... I mean, it's substantial.
VISITOR: And the electricity, the water, the drains?

The salesman then puts in another ready-prepared sequence: *You'll-know-*

> 158

that one should adapt sales strategies to individual cases. And the salesperson's ascendancy over the situation, which gives them impetus, will do the rest, the salesperson being sufficiently close to the clients socially that the transition to 'personal' relationships will occur and, with it, the confusion of 'personal' information and information useful to the bank.

As was shown by the study we carried out in 1963 at the Compagnie Bancaire, even the semblance of an interest in the 'person' of the client tends to disappear as the process of drawing up the contract progresses. Beyond the first contact with the receptionists, all the phases of the administrative process – assessment, drafting of the contract, payment and management – take place outside the presence of the clients, with the bank staff calling on them only when the loan application is incomplete, excessive or poorly supported, or sufficiently complicated to require detailed examination. Those responsible for dealing with the loan application have no contact with the clients, or even with the people who first met them. After the initial selection process carried out at reception, the bank proceeds on the basis of the file alone: the real decision is taken at this level, that is to say, *outside of any personal contact*. It is exceptional at this stage for the client to be interviewed, and indeed the managers argue that it might lead the officials concerned to infringe against their standards of objectivity; out of sympathy or kindness, they might forget the strict rules of financial equilibrium, be won over by the client's optimism and make overfavourable financial estimates, which are likely to involve them in excessively heavy costs. In the file, the 'person', defined as the point of intersection of a multiplicity of abstract classifications, is reduced to a finite set of isolable, codable statistical characteristics, on the basis of which the individual's value, that is, his or her future monetary yield, is assessed. And it is the bank that will alone decide on the particular conditions to be applied to the loan, employing for this its own undisclosed knowledge and rules known to it alone (its own scale or 'ready-reckoner') on the basis of the in-depth knowledge it has of the client.

The ambiguity objectively built into the institution finds expression also in the linguistic strategies of the clerks and salespeople who, having two languages available to them when the client most often has only one, can switch between the neutral language of the banking bureaucracy and the personal, familiar language of ordinary existence. So a question like 'Should I buy an existing house or go for new-build?' can bring two possible answers. Either: 'We always advise our clients to buy a new house, because they can then avail themselves of the discount offered by the Bank of France.' Or: 'You know, I'm not really the person to tell you that, because I bought an old house.' In the first case, the employee is

> 159

to-the-penny-what-you-have-to-pay (another salesman's variant of this: 'We count everything so you don't have any *surprises* at all').
SALESMAN: So, the houses are exclusive of connection charges, the price of the house ... But we take account of this in the finance plan. Which means that when you walk out of here, *you know exactly to the penny how much you're going to pay.*
VISITOR: And can we choose the wallpaper?

The salesman moves on to the *three-levels-of-finish* sequence:

SALESMAN: We have what we call *houses ready for decoration*, where you put up the wallpaper and do the painting yourself. That's the first one. Then we have what we call a *standard package*, which is a package where the house is wallpapered and painted, with needle-loom carpeting in the bedrooms. Then you have what we call the *luxury package*, where the house is fully tiled, there are luxury carpets in the bedrooms, tiles around the sink and bath and wallpaper everywhere. There are three levels of finish.
VISITOR: Do the houses have tiled roofs? Which of them do you recommend?
SALESMAN: This one. (He shows him a model: this is the latest house to come out, which is the one he always recommends. His builder has recommended it to him and he likes it: there are cupboards and storage space everywhere.) It hasn't got five bedrooms, but I'm proposing an extendable model. *Anything's feasible for us.*
VISITOR: What are your guarantees?

The salesman replies with the *Guarantees* sequence (there's a two-year guarantee covering the house and installations, plus a ten-year structural guarantee and the supplementary guarantee).

VISITOR: Will the plot be isolated or is it on an estate?
SALESMAN: It's as you wish. I mean you have the financial capability to do it, *so you can choose* the plot yourself.
VISITOR: How much would that one cost? (He points out a model.)
SALESMAN: I'll give you the *entirely finished price*. By that I mean, as I was saying just now, you just take off your coat and live in the house.

The salesman gives him the price. The visitor asks how long it would take. They could start right away, replies the salesman, announcing at the same time that *he can find the plot before the end of the week.* He then goes on to deluge the visitor with a new sequence on '*the-length-of-the-administrative-procedures.*'

Third and last phase. The salesman regains control of the situation and prepares to close by coming back on to his most favourable ground. He lets

> 160

speaking as an authorized spokesperson and official representative of knowledge; in the second, behaving as one ordinary individual advising another. Bank employees ought, in theory, to indicate by their language and tone that what interests them is not the client's private life, but certain generic, abstract characteristics of their property transaction, which are necessary to put them in a particular class and hence to apply the appropriate scale to the case. And, indeed, this is how things are done with the specialists (bankers, employers, agency directors, consultants) who telephone on behalf of a third party: the technico-bureaucratic language, larded with specialist terms designed to confer a tone of technical neutrality on what is said (mortgage, delegation of privileges, etc.), and 'noble' equivalents of ordinary terms (third party, enjoyment, housing development, residential building, acquisition, complementary loan, execute [an operation], etc.) is what makes it possible to 'meddle', as the expression goes, in clients' 'business' as much as the situation demands, while maintaining a proper distance and not impinging on their private lives.

Matters are quite different in exchanges with 'ordinary' clients. The inherent force of the expert language no doubt continues to have its effects even when employed by agents who do not possess all the competence it is supposed to underwrite. (Though it can happen that the somewhat forced character of their use of this managerial language betrays itself in the strains and cracks that appear when they find themselves, exceptionally, confronted with clients who have a total mastery of economic language, as in one case we observed involving a professor of law.) Economic language, when coming from bank receptionists, who use it in what is often an approximate and mechanical way, can be a distancing tool, intended to disarm clients by disconcerting them and weakening their defence systems: the impersonality of technical language is one of the means of getting clients to leave aside all personal reference to their 'personal' problems while providing the (falsely) 'personal' information required to draw up a contract.[1]

However, the speakers of the dominant language may allow themselves changes of linguistic register when clients unable to maintain this technical parlance in quite such a sustained way translate the receptionist's remarks into the language of personal relations. 'Our offices are open without interruption,' says the receptionist; and the client picks this up with a translation game that helps him to understand and enables him to check that he has properly understood, while also expressing an effort to reduce the distance (and anxiety): 'Right, you're open all day.' 'Yes,' says the

> 161

rip a series of sequences on the financial aspect of the transaction: 'You know, the *notary's fees* are 3 per cent and can only be taken from the deposit'; 'You'll have updating charges to pay to cover the various rises, but the actual prices are final, firm and can't be varied'; 'You might possibly make *savings* if you do the mains electricity connection between the street and the house yourself, but you'll have to pay for the materials'; 'If you're not building a garage, but just a car port, you have to tell me at the beginning, so that it's included in the planning permission.'

He then comes to the question of the plot, which allows him to involve himself personally.

SALESMAN: Currently I have a number of plots available in the département you're interested in. In fact, *I'm head of sales for the next département* and I know the Continent hypermarket down there. It's *close to the countryside* and to [name of town], which is very nice and very well known ... I've been with [name of builder] for four years and *in fact I'm currently having a house built* by [name of builder] myself. (He closes with an appeal to conclude the contract definitively:) So, tell me, when will you be making your decision? If you were to make up your mind within the next few days, the house would be ready for when your children go back to school in the autumn.

The salesman hands the visitor the catalogue, together with house plans, his project schedule and the price lists. He shakes him by the hand, saying 'See you soon' and watches him leave.

Monsieur and Madame F.

Monsieur and Madame F., who are looking to buy a house, have for some time been spending most of their weekends on that undertaking and regularly visit the show village of Florélites Nord in the Paris suburbs, where all the various builders are to be found. This Sunday, accompanied by their two eldest daughters, aged 11 and 7, they decide to focus on builder G, who, for the moment, is known to them only by name. After having some difficulties locating the house in the middle of the village, they set about visiting it. Going from one room to another, they stop in the kitchen where models of houses are on show, suspended in glass bubbles. The saleswoman who is there is just finishing a conversation with another couple and turns, then, to them.

MONSIEUR F.: It's like this, we have three children and we'd like some information on buying a house.

Very relaxed, sitting on the edge of the sink, the saleswoman sets about very quickly testing the seriousness of M. and Mme F.'s request, by asking the first questions: 'Do you know where you want to build?' 'How much

> 162

receptionist, 'come when you want.' (The receptionists, who always have to give their names at the beginning of the conversation, lay great stress on the almost 'friendly' aspect of the relationships they form with the clients: 'The first contact is crucial. You have to put the customers at ease and let them talk. Usually, they're tense when they come in. All it takes to relax them is for you to be friendly. Generally, with those clients who stay with us, we follow them through to the point where their application is assessed. I don't say we become friends with them, but it gets a bit like patient and doctor: they ask us our names etc.')

Similarly, as if to encourage the customers' propensity to mistake the entirely professional interest in their personal characteristics for an interest in their private lives, the salespeople often themselves adopt the clients' ordinary-language translations or make such translations spontaneously on their behalf. For example, to the client who complains about co-ownership, the salesperson declares: 'I know what it is, I've got it myself.' The pursuit, more spontaneous than calculated, of personal complicity often leads the salespeople to introduce into their remarks anecdotes or snippets of common sense designed to show they can put themselves in the customers' place. This mechanism is seen most clearly in the extreme case in which the salesperson, to break down the resistance of a client who does not at first play the game, provides both questions and answers: 'In that case, you're going to ask me why ... And I'll tell you ...' But when the structure of the relationship with the client does not permit of the 'relaxed personal' exchange, the employee can arrive at the same ends by resorting to technical-bureaucratic language which, by way of the technical competence its use is supposed to underwrite, makes it possible to establish its user as an expert and induce the client to behave as a seeker after technical advice.

In fact, the duality of linguistic registers opens up the possibility of rhetorical manoeuvres, doubtless more unconscious than conscious, by which the social distance between the interlocutors can be manipulated, whether this takes the form of greater closeness and familiarity, achieved through the use of a familiar mode of expression or, conversely, of a standoffishness produced by the use of the most 'formal' mode of expression; alternate use of the two strategies giving a more or less complete mastery of the exchange situation. Thus, for example, when clients speak in favour of mortgage credit, the elements of popular wisdom they draw on are often taken over in precisely the same terms by the receptionists. To one client, complaining about the rent he has to pay, a receptionist says: 'You don't have to tell me. My mother pays so much ... and in

> 163

can you put in for the plot and the house?' 'Where do you live?' 'What station do you want to use into Paris, the Gare du Nord?' She will then answer the randomly ordered questions of M. and Mme F. one by one, before closing with: 'Would it interest you to meet a *colleague* who could offer you various styles of house and, most importantly, plots to go with them?' With the acquiescence of M. and Mme F., she takes them into an adjoining room that has been turned into an office and offers them a seat. A few moments later a man makes his entrance:

SALESMAN: Good day to you. You want some information, I presume? (He sits down at a desk.)
M. AND MME F.: Well, we're possibly interested in a house, a house here ... somewhere round here. And your colleague said we should talk to you about plots.
SALESMAN: We have to look, er, we have to *look at the whole thing*: what kind of house you want, what budget you have available, and then the plot on which, well, in what part ... well, in what area you want to build.

He then begins to ask the first questions. 'Whereabouts are you living at the moment?' 'Where in Paris do you work?' Then he continues: '*In terms of the financial package*, in terms of your budget, the plot plus the house, do you know exactly what you can get?'

M. F.: Yes, we've been to see [he mentions the name of another builder]. They did a financial assessment, we were ...
SALESMAN: You've been to see the opposition. O.K. And what kind of a figure did they come up with? 50 ... 60 ...?
M. F.: Well, 65 million old francs [650,000 new francs].
SALESMAN: 650,000 francs plot and house, all inclusive. Are you going to finance this by a PAP or a covenanted loan? Have you looked at that?
M. F.: Well, he did some calculations for us ...

The salesman then launches into a very succinct explanation.

SALESMAN: There are currently *two modes of financing*. You can have, through your family circumstances – number of dependents and your tax status – you can get a state loan, the PAP loan. Either, on the one hand, your family circumstances and your tax status allow you to get a state loan at 9.6 per cent interest or you have to go for a covenanted loan. These are two types of finance, but they make a difference when it comes to what you can afford.

Then he sets about a very detailed questionnaire, to which M. and Mme F. reply alternately while the salesman notes all their replies on a form: The amount of deposit they could pay? Are they homeowners or do they rent? Number of children? Income? Family allowance? ('But be careful, the banks don't count that.') He checks the figures provided by the

> 164

the end, it's money wasted …' By contrast, the client who seems opposed to credit gets a reply couched in technical language, designed to impress upon him that he does not understand it in the slightest. This language play exists as a possibility in any bureaucratic interaction. All individuals who find themselves invested with the status of representative of a higher authority (a status marked quite often by the wearing of a uniform or some distinctive mark) are 'dual' figures: they are permitted, or condemned, to engage in that self-duplication or double-dealing that underlies many of the most typical strategies of the bureaucratic management or manipulation of the lay public. Like the policeman who, when called upon by the offender to personalize the interaction, replies that 'rules are rules', they may identify purely and simply with their position, with the social definition of the functionary that is inscribed in his function. This is what the salespeople do spontaneously when, arming themselves with usurped authority, they behave as legal and financial experts, as mouthpieces of the law and the state, charged with revealing the law or the regulations to the client and, more precisely, with determining very exactly his or her entitlements by introducing into the universal formalism of the legal stipulations the numerical values of the parameters provided by the interview (number of children, family income, etc.). Playing, more or less consciously, on the representation the clients, particularly the most deprived of them, have of the law and, in particular, of the *contract* as an immutable straitjacket, they do everything in their power to deck out their conclusions in the apodictic certainty of a logical deduction or legal verdict; manipulating a technical vocabulary they never explain – or explain only in terms that show they have not fully mastered it themselves – and which, as the subsequent setbacks suffered by excessively indebted house buyers attest, is doubtless more designed to impress than to communicate useful information, they transform information about the conditions of access to various benefits – APL or progressive loans – into a peremptory statement of duties. (We can see here, in passing, that it is not easy to determine concretely where the state ends and 'civil society' begins. Apart from being in everyone's mind, in the form of common patterns of thought, the state is in a sense present in the person of the Bouygues or Phénix salesperson, who usurps a form of official delegation to impose the legal norms of the property transaction or, in other circumstances, it is present through the representatives of the bankers, estate agents or property administrators who, without being full-fledged members of the state, have a voice on the commissions where state regulations are elaborated. In fact, abandoning the dichotomy, which may

> 165

competitor ('A third of 12,000 francs, that's 4,000. Yes, that's right') and goes on with his questions: 'Is there a possible loan from your employer?' 'Do you have your tax assessment?' 'How long have you worked at the same company?' He asks if the other builder didn't offer them a PAP loan and decides 'Right, *we*'ll do a PAP loan spread over 20 years, and a complementary loan ... Yes, that's it. We'll do an enhanced PAP loan, no problem ...'

M. and Mme F. can only agree. The salesman goes on: 'So, now, what are you looking for *in terms of a house*, what do you need?' M. and Mme F. state that they want one bedroom per child 'at least', 'somewhere around 100 square metres surface area; that kind of figure', 'all on one level ... with a garage'. The salesman acquiesces. 'All right. Now what can I offer you of that kind at the moment?' He flicks through a catalogue.

M. F.: We saw one in your adverts in the kitchen that seemed all right ...

He names it, referring to one of the latest houses produced by the builder, a house unanimously regarded as unsaleable by the sales staff who, since they regard it as too complicated and generally unsuited to the demands of their clients, never propose it.

SALESMAN (carrying on with no reaction, going through the pages of the catalogue): As a possible house, 100 square metres, with a garage ... there are several possibilities ... (turns the pages) ... Well, here's one example. (He shows them the plans. It is the latest house the builder has brought out and one that, unlike the previous model, has won approval from the sales staff.) We'll add you in the garage here ... So many possibilities, eh? *We can do anything.*

As they look through the catalogue, M. and Mme. F. attempt unavailingly to get the salesman to talk about other models. He just carries on filling in his form, making financial calculations about the garage ('that makes so much'), adding in the Personalized Housing Allowance (APL), the amount of the PAP loan, and airily answering the questions M. and Mme F. try to put to him, mainly on the technical aspect of the house.

MME F.: How did the clients you have round here get on in that cold snap we had a while ago?
SALESMAN (takes advantage to *involve himself personally*): Naturally, I had no trouble with that at all. I have a G house myself.

A long technical description of G houses follows.

M. and Mme F. then learn that their loan 'will be progressive', without the terms being explained to them.

M. F.: At any rate, there'll be other expenses, of course, but to have a nice little place of our own and all that, we can make sacrifices, no problem ...

> 166

produce its effects in 'debates on the state of society', we have rather
to speak the language of differential access to specifically bureaucratic resources – law, regulations, administrative powers, etc. – and
to power over these resources, which the canonical distinction, as
noble as it is empty, leads us to forget.)

The relation between the occupants of bureaucratic positions – or
the occupants of comparable positions, such as salespeople – and the
users of their services is characterized, very generally, by a profound
dissymmetry: the functionary, benefiting from the experience
provided by thousands of similar cases and the information each
of his or her clients unwittingly provides, which enables him or her
to anticipate their expectations, preferences and even their defence
system, which is itself entirely commonplace and predictable (like
their supposedly 'trick questions' or their shows of false competence), is able to deal with situations that are for him or her
repetitive and standardized with standard strategies and instruments,
such as forms, questionnaires or crib-sheets providing the answers to
all possible questions (see appendix I on p. 176), whereas the user of
the service tends to experience these situations as unique and
singular and to find them the more generative of anxiety the greater
the stakes and the less readily available the information (as, for
example, at the hospital).

But the bureaucratic agent can also draw on the generative
capacities of his or her habitus to establish a personal relationship
that may, in some cases, go so far as to transgress, at least in
appearance, the limits laid down by his or her function: this is the
case when the salesperson points out in confidence, if not indeed in
conditions of secrecy, some particular advantage that is to be gained,
or when, as a favour, he vouchsafes some valuable, confidential item
of information – for example, regarding the building plots still
available on an estate, or the particular quality of a certain type of
house; or when, playing on the frustrations and expectations which
anonymous, depersonalizing treatment produces in the client, the
bank offers him *personal attention*, which he will gladly seize on (at
the second visit, the client is directed towards the clerk who saw him
the first time: he is called by name; and knowledge of his particular
case is displayed in various ways, thus indicating the very special
interest in him, etc.). It is, in fact, the salesperson's duty to create a
relationship of symbolic domination that is destined ultimately to be
cancelled and consummated in an act of identification with the
reasoning and interests of the bank which, possibly, under cover of a
'personal' identification between the salesperson and the client, will
be presented and experienced as totally identical with the reasoning

> 167

SALESMAN (protesting): Oh, no, no. As they say: everyone to his job ... I ask questions and that enables *us* to agree about the financing ...

He announces the total cost that comes out of his calculations, before asking whether M. and Mme F. were given the same figures by the competing builder. Monsieur F. cites a higher figure and the salesman plunges back into his calculations but ends up saying, with a laugh: 'Oh, no, no. *Mathematically,* that's not possible!' He then tots up *'what's left over for the plot'.*

M. and Mme F. would like a certain area of land. The salesman replies by referring to a specific plot. 'I have *one* plot there, on this estate. Otherwise ... It's just become available. We've sold everything ...' And he points out the advantages of 'the station right on the spot': 'it's a little village'; 'you've got the schools which are here'; 'there's nothing but fields immediately behind ... It's 500 square metres.' The salesman tries to position the house he has recommended on this plot, but cannot do it. He suggests another plot, behind Roissy airport, which M. and Mme F. reject 'because of the noise of the planes not far away', and he ends up suggesting a third one, a bit further out and more expensive, that seems to suit M. and Mme F. better. He then adds, 'Be careful. It's the last plot on the site. It'll soon be gone. We're already getting the planning permission.'

Second phase. M. and Mme F will ask questions to which the salesman will reply in ad hoc fashion, interlarding his replies with prepared sequences.

M. F.: The planning permission and the administrative procedures – do you do all those?
SALESMAN: From A to Z. You don't have to do anything. That's our problem. You can take it easy. We'll simply phone you from time to time ...
M. F.: Are you building the whole of the estate?
SALESMAN: It isn't just us. But we have a very precise building method ... What I mean by that is that we have distinctly more rigorous methods of fabrication, since we don't contract work out to other builders or craftsmen.
MME F.: So, when there's a problem, we call you ...
SALESMAN: There are no problems. No, it's true ... Our materials are the materials developed for *building dams.* So we're sure of our stuff, eh? That's some guarantee, isn't it? (The salesman then runs through the *Guarantees* sequence.) In fact, that's why we can guarantee our houses for 30 years for the exterior (plus the three-year guarantee on the fittings, called the supplier-guarantee).
MME F.: And the windows – when they close badly?
SALESMAN (technical sequence): No ... And then, after all, we've 40 years practical experience behind us. There's even a special department that takes care of ... [he quotes the name of his builder]. You can modify your houses later, there's a Home Improvement department which provides a full after-sales service. There are people ...

> 168

and interests of the client. The salesperson must use the advantage afforded him by the fact of being informed about the product, about loan terms and, most especially, about the traps those terms may contain, to generate or reinforce anxiety which, when taken to its extreme limits, can be resolved only by the client placing himself in the salesperson's hands.

The salesperson, who expects the client to defer to him and delegate to him the power to decide on the nature and form of the contract, must then allow the client to form a clear sense of his incompetence, while offering him assistance proportionate to the turmoil into which he is throwing him, and presenting himself to the client both as genuinely attentive to his concerns and capable of identifying with them, and, at the same time, as more able than he is himself to 'look after his interests'. The buyer, who is faced with a decision of very great moment without the minimum information required to make it (either regarding the technical qualities of the product or the financial terms of the credit), is inclined to hang on to anything that can seem to him like a personal guarantee; he looks for a contract of total trust, capable of dispelling his anxiety by providing at a stroke and for all time complete assurances regarding the uncertainties of the transaction. This is something the sales staff themselves feel, and they get caught up in the game themselves: 'We don't sell our houses. We sell plot-and-house. Well, no, we sell our finance and the plot ... and our faces. It's true, the house doesn't come into it This is how it is: we sell the plot and our faces and, if you like, as a bonus, they end up with a house (laughter) ... It's not often they ask about how the house is built. Very rare, that.' And the social affinities that bind them to their clients provide the basis for this relationship of reciprocal identification.

The structural homology between the spaces of the various builders and the spaces of the social characteristics of their agents (mainly the sales force), or, in other words, between the spaces of the products offered and the spaces of their respective client bases, has the effect of ensuring an 'automatic' fit (not without some local, partial mismatches) between the commercial strategies of the various salespeople and the socially constituted expectations of the corresponding client bases. According to a survey of 571 owners of Phénix houses carried out by the Institut Français de Démoscopie in 1981, Phénix's clientele includes 45.3% blue-collar workers, 2.2% domestic and maintenance staff, 18.6% white-collar workers, 15% middle managers, 17% craftsmen and small shopkeepers, 1.5% farmers, 2.2% other employees, 10.6% retired people and 3.5% senior managers and professionals. And, for the same socio-professional categories, the owners of Phénix houses are older and, above all, less educated than the owners of

> 169

M. F.: Is there a [name of builder] owners' club?
SALESMAN: No, there isn't a [name of builder] club, but all the same, a club could be started, as we've built 150,000 houses.

Third phase. The salesman no longer attends to what Monsieur and Mme F. are saying, but takes control of the conversation to get his last arguments over and attempts to force them to make a decision.

To a practical question put by Mme F., 'Can we add a little lean-to beside the garage?' the salesman makes a reply that relates to 'the whole of the project': 'Of course, that depends on the frontage of the plot ...' And he goes on: 'Now, for the plot, I have something I can offer you at this spot here that matches up well with the finance you have.' Monsieur and Mme F. then suggest 'going round to see it on their way home'. The salesman now begins to press them:

SALESMAN: If we're talking about this plot at ... I think you'll have to move a lot quicker than that ... Er, yes, *there's only one left.*

Monsieur and Mme F. now show reticence at so much hurry. The salesman then tries to get a sense of whether he has at least managed to interest them.

SALESMAN: On the other hand, in terms of finance, in terms of houses, does this match up with what you're looking for?

Monsieur and Mme F. agree that it does. The salesman now tries to draw up an order for them.

SALESMAN: ... Er ... What I mean by that is that there'd be a procedure to go through ... It's to fix the price. If it's that house you're interested in, then we can make out an order for that house, freeze the basic price of the house, and working from there I can sort out the finance details and do a search for the plot. *I myself* ... If you like, today we can make out the building order and reserve the house. So the price is fixed. Now, to do that, we need a payment of 2,000 francs. If there were a problem, you would get that back, and with that, that would allow me to start looking for a plot.

Given the reticence of Monsieur and Mme F. ('Perhaps we'll wait until the weather's a bit nicer to go and look'), the salesman ventures to insist: 'It would be a pity for you, if you're ready, to miss out on a *basic house price* ... You know, you're not acting in haste here. There are so many protective clauses ...' And he goes on: 'We can't do everything in one go. We have to move forward bit by bit.' Monsieur and Mme F. reply: 'We'll take a calm look at it all ... Right, we'll possibly come back another weekend.' The salesman closes the interview leaving them his contact details, together with the financial assessment he has done, to which he adds the catalogue including the different house models, then shows them back into the adjoining room.

□

houses built by close competitors within the field (such as GMF, Bruno-Petit and Châlet Idéal), not to speak of the owners of houses built by firms offering 'top-of-the-range' houses.

Now, we observe similarly that the cultural level of the salespeople is distinctly lower in the big industrial companies, which offer the least technically and aesthetically refined products, and which have the least well-off and least educated clienteles. For example, among the salespeople of Maison Phénix, 22% possess the CEP or the CAP, 24% have the BEPC, 12% claim to be of baccalaureate level, 13% have the baccalaureate or the BTS and 5% have had some higher education (24% did not provide information on this point). We know, moreover, that a number of salesmen with Maison Phénix began their careers as factory workers. It seems very likely that the different firms' sales staff are differentiated, both in terms of their educational backgrounds and their career paths, on identical lines to their respective firms. Thus, at Kaufman and Broad, for example, an international firm building 'top-of-the-range' properties, we find a significant proportion of salespeople who have received higher education, some of them even having attended the École des Beaux-Arts.

The salespeople occupy a strategic position in so far as it is largely through them that the *fit* between the product and the purchaser, and hence between the firm and a certain clientele, has to be made. Among other factors of the success or failure of a commercial policy or a product, one of the most crucial is undoubtedly the 'harmony' between sales personnel and clients and also, within firms, between the sales staff and the commercial managers and the marketing or advertising departments whose job it is to define how the product is promoted in the marketplace. As much as remuneration, which obviously counts for a great deal, particularly in the competition between the various producers to have the best salespeople, it is the fit between the dispositions the salespeople in practice bring to their task and the arrangements conceived by the specialists (who are often regarded by the sales force as mere theorists with no real knowledge of work in the field) which means that the salespeople do their work *happily*, that is to say, with both objective efficiency and subjective satisfaction. The salesperson does, in fact, *contribute crucially to the production of the product*: what the buyer is offered is not just a house, but a house accompanied by the discourse surrounding it, that of the friends or acquaintances who, as the survey shows, often prompt the choice of a particular builder, and, most importantly, that of the salesperson who very often stands warranty personally ('You know, I've got the same one and I'm very happy with it').

The reversal of the initial relationship that results from the transformation of a house purchase transaction into a loan purchase negotiation, and from the assessment of a house on offer into the financial assessment of the person desiring that house, can succeed and lead to the signature of a contract (rather than to the client backing out of the transaction) only if the salesman succeeds in transforming the definition of the situation and of his own image, and at the same time the image the buyer has of himself and the situation, in such a way that the relationship of anxious mistrust is turned into a relation of total trust, based on a certain form of identification. By drawing on an ethical and emotional complicity, linked to an affinity of habitus, the salespeople can combine the authority of the expert and the closeness of the adviser or confidant to bring clients freely to recognize the bank's judgement as representing the inevitable constraints of economic necessity or, to put it another way, to bring them themselves to adopt the bank's point of view, by identifying with the singularity of a person who is the bank personified: 'One must always have the clients judge for themselves the possibility of providing them with credit or not,' remarks a bank official. The prior examination of financial guarantees by which the lender protects himself from the borrower can be presented as arising from a concern to protect the client from imprudent decisions, that is, to protect the client from himself (and from an urge which, as a legal adviser in the Housing Information Association (ADIL) of the Val-d'Oise remarks, would be easy to exploit: 'They so want to hear that they can buy their three-bedroomed house and garden, and that it won't pose any difficulties for them, that they tend to distort reality ... We saw a lady who so much wanted to buy that she assured us she didn't spend more than 500 francs a month – a ridiculous figure – on feeding five people. She was so keen to say, to show that she could buy, that she went so far as to tell us: "No, there's no problem, because Mr So-and-so gives me vegetables and we only eat pasta; we only have soup in the evening because the children get meat at lunchtime at school." You hear such amazing things! You see people who clearly won't face up to reality, people convinced they can get what they want if only they tighten their belts. And you also see families going without holidays to buy a house. It's something that's so important!'). And if the bank employees, with the economic and informational capital at their disposal, are able to conceal their activities as lenders behind a mask of disinterested action on the part of advisers who, like doctors or lawyers, are making a stored knowledge available to their clients, this is because they are simply protecting the interests of the bank when they protect the clients from themselves, as when they advise them, for example, against concealing prior commitments (alimony payments, other loans, etc.) or against getting into debt beyond a certain level.

Given that he can sell his houses only if he manages to sell the necessary credit, the salesman is in a 'double-bind' which simply takes to extremes the contradiction inherent in the strategies of the bank: as the seller of a product, he may be tempted to exploit the impatience, imprudence or illogicality of the bad arithmeticians; as a seller of credit, he must, in order to protect the bank's interests, protect the client from excessive borrowing. He has, then, to steer between the temptation to 'push things', which would lead him to drive the client's housing expense ratio (the ratio of repayment levels to the client's current or permanent income) as high as possible, and the fear of insolvency or overindebtedness, which incites him to check carefully on the client's resources, and also, possibly, on other forgotten or concealed expenditure. He must both personify the pleasure principle, evoking, as the promotional leaflets do, the family's happiness, the comforts of the future house and so on, and the reality principle, reminding the client of all the various financial constraints.

As a captive of constraints and commands that leave him little freedom, it is perhaps ultimately his main task to guide and assist the clients in the work of psychological disinvestment they have to accomplish to adjust their hopes to their capacities: by obliging the clients to fit their projects within the constraints of a finite budget, he brings them to the discovery that, though all the properties of the hoped-for house can be magically reconciled in dream logic, they are actually interdependent, and unforgiving calculations of the economic optimum mean that all concessions to one's dreams in one sphere (surface area, for example) have inevitably to be paid for in another (usually, the distance to town or to one's work). If the salesman can help the clients effectively to accomplish this work of mourning without quenching all desire for home ownership, this is because, while submitting completely to economic and legal necessity, it is also in his interests to draw on all the resources of his economic and technical competence to ensure that as great a degree of the client's dream is fulfilled as is accessible within his means.

The strength of the aspiration to the ownership of a single-family house is such that unreasonable purchases, which are eventually punished by excessive indebtedness, would undoubtedly be more common if the sellers of credit were not able to impose on borrowers economic constraints that reinforce the *reasonable* (rather than rational) *anticipations* most of their clients would spontaneously

engage in their economic behaviour.[2] The injunctions and recommendations of the salespeople are, in fact, more likely to lead to
ultimate identification, culminating in the signing of a contract,
where the client is more completely geared in advance to the
expectations of the institution. This 'ideal client' is the lower or
middle-ranking civil servant who has just enough financial resources
to provide sufficient guarantees and who is sure enough of his future
to be provident, without being so well off as to be able to manage
without a property loan; he has just enough cultural resources to
understand the bank's requirements and identify with them, but not
enough to mount organized resistance to its manoeuvres. The career
of the civil servant is, in fact, the twofold root of the behaviour that
is regarded as rational, that of a being who is both calculable and
capable of calculation: it is the career which, as we have seen, confers
fully guaranteed existence on the permanent income, a sort of
potential capital which credit makes it possible to realize in part; and
it is also the career which establishes and makes possible the
dispositions without which there is no rational use of this form of
credit.[3]

Moreover, the banks' liking for this 'middle of the road' client is
clearly expressed in their explicit rejection (through the statements of
their officials and agents) of two opposing categories of clients, who
each sin by excess, though in opposing ways. The first of these is the
client who is 'not worth bothering about', who, lacking economic
and cultural capital in equal measure, will go to any lengths to fulfil
his dreams and is inclined to make financial commitments that
cannot be met (according to some studies, these can rise to more
than 40 per cent of income), mainly because he does not have the
minimum of necessary information to take advantage of the
information provided by the bank staff (and does not understand
the mechanisms of APL or progressive loans); the other is the client
described as 'a pain in the neck', who is excessively well informed
and, knowing his rights and interests only too well, does not allow
himself to be manipulated and intends to exploit the possibilities
afforded by the personalization of credit to obtain all the financial
advantages attaching to the fact that he is providing very substantial
guarantees. The first type, often driven by a sense of urgency, has
very little to put down as a deposit and provides a low level of
personal guarantees; he wants long-term credit; falling short of the
scale of calculability, he has a poor idea of what he is worth and
hence wants more than he is worth. The second, not being too badly
housed, can afford to wait; he can put down a substantial deposit
and provide genuine guarantees, which leaves him assured of a

favourable reception anywhere; he does not need a very long repayment term; he has the intellectual resources to make the best use of his assets, which he understands well.

As for the agents of the bank, they have all the requisite means at their disposal to 'make the client see reason'. The 'personal credit' formula means that the procedures for drawing up the contract act as a 'revelation mechanism', to use the language of the theory of contracts:[4] they effectively oblige the client to supply almost total information (give or take a few acts of concealment) for a very low 'truth extraction cost'. The bank therefore has all the means it needs to act in conformity with its interests in 'discriminating between agents' in such a way as to establish a specific contract for each of them. It holds all the necessary information to choose the clients presenting no hidden defects and to exploit these profitable clients without going beyond the point where the risks would become too great. It is, therefore, almost totally protected against the risks of 'adverse selection' associated with ignorance of one of the client's characteristics that might be such as to lead them to reject the contract: with the borrower who might be tempted to hide some other loan or financial commitment which might, in the long term, threaten his or her solvency, it is in fact able to dissuade him or her from taking that course of action. The bank is also safe from 'moral hazard', that is, from the dangers associated with a change in the agent's behaviour, such as might be caused by discovery of the latent defects of the contract or of the purchase, or both. One can see why excessive debt affects only a very small fraction of the indebted population.[5]

Being constrained to be rational in the negotiation of the loan contract which defines the limits of his legitimate aspirations, the borrower is also constrained to be reasonable in the management of the existence he has allotted himself, without entirely knowing it, by signing a contract which, in more than one instance, entailed a whole series of hidden consequences (such as increased transport costs, the acquisition of a second car etc.). The work of disinvestment that is accomplished, with the salesman's assistance, through the discussion of the payment plan, continues far beyond the moment of signature (which itself, very often, ratifies a moment of resignation): nothing is more reasonable and realistic than that long series of justifications one often garners when one enquires into the history of successive dwellings ('but at least you're in your own home ...', 'there's nothing like the horizontal', etc.), which are the product of the immense *work of mourning* that must be accomplished (so as to manage to *content themselves* with what they have) by buyers who discover all that their purchase entailed: the noise of the mowers at the weekend, the barking of the dogs, conflicts over shared charges etc. and, above all, the time costs of daily commuting.

Among house owners, it is the members of the middle-range occupations in business and public bodies, the technicians and clerks, who spend most time travelling to work, and the professionals and entrepreneurs/corporate managers who spend least: of house owners in the Île-de-France region, 13.5 per cent of those in middle-range occupations in the public sector, 12.5 per cent of technicians and those in middle-range occupations in companies and 11 per cent of white-collar workers spend at least three hours a day in travel between their residence and their place of work; no entrepreneur/corporate manager or professional spends as long as this. Among those who spend two hours or more are 48.5 per cent of senior managers in the public sector and 35.5 per cent of engineers. Among blue-collar home-owners, the foremen and supervisors have the longest travelling times, with semi-skilled workers having the shortest.

Thus, after so much deliberation and consultation, house buyers, who are rational calculators in spite of themselves, are forced to submit to the constraints which, through the new forms of financial assistance, govern the property market – the one major choice left to them being that of deciding on the aesthetic or technical quality of the dwelling and how far out it is, that is to say, they can choose between a mediocre house close to their workplace and a more spacious, more comfortable dwelling further away. For this, they have to 'lower their sights', both before and after their decision, and strive to achieve that kind of *amor fati* which allows one to make a virtue of necessity, of which allegiance to a particular brand of automobile is another example. But they have also to leave out of account, in an enormous gamble, all the unknown factors in the world of the economy – lay-offs, transfers, etc. – or in the domestic life-cycle – the permanence of marriage or divorce, children remaining in the household or leaving it, etc. – which they implicitly engage in their 'choice'.

This being said, however pressing the necessity that weighs upon the transaction, things are never decided in advance, and both the sales staff and the purchasers can play on the freedom afforded them by the structure of the economic relationship, the one group to tighten the structural constraint or, conversely, to relax it strategically, in order to allow it to return all the more strongly at a later stage, the others to escape it, by resistance or flight. And it is only through the series of interactions, all equally unpredictable and random (a particular couple who might not have stopped, or might have passed on to another stand, or have moved off saying they would come back, etc., find themselves there signing an undertaking conforming to the objective life-chances their characteristics assign to them), that, in the last analysis, the system of economic and demographic factors revealed by statistical analysis 'acts' or, better, actualizes itself. Far from being a mere ratification of the structure of the economic relation, the interaction is an actualization of that structure – an always uncertain actualization, both in its course, which is full of suspense and surprises, and in its very existence: observation and ethnographic description thus offer the only way of apprehending and reconstructing the form assumed, in the lived experience of the actors, by the action of factors that can act only by realizing themselves through that form. The exchange cannot be reduced to a mere process of revelation, in which the buyer might be said to be unwittingly collaborating with a salesperson seeking to extract information. The salesperson contributes to producing the need and the taste of the buyer at the same time as he or she evaluates the buyer's aptitude to meet the repayments and contributes to producing that aptitude: the buyers learn about themselves, about their tastes and their interests, and they accomplish the psychological work necessary either to go ahead with the purchase, at the cost, most often, of a considered restriction of their aspirations and expectations or, conversely, to delay a decision or give up the idea. In short, what observation reminds us, and what the logic of pure models might lead us to forget, is that *the act of purchase is not logically implied and practically included in the set of conditions that have to be fulfilled in order for a purchase to occur.* And, more broadly, that the action or interaction cannot be understood either as a mere mechanical effectuation of the structure (here the unequal relation between the salesperson and the buyer) or as a communicative action that could be explained without taking account of the structural necessity expressed in it. To sum up, the economic act is not the effect of a quasi-mechanical necessity working itself out through agents who might be replaced by machines; it can be accomplished only by assuming a particular social form, which is bound up with the social particularities of the agents engaged in the exchange and, most particularly, with the effects of trusting closeness or hostile aloofness that ensue from it.

APPENDIX I

THE SALES SCRIPT AND ITS USE

Madame A., a young secretary with a national builder, is responsible for answering the telephone and arranging the salesmen's appointments. 'Our company sent us ... well, someone who's in charge of staff training sent us sales scripts.' She pulls from a drawer a dozen or so stapled sheets which have come from the management. At the top of the first page you can see the words 'Sales Script'. She puts the document down in front of her and begins to read aloud, spelling out the prescribed script for each of the situations which may arise:

MME A.: **When a call is received:*** *Yes, of course. Could I ask your name please? Your address? Your phone number? I'm going to give you an answer that won't entirely satisfy you because I presume you wanted an exact price? I can say it will be between so much and so much* ... (She comments:) So that doesn't mean much. You try to ... to talk a bit about the financing ... (She goes on reading:) **Details regarding financial matters:** *I see you're concerned about the financial side. You're right to be, it's very important* ... I use those two sentences. *Right, well, our financial expert will answer all your questions. I suggest you meet him on* ...

    A request for prices: When they request a price, I always keep it vague. It's between ... and ... I don't give a price. That's to leave it a bit hazy for people, so they want to see someone to get some more information. If I give them a price, they'll say 'goodbye' and call round several other builders and then sort them out for themselves later ...

INTERVIEWER: But you know the prices ...?

MME A.: Of course, of course. I have the price lists, naturally ... But I say, for all the models, between 250,000 and 300,000 francs ... 350,000 sometimes. If they ask what a five-room house would cost, I say 'Right, five rooms. We have that as 90 square metres or 80 square metres or L-shaped or a two-storey house. They're all five-room houses.' So the client feels that's getting too complicated and he wants to see what it looks like. That way I get his address and phone number.

    Reviving client interest: There's also what the clients are likely to reply ... *You were in touch with us a while ago. So I'm calling to see where you've got to with your building plans.*

INTERVIEWER: So what does he reply then?

MME A.: *He says, 'we've given up on the idea.'* Then I reply, *'Monsieur So-and-so, why have you put off your building plans?'* Then, if the reasons are financial: *You had a meeting with one of our experts at the time. Did he*

---

* Italics (including those in bold type) have been used here to distinguish the words of the script from the employee's own words.

draw up a payment plan for you? If they say 'yes', I say 'How much did that come to? Has your financial situation changed since then?' If he says 'no', then I go on: 'Can I ask you some questions about that? Do you have children? How old are they? What's your monthly household income?' Then, first scenario: if the assessment is equal to or higher than the amount in the plan, 'Do you have some money for a deposit or some family savings you can put down?' if the answer is yes: 'Do you have a plot?' If the reply is in the affirmative, 'Where is it?' If not, 'What area do you want to build in?' In the second scenario: if the assessment is lower than the figure in the plan, 'Can you get hold of some money to help you get the project started?' The answer is no. Then I say I'll first send them another copy of our catalogue and I'll be in touch again in a few months' time. But if they have anything they want to ask us in the meantime, we are here to help ... Last month, I went back to all the leads that had gone cold. Out of some forty or so calls I got three appointments. That doesn't seem much, eh? Out of that there were two sales, but let's say that, by comparison with the number of people, er ... with what they tell us ... So what we did, and this worked reasonably well ... the proof is that when I managed to get an appointment with people who hadn't signed for one salesman, we gave them to someone else, and the other salesman managed to get them to sign.

Cancellation of appointments: Now, this is very hard ... a very hard situation to retrieve ... The client says, *'Oh, I'm very sorry about this, but I'm not going to be able to make the appointment with your salesman.'* Now, that's where I try to be a bit crafty when it's an appointment that same day. For example, the boys have appointments at 6 p.m. and 8 p.m. and a client calls me in the morning to cancel. So, then, trying to be a bit crafty and hold on to the appointment, I say they're not here now and I won't be seeing them today ... 'That's very awkward for me, because I won't be seeing him' or, at a pinch, if it's the day before, I say (Mme A. reads from the sheet:) *'Ah, I've got a big problem there, because unfortunately I'm not going to see our representative before this evening (or tomorrow evening)'* ... Right ... *'I know he talked to me about your plan because he had some important things to say about it.'* Well, there, I actually say: 'Oh, that's a pity because we were just talking about you yesterday and he had a proposal to put to you.' That's good because people then think to themselves, 'Good, they're talking about me.' That hits the mark.

(Mme A. picks up her script again and reads:) *Cancellation of a sale:* Now that's very hard as well...

INTERVIEWER: Is it?

MME A. (reads): *So, Monsieur So-and-so, what we need to do to cancel the sale, to return your deposit to you and close your file is for you to meet [salesman's name] as soon as possible. He'll show you how to proceed and will carry out the formalities.* So I try that. That way, the salesman gets a second meeting with the client.

INTERVIEWER: And does that work?

MME A.: ... Yes, it works. Because, as the people have given us a cheque, and their wage slips and tax returns and so on, we have personal papers relating to them. I'm counting on that having an effect. But, on the other hand, you do have to move very quickly there ...

INTERVIEWER: You do?

MME A.: Within 48 hours at the outside. Within 24 hours is very good. If the client calls, you drop practically everything and get after him. Because it's a sale to retrieve ... particularly if they tell you there's another competitor more or less ...

INTERVIEWER: And does that do the trick?

MME A.: Er ... it depends ... No ... well it's a hazy area. Sometimes it works, sometimes it doesn't! We had some cases last month and tried to retrieve them, but we didn't manage it with any of them. One instance of someone losing their job. Another was a divorce that didn't go through ... It wasn't retrievable at that moment. Perhaps in a year's time!

 A deal falls through (the client cancels his contract with the builder).

MME A. (reads her script): *Did you meet with one of our experts at the time? Monsieur So-and-so, I'm going to ask you a favour. Can you tell me what you found elsewhere which we weren't unfortunately able to offer you?*

INTERVIEWER: And what answer do you get?

MME A.: Ah (laughs) ... All sorts. Sometimes they say they didn't like the salesman ... Or ... he didn't tell us this or that ... etc.

INTERVIEWER: And what do *you* think of this sales script?

MME A.: Er, well, I'm not particularly keen on this kind of thing. I talked about this with my area manager last week because I don't know how it feels to the client on the phone, but for me, when I'm talking to the client, I feel like I'm reading. So I have some problems with it. It's not spontaneous as regards what the client says to me. I follow my lines (Mme A. reads from the pages:) *Then, yes. 'Do you have a preferred locality?'* So I say that in the conversation, but once we've spoken about that I've gone off the script. I don't know where I am any more. Do you see? But it's also difficult because it depends on what the client asks you at any given moment. You're following a different agenda to the client. So it gives me some problems because I feel I'm reading too much.

INTERVIEWER: But are there things this script makes you say that are opposed to what you would say if you were left to your own devices?

MME A.: Er ... (she reads from the page in front of her) *Hello, is that Monsieur or Madame X's? Is that Monsieur or Mme X? Hello, this is [builder's name]. You wrote to us. That was very kind of you. Thank you very much. I've noted the information you supplied, but there is one thing we need to know regarding a plot. You say you don't have a plot, but which area do you want to build in?* Right, I don't have any problem with any of that. *Do you have a preferred locality?* All right. Well, actually I try not to ask if they have a preferred locality, because I have a fair idea that if people live in Meudon, they want to build in Meudon or if they live in the 16th arrondissement of Paris, that's where they want to build. Well, there's a problem there (she laughs), first because there aren't any plots and, second, because very often the poor souls don't have any money. So rather than tell them it isn't possible well, that's not my role in any event. That's for the boys to follow up, but my aim is to get appointments. So instead of saying *'Do you have a preferred locality?'* I ask them what area they intend to build in?

INTERVIEWER: You keep it more vague ...

MME A.: Yeah! I prefer to remain more vague. No, but it's true. That particular phrase there – *'Do you have a preferred locality?'* – I never talk about that. That, er, that's something I can't imagine myself saying because it isn't our job to convince the client to take a plot elsewhere.

INTERVIEWER: Are there other phrases you wouldn't ...

MME A.: *So, what I suggest, and this doesn't commit you to anything* – well, I always say that because people are always very afraid – *is to meet our expert who will answer all your questions, first on the financial side of things, that is to say what kinds of benefits and loans are available to you* – well, normally people know that because they've, er, been to see several companies – *then regarding the land, that is to say what plot you can get, what precautions you have to take* – I never talk about that ...

INTERVIEWER: Oh, why not?

MME A.: Because ... no, because ... it's like with the preferred locality ... what plot, what precautions they have to take ... the thing is I wouldn't know how to follow it up. Because the client's going to say, 'What does that mean, the precautions you have to take?' And I don't know.

INTERVIEWER: What do you say instead?

MME A (laughs): I miss that out completely. As a rule, everything to do with land ... Er ... well, I stick to the housing side. I don't talk about the plot ... (Mme A. goes back to her script) *You will, of course, tell him what kind of house you want, what choices you've made and he'll answer all your questions. So I suggest you could meet him either ... Or ...* (Then, if the appointment is at a late hour) *Is there a day when your husband could see him at an earlier time?* (Then you rearrange the appointment and that's it.) The area managers have done some test runs and they claim to have found that out of ten addresses they could get five appointments in mid-afternoon. Well, perhaps they have, but that's not my experience. I rarely manage to make afternoon appointments. People are at work. I get appointments from 6 or 8 p.m. onwards. Generally, I adopt the approach of asking if they are, by any chance, free early or late in the week, and if they prefer us to come to them in the morning or the afternoon. And when I do that, they say after six o'clock ... Since the aim is for both the husband and wife to be there, so that they can't use the partner's absence as an excuse, I also try to ask if they'll both be there ...

INTERVIEWER: Are there other things in this script you don't manage to say?

MME A.: Oh yes! (She looks at the sheets) *The client's objections ... 'Hello, I just want some information.'* So you try to get an appointment, but there's no way because the client says they 'just want information'. Then, er, I'm reading from my crib-sheet still ... and, er, I always find it a bit hard to say: *So yes, of course, Monsieur So-and-so. I understand totally. Only, all the same, a building project isn't something import ...* Er ... (Mme A. begins again) ... *all the same, it's something important. You're making a commitment for many years and that deserves in-depth consideration. Here at [builder's name] we're serious about what we do. We think an interview with our expert is decidedly preferable to give ...* Er ... *to give you a response. You're not committing yourself to anything by doing this, of course. It's for that reason I suggest an appointment on ... Or ...* Well, I don't say all that part myself.

INTERVIEWER: No? What do you say?

MME A.: In my opinion, the client doesn't want to sit through a long spiel from me. So I just say, 'Listen, if you want to get ... really ... accurate information on what you want or what you're looking for, a meeting's essential.' I don't have too much of a problem making appointments like that, because if people call you up they do it because they really want to know something. So, I use this script as a basis ...'

INTERVIEWER: Which sentences here, for example, do you keep in?

MME A.: Ah, well. There ... Er ... *Here at [builder's name] we are serious about what we do.* I keep that in. Obviously ... [laughter]. The rest I boil down. (Mme A. continues to read the pages of her script): *Potential questions: how are your houses built?* Then I keep this sentence that comes next: *I can see you're interested in the technical aspect, and you're right to be, it's very important.* I say that one because it's too good to leave out. But, after that, on the other hand: *Well, our expert will answer all your questions. For that reason I suggest an appointment on ... Or ...* I say all that too, because it's in short sentences. It's to the point. So I don't change anything, because what's there works better ... On the other hand, I never say this bit where there's a cancellation: *Monsieur So-and-so, what I'm going to ask you is to make an effort and give us a few moments ...* I never say that because, if the client has called, I find it ridiculous to ask him to give me a moment when he's already made the effort to call to cancel, because then the people would tell us where to get off ...

INTERVIEWER: In fact you've never said the whole of your script ...

MME A.: No, I've never tried, because there are quite long sentences in there too. And ... having the person on the phone then and there, you want to move quickly. I try to go as quickly as possible, not to get too wordy. Because if you begin to get wordy, er, it's no good me telling them I'm a secretary and I don't know things. I have to stay a bit vague – do you see? – because I'm a secretary, not a saleswoman. So if I begin telling them my life story, they say, 'Oh yes, but do you think I can ...' or 'Yes, do you think I can get a plot for this price ...' In a word, they start asking me lots of questions. So I try to keep it as vague as possible! If you like, the aim of the script – and it's fine that way – is always to say yes. They say, 'We're not in a hurry' and you reply, 'Yes, of course, I understand.' Then, afterwards, the client's very happy because he thinks to himself, 'The lady understands ...'

(She bursts out laughing.) I ought to follow this script all the time, but each time I tend to slip into my own natural style and then ... there it is, I've shortened it!

APPENDIX II

TWO INTERVIEWS

'A REAL NIGHTMARE'

Monsieur L. and his family have decided to set about buying a house. He is 32 and works as an operator with a computer firm. She is 30 and is an accounts software operator in an insurance company. They have two children, aged seven and three. Speaking of the building of the house, he says: 'It's a grind, a real nightmare. You have to really want to do it. Yeah, it's crazy! I don't know how to put this. It's so easy to get loans now for cars and other things, but, with a house, you wouldn't believe the paperwork that's needed and the general lack of coordination. In the end, I took charge of it myself. Normally, it's the builder who takes care of the loans and all that. Well, I may perhaps have made life difficult for myself, but, when it comes to the documents, everyone's dependent on everyone else. You waste months and months. Here we had the problem that the services weren't laid on yet, but we had to get a finance package together, see how much we could raise. That's the problem at the beginning. You don't know how to set about things, where to start. For instance, should you go and see a builder? But he asks you if you have a plot. Should you find a plot and then go and see a builder? To do that you have to know how much money you can put up.

'At the beginning you're lost. In fact, you set about everything the wrong way round. That's what happened to me. I went to see the builder and he said, "do you have a plot? You don't?" He had plots, but would the ones he had match what we wanted? There wasn't any reason why they should. You can find a plot elsewhere. So, all that's a problem. After that there's the business of finding a loan and coordinating everything. It's hell on wheels from beginning to end. For instance, we're stuck now because we haven't got planning permission. We're waiting for permission right now. When I get that I can make the application for a 1 per cent loan, a *prêt patronal* [employer's loan], etc. You also have to sign the documents with the notary. Nothing's made easy for you. All in all, it's going to take a year and a half to build a house. It's a nightmare! You spend almost as much time on the paperwork and all that as you do on building the house. It doesn't make sense!

'Afterwards, you have to monitor the building work. I'll be the same with that. Since I'm pretty pernickety, I'll do that myself too and it's going to take a lot of time. And I want the work to be done well, so I'm going to spend a lot more hours coming and going, seeing how it is and so on – making sure it's done as I want it. Because it's pretty rare that the work is done exactly as it should be. You really have to have the will.

'[...] Always the impression we're not going to get there. Certainly,

someone who has a good salary and other sources of finance, well ... But, with us, we've nothing from family sources, we've always got by on our own. Then, to be faced with a load of problems, it became demoralizing in the end. We were up for it at the beginning, but after a while we were in despair. We thought, it's not going to be possible, we'll never do it. That's the side, we were demoralized. At one stage, I said, it's impossible; we're never going to do it. And, as I'd got the idea of the house into my head and wanted it, I was frustrated and angry. I'm very happy we're getting there now. All the people I've seen who've bought a house found it pretty hard all the same in the first two years because you have to adjust to the rhythm, but it seems that afterwards it's no ... At any rate, the way things are going, rents ... But my lasting memory will be this sense of battling with the wind, it's crazy! The sense of not making any headway is so frustrating. Really, unless you have the resources, you can't always do what you want. I realize that, what with the dreams I had, what I wanted to do in the beginning, it's hard to do even a part of what I dreamt of doing. In fact the house has shrunk for me. It isn't the house I envisaged any longer. I was looking at a big house, big rooms, a big fireplace, sort of thing. When I was young, I had lots of mates who lived in Enghien who had quite nice houses. I always said to myself, that's great, that's what I'd like to have. And then the sad reality sets in (laughter).'
(Extract from an interview with a purchaser of an industrially built house at Taverny, Val-d'Oise, in late 1987.)

'LOWERING THE TEMPERATURE'

SALESMAN· When, as a client, you've just signed the agreement with the salesman and you go home in the evening, the next two days are going to be terrible for you. So we need to give them a little reassurance by telling them: 'Right, we've got your application for finance sorted out; it's gone off to such and such a bank; we've seen the person dealing with it; we already have a positive response from so-and-so.' 'Oh, right,' they say and things feel better. But then, afterwards, they get pretty edgy again. So you reassure them again, and actually go back to see them when the loan application's accepted. Things are still pretty feverish at that point. After that, there are the problems around planning permission. They have their loan, but are they going to be able to build what they really want, because there are also standards to conform to ... set by the DDE? Admittedly, the tension's gone down a bit now, but there's still a degree of apprehension, relating largely to the possible modifications; for somebody who wants to make architectural modifications, it isn't certain, among other things, that they'll be approved by the architect ... But the pressure isn't so great at this stage. The real pressure is around the loan, when the application is borderline. That's when it's difficult. But once it's been accepted, things are a lot better, because they know they're going to get finance and they can build, come what may.

INTERVIEWER: So your job at that point is to ...

SALESMAN: Reassure them ... make them accept the ... reassure them they've made the right choice ...

INTERVIEWER: But how do you set about doing that?

SALESMAN: There certainly are people who are frightened by the financial side, by borrowing over 15 or 20 years. And when you get your loan offer and it shows you the interest over 20 years, with all you have to pay! You've got to remember that even 10 per cent is 10 per cent a year. And, over 20 years, that makes 200 per cent. You're tripling the cost of your house ... So, it's incredible! And we reassure them first of all about ... about the value of the money intrinsically. But those are abstract notions. You can reassure them much more by telling them they don't have to feel *obliged* to spend 20 years paying for it ...

INTERVIEWER: They shouldn't feel obliged to spend 20 years paying for it?

SALESMAN: Certainly not. They can sell it ... And since property prices are ... I don't know anyone who loses money on property ... You buy something for 200,000 francs and even if you don't make a great gain, ten years on you can sell it on for 400,000 or 500,000. And then you have a new deposit and you can make a fresh start ... It isn't a house for life these days ... You have young couples, young households with a little toddler who want a five- or six-room house right away because it's *their* great purchase. Well, if they can raise the finance, if it fits in with their budget, then all well and good. But if it doesn't, then you have to take the drama out of the problem. Why do you want six rooms for three of you? What do you want to do with them right now? Right, well you can raise a deposit of so much, you have so much income that allows you to gain ownership of a detached property. But how are you going to do it?

INTERVIEWER: I didn't know you used that kind of argument as a selling ...

SALESMAN: It's not an *argument* as such, but it is perhaps a *counter-argument* to a possible objection about price, about the length of the loan, the space or the size of the house. You can ... er ... use this angle, of course ...

INTERVIEWER: You say 'counter-argument'?

SALESMAN: And the person who dreams and wants their house, they see it in their mind's eye. Getting them to accept a project *less than* what they want isn't easy. The opposite is always easier.

(Extract from an interview with a salesman working for a national builder, Salon de la Maison Individuelle, Paris, October 1984.)

Conclusion: The Foundations of Petit-Bourgeois Suffering

What we have addressed throughout this work is one of the major foundations on which the suffering of the petite bourgeoisie is built or, more exactly, on which are built all their little troubles and adversities, all the infringements of their freedom, the blows to their hopes and desires which load their existences down with worries, disappointments, frustrations, failures and also, almost inevitably, with melancholia and resentment. That suffering does not spontaneously prompt the sympathetic, compassionate or indignant reactions inspired by the great hardships of the proletarian or subproletarian condition. No doubt because the aspirations that underlie the dissatisfactions, disillusionments and tribulations of the petite bourgeoisie, who are pre-eminently the victims of symbolic violence, always seem to owe something to the complicity of the sufferers themselves, and to the mystified, extorted, alienated desires by which these modern incarnations of the *Heautontimoroumenos* conspire to bring about their own unhappiness. By embarking upon projects that are often too large for them, because they are measured against their aspirations rather than their possibilities, they lock themselves into impossible constraints, with no option but to cope with the consequences of their decisions, at an extraordinary cost in tensions, and, at the same time, to strive to *content themselves*, as the expression goes, with the judgement reality has passed on their expectations: they may thus spend their whole lives striving to justify misconceived purchases, unfortunate schemes and one-sided contracts both to themselves and to their nearest and dearest; or, on another favoured terrain for their investments, the terrain of education, to justify their failures and semi-successes or, worse, deceptive successes leading to complete dead-ends which the education system often reserves for its favoured sons and daughters, the most noteworthy of which is surely a career in teaching itself, doomed as it is to structural decline.

This 'people', simultaneously petty-minded and triumphant, provides no source of comfort for the populist illusion and, being both too close to home and too distant, attracts only sarcasm and disapproval from the social commentators, who criticize it both for its *embourgeoisement* and for the failure of its efforts to achieve bourgeois 'freedoms', jointly condemning its mystified aspirations and its incapacity to satisfy them in ways that are anything other than illusory and derisory; it is, in short, the butt of all the denunciations of the 'semi-detached dream' and of the condescending discourse on the 'consumer society', in which certain inadequately socioanalysed 'philosophers' or 'sociologists' have come to specialize. And yet, because they find themselves drawn to live beyond their means, on credit, they discover the rigours of economic necessity almost as painfully as did the industrial workers of a different era, particularly through the sanctions imposed on them by the banks, to which they had looked to work miracles on their behalf. It is no doubt this which explains why, though they are in part the products of a liberalism aimed at tying them in, by bonds of home ownership, to the established order, they keep faith, in their voting patterns, with parties that regard themselves as socialist. Though they are, ostensibly, the great beneficiaries of the general process of *embourgeoisement*, they are shackled by credit to what is often an unsaleable house, if not indeed unable to meet the costs and commitments, particularly in terms of lifestyle, that tacitly formed part of an initial decision that was often obscure even to the decision-maker. 'In a contract not everything is contractual,' said Durkheim.[1] Nowhere does this formula apply so much as in the purchase of a house, in which an entire life-plan and style of life is often implicitly engaged. If the act of *signing* a contract is so harrowing, this is because there is always something fateful about it: the person signing the contract brings down a largely unknown destiny on himself or herself and, like Oedipus, unleashes a host of hidden consequences (hidden, largely, by the action of the salesperson), consequences built into the web of legal rules to which, without the signatory realizing it, the contract refers, and also all those consequences which he or she, with the connivance of the salesperson, refuses to see: these latter, contrary to what is feared, have less to do with the 'hidden defects' of the product and more with the implicit commitments into which he or she is entering and which will have to be seen through to the end, that is to say, far beyond the last due date for the last payment.

This is what so many accounts, all of them equally dramatic, tell us unremittingly.

Béatrice, aged 40, is an office worker in the Direction Départmentale de l'Équipement at Cergy-Pontoise. Her husband (it is a second marriage) is a maintenance worker in a ministry building in Paris. She is the eldest of 12 children. With her first husband, by whom she had two children, she ran a mobile chips and waffle stall in the forests north of Paris. At that point, business was good. They had 'good sites for the van' and lived in rented accommodation. After her divorce, her current employer let a state-requisitioned house to her at a very low rent: 'A very old house, really splendid ... a very big garden ... but building work to do ... the roof was falling down ... and doing building work on a house that isn't yours ...' They could, however, have stayed there 'indefinitely'. She was expecting a fourth child. At that point, the firm GMF mounted a promotional campaign in Cergy-Pontoise. Tempted by the advertising, they dreamt of having a house of their own. Before making up their minds, they went to see other housing estates in the region. 'Near Cergy, at Puiseux, Maisons Bouygues and France Cottage, which we quite liked. But it was too expensive. Given the financial situation, we couldn't possibly have one ... We didn't have anything to put down as a deposit.' GMF offered them a preferential '*prêt ami*' loan, covering the deposit normally required. After hesitating ('it was a long way out ... particularly for my husband'), they settled, 'under pressure' from the saleswoman, on a six-room house in a development at Bernes-sur-Oise. 'It was reasonably priced.' And 'the people selling the houses take care of everything. There's no problem.'

They were able to obtain a substantial PAP [first-time buyer] loan because the amount of the loan is fixed according to the income indicated on one's tax return. Since they married in 1981 and had three dependent children, they paid practically no tax at all. 'The personalized housing aid allocation is a fantastic amount', but as a result the repayments are enormous. Not to mention the *prêt ami*, which they are not entirely sure when or how it is to be repaid. 'Because if the interest runs over 20 years ... The lady should have told us. We, let's say, we didn't think about it, you're rather in cloud-cuckoo land when you're buying a house. You're not really on the ball. You see the house and imagine the kids in it. Then we'll manage somehow, after all.'

Before making up their minds, they sought advice. Most people were favourably disposed towards GMF. Her husband made enquiries. He watched the TV programme *50 millions de consommateurs* [50 Million

Consumers] a lot: 'With the limited choice we had, between Phénix, Socova and GMF, he decided, all the same, that we should opt for GMF.' When the building work began, they went to see 'if they were doing everything that should be done': 'We had some unpleasant surprises, for example, over the insulation, the plumbing and so on ... We didn't know if we could take them to court over this. Anyway, that ... if you want to do it ... costs money.'

The house is a little too big ('At the outset we would have liked one room fewer, but they said, "with four children, have this one. It'll be better ..." '). 'Otherwise, it's great. Well, it's the bare minimum, as my husband says. Inside, you can hear everything. The walls are very thin. But I'm happy in my house.' Yet Béatrice is worried: 'We don't have any regrets ... but we find it very hard to keep up the payments now. It's very hard ... We've cut back on lots of things so that we can meet the monthly repayments.' Two years after the purchase, they have still not received the finance plan. 'We don't know where we're headed ... We're in a little bit of a panic ...'

It's the same for a lot of people on the estate: 'It's a catastrophe ... Most of the people have been forced to leave ... They were like us, they couldn't keep up with the heating costs, they couldn't do anything ... There are a lot of working people who don't take notice of these things ... They don't grasp that there are shared charges.' A lot of people came from 'the council flats over by Aubervilliers. They weren't used to living in a house ... In the first year, you should have heard the shouting ... They were holding conversations from one house to another.'

Béatrice gets up at six, gets the children ready, takes the youngest to the childminder and catches the eight-thirty train. She has problems with her work colleagues because that 'gets her in at half past nine instead of nine o'clock'. Her husband has four hours' commuting a day. 'Persan-Beaumont is the worst of the lines.' In the evening, Béatrice picks up the youngest children from the childminder on her way home. There aren't enough places in the schools because 'in little communes like this, they don't make provision for people coming in'.

Every year they go to stay with Béatrice's mother-in-law in Perpignan for their holidays. There would, however, be 'no holidays' this year, as they have to put up a garden fence: 'Just doing that is going to cost us 8,000 francs.' She likes white, American-style fences: 'For the gates alone, you're looking at 5,000 francs.'

'If we're still in this position when we've been here ten years, we're going to stop spending on the house. Even if we lose everything. I don't want to end up dying at 60, for a house my kids are just going to fight over ...'

But there is no need to go as far as the extreme cases, even more dramatic than this one, in which the gamble on the stability and permanence of things and persons, and of the relations between things and persons, that was tacitly involved in the decision to purchase a house has not worked out, either as a result of an enforced move, unemployment, divorce or separation. We need cite only the statistically ordinary case of all those inhabitants of prefabricated houses in the so-called residential areas who, lured by the mirage of falsely 'individual' housing (like the semi-detached houses on estates, which have almost all the same restrictions as a council flat), experience neither the solidarity of the old working-class districts, nor the isolation of the better-off areas: these people, who spend hours each day commuting to distant workplaces, are deprived of the relationships that formed within their neighbour-hoods, particularly in and through trade union campaigns, without being able to create – in a place of residence where socially very homogeneous individuals are gathered together, but without the community of interests and affinities that ensue from belonging to the same world of work – the elective relationships of a leisure community.

The single-family house thus functions as a trap, and it does so in several ways. As can be clearly seen from the interview below, it tends gradually to become the exclusive focus of all investments: those involved in the – material and psychological – work required to come to terms with it in its reality, which is often so far removed from anticipations; those to which it gives rise through the sense of ownership, which determines a kind of domestication of aspirations and plans (these now end at one's own doorstep and are confined to the private sphere – as opposed to the collective projects of political struggle, for example, which always had to be carried on in the face of the temptation to retreat to the domestic sphere); those it inspires by imposing a new system of needs, inscribed in the exigencies it contains in the eyes of those who seek to live up to the (socially formed) idea they have of it.

Denise is a little over 30. She is a secretary. Her husband is an accountant with UAP. She bought an industrially built house on a 97-house estate at Éragny in the Val-d'Oise, near Cergy-Pontoise. She has lived there for seven years. She 'opted for a house' when she saw that 'in the Paris region, closer to Paris, flats were as expensive as a house was there'. Before that, she lived in rented accommodation – a nominally three-roomed flat, where she was 'short of space'. 'There were about to be four of us. And with just the one bedroom.' She had a savings scheme, which she had to curtail 'because the child arrived a little ahead of time': 'So that restricted us a bit in terms of the financial means at our disposal. We couldn't get a Savings Bank loan ... So that more or less forced us to look at new-build. And the covenanted loans were a better deal than the ones we were offered by the banks.' For want of financial resources, they had to look for something 'in this suburb in the Hauts-de-Seine, which [they] didn't really like'. They would have preferred an old building. But, 'even in this region, that poses a lot of problems on account of the loans which are at distinctly higher rates': 'otherwise, I do think we would both have preferred to go for something with a lot more character, in fact, than this house in a new town where everyone is the same age, and is more or less on the same level ... It's too samey.'

Denise and her husband chose this region 'because, in spite of the distance, it had the best communications with Paris' where they both work. Before making up their minds, they mainly studied advertisements ('But when we saw the prices, we didn't look at any old houses. We didn't want to be tempted ...'). They went to look at building sites, at estates.

They were urged on by friends who had just bought a house: 'They took us around, because they'd already been round all the other sites, the new building sites.' In fact, if they did make their minds up to buy, it was because no one around them had advised them against it. And then they thought that 'if we can't find what we'd want ideally, at least it would enable us to get a foothold on the property ladder ... so we could try and find something better afterwards.' Perhaps a house 'standing entirely alone' or a house in an area that is not so new. The house they chose was the cheapest and it was 'ready to move into'.

There were lots of disappointments in the early stages. 'The finishings were pathetic.' There was very little choice – only three or four wallpapers, 'and it was really council-flat wallpaper'. They had to have the ground floor retiled. They did lots of work 'bit by bit': 'we totted up each year what we could do.' Then they discovered the noise from the lawnmowers during the weekends, until the residents' association regulations prohibited them. 'And then, as we're between two houses, the bathroom and kitchen plumbing are shared with the adjoining house and you hear all their pipes.' The fireplace, made 'by a company which was in cahoots with the property company', was very expensive.

They bought furniture 'bit by bit', from private individuals, whom they contacted through local newspapers such as the *Centrale des particuliers* or *Le Bichot*. 'We'd been looking for a bookcase for two years. We finally found one a month ago, from an advert in *Le Bichot*.' They have acquired the habit of searching ('much more than in the past') at flea markets or among the second-hand dealers of the region 'wherever ... old things are sold. Before that, we never thought about it. Now, on Sundays, since there isn't so much entertainment here, being further away from Paris ... well, on Sundays, if we want to go out, we happily go either to a local sale ... or to dealers or private individuals. Sometimes we make that the destination of a walk.'

They have tried to plant up the garden, a little patch of land measuring a hundred square metres: 'just enough to have a bit of greenery, and a little fruit all the same' – strawberries, two pear trees, then a cherry tree. 'But these are all young. We haven't had much fruit yet.' 'The advantage of plants is that they've grown and we're a bit less aware of having so many neighbours.'

Denise gets up at six thirty every day, while her husband rises at quarter to six. She breakfasts with him, then goes off to the bathroom while her husband leaves to catch his bus. She takes the girls to school by car, at around eight o'clock, then catches the train at Conflans. She gets to work around nine thirty. She is never home in the evening before quarter past seven. They don't feel up to going back into Paris at weekends. 'We've noticed as we've gone on that we don't go into Paris very much at the weekend.' Going out is undoubtedly the thing she misses most. 'I like the cinema a lot. My husband would like to see *Amadeus*, but we can't ...' She is not sorry to have bought the house, in spite of the length of their journey times. The positive aspect of living on the estate is that the children are safe. They can cycle and roller-skate; they go to each others' houses. But will things be the same when they're 15 or 16? 'The older girl likes to go out, to go to galleries and that sort of thing. That's not something she can do at Éragny. For sporting activities, it's all right – skating, swimming, dancing and so on.'

Denise has three hours' travel each day. She 'makes use of it to knit. That's what a lot of women do on the train. It's quite possible to read when you're not too tired. But there are moments when you're so tired that knitting is ... well, it's more mechanical. You switch off while you're knitting. Reading is more difficult. In the train, you can only read magazines – or undemanding novels.'

'What are you reading at the moment?'

'At the moment ... I'm not, er ... (silence)'

'The last thing you read?'

'The last thing was a book called   let me see – *Les Enfants de Jocaste*[2] ... I haven't finished it yet. It's a book on Freudian theory.'

What emerges from this entirely ordinary account, chosen precisely for its representativeness, is the effect of a policy that was intended to provide house builders with a market, while producing homeowners attached to their property, and that has, in a sense, succeeded. However, those who found themselves constituted as suburban homeowners in most cases gained access to these satisfactions only at such high costs that, even if it fostered a profound transformation of the social order, and one profoundly in keeping with the desires of its promoters, liberal policy has undoubtedly not brought its promoters the political benefits they expected. The family unit, centred on the upbringing of the children, which is seen as a path of individual social ascent, is now the site of a kind of collective egoism that finds its legitimation in a cult of domestic life permanently celebrated by all who live directly or indirectly by the production and circulation of domestic objects.

And, without exaggerating the importance we should accord to such indices, one cannot help seeing it as what is sometimes called a sign of the times that the production and distribution of televised images has now fallen into the hands of the firm and the entrepreneur who, having shown themselves more skilled than any at exploiting the aspirations to private happiness hooked up to the age-old ambition of owning a piece of transmissible heritage, are able to imprison the petite bourgeoisie of suburban 'semi' land in the specious world of dubious advertisements for domestic products, of game shows glorifying the same products and shows in which a fake conviviality is established around a kitsch culture – in short, in the very family-centred, skilfully domesticated amusements that are mass-produced by the cultural industry of professional entertainers.[3]

Part II

Principles of an Economic Anthropology

To break with the dominant paradigm, we must – taking note, within an expanded rationalist vision, of the historicity constitutive of agents and of their space of action – attempt to construct a realist definition of economic reason as an encounter between dispositions which are socially constituted (in relation to a field) and the structures, themselves socially constituted, of that field.

The structure of the field

Agents, that is to say, in this case firms, create the space, that is to say, the economic field, which exists only through the agents that are found within it and that deform the space in their vicinity, conferring a certain structure on it. In other words, it is in the relationship between the various 'field sources', that is to say, between the different production firms, that the field and the relations of force that characterize it are engendered.[1] More concretely, it is the agents, that is to say, the firms, defined by the volume and structure of specific capital they possess, that determine the structure of the field that determines them, for example, the state of the forces exerted on the whole set of firms engaged in the production of similar goods. These firms, which exert potential effects that are variable in their intensity and direction, control a section of the field ('market share'), the size of which increases with the size of their capital. As for consumers, their behaviour would be entirely reduced to the effect of the field if they did not have a certain interaction with it (as a function of their – quite minimal – inertia). The weight (or energy) associated with an agent, which undergoes the effects of the field at the same time as it structures that field, depends on all the other points and the relations between all the points, that is to say, on the entire space.

Though we are here stressing the constants, we do not overlook the fact that capital in its various species varies depending on the particularity of each subfield (corresponding to what is ordinarily referred to as a 'sector' or a 'branch' of industry), that is, depending on the history of the field, on the state of development (and, in particular, on the degree of concentration) of the industry considered and on the particularity of the product. At the end of the huge study he conducted of the pricing practices of various American industries, W. H. Hamilton related the idiosyncratic character of the different branches (that is to say, of the different fields) to the particularities of the histories of their emergence,[2] each being characterized by its own mode of functioning, its specific traditions, and its particular way of making pricing decisions.[3]

The force attached to an agent depends on its various 'strengths', sometimes called 'strategic market assets', differential factors of success (or failure), which may provide it with a competitive advantage, that is to say, more precisely, on the *volume and structure of the capital* the agent possesses in its different species: financial capital (actual or potential), cultural capital (not to be confused with 'human capital'), technological capital, juridical capital and organizational capital (including the capital of information about the field), commercial capital, social capital and symbolic capital. Financial capital is the direct or indirect mastery (through access to the banks) of financial resources, which are the main condition (together with time) for the accumulation and conservation of all other kinds of capital. Technological capital is the portfolio of scientific resources (research potential) or technical resources (procedures, aptitudes, routines and unique and coherent know-how, capable of reducing expenditure in labour or capital or increasing its yield) that can be deployed in the design and manufacture of products. Commercial capital (sales power) relates to the mastery of distribution networks (warehousing and transport), and marketing and after-sales services. Social capital is the totality of resources (financial capital and also information etc.) activated through a more or less extended, more or less mobilizable network of relations which procures a competitive advantage by providing higher returns on investment.[4] Symbolic capital resides in the mastery of symbolic resources based on knowledge and recognition, such as 'goodwill investment', 'brand loyalty', etc.; as a power which functions as a form of credit, it presupposes the trust or belief of those upon whom it bears because they are disposed to grant it credence (it is this symbolic power that Keynes invokes when he posits that an injection of money is effective if agents believe it to be so).[5]

The structure of the distribution of capital and the structure of the distribution of costs, itself linked mainly to the scale and degree of vertical integration, determine the structure of the field, that is to say, the relations of force among firms: the mastery of a very large proportion of capital (of the overall energy) in effect confers a power over the field, and hence over the firms least well endowed (relatively) in terms of capital; it also governs the price of entry into the field, and the distribution of the opportunities for profit. The various species of capital do not act only indirectly, through prices; they exert a structural effect, because the adoption of a new technique or the control of a larger market share, etc., modifies the relative positions and the yields of all the species of capital held by other firms.

By contrast with the interactionist vision, which knows no other form of social efficacy than the 'influence' directly exerted by one enterprise (or person entrusted with representing it) over another through some form of 'interaction', the structural vision takes account of effects that occur outside of any interaction: the structure of the field, defined by the unequal distribution of capital, that is, the specific weapons (or strengths), weighs, quite apart from any direct intervention or manipulation, on all the agents engaged in the field; and the worse placed they are within that distribution, the more it restricts the *space of possibles* open to them. The dominant is the one that occupies a position in the structure such that the structure acts on its behalf. It is through the weight they possess within this structure, more than through the direct interventions they may also make (in particular through the 'interlocking directorates' which are a more or less distorted expression of it[6]) that the dominant firms exert their pressure on the dominated firms and on their strategies: they define the *regularities* and sometimes the *rules* of the game, by imposing the definition of strengths most favourable to their interests and modifying the entire environment of the other firms and the system of constraints that bear on them or the space of possibles offered to them.

The tendency for the structure to reproduce itself is immanent in the very structure of the field: the distribution of strengths governs the distribution of chances of success and of profits through various mechanisms, such as the economies of scale or 'barriers to entry' resulting from the permanent disadvantage with which new entrants have to cope or the operating costs they have to meet or the action of all kinds of 'uncertainty-reducing institutions', to use Jan Kregel's expression,[7] such as wage and debt contracts, controlled prices, supply and trading agreements or 'mechanisms which provide information on the potential actions of the other economic agents'. It follows that, by virtue of the regularities inscribed in the recurrent games that are played out in it, the field offers a predictable and calculable future and agents acquire in it transmissible skills and dispositions (sometimes called 'routines') which form the basis of practical anticipations that are at least roughly well founded.

Because it is a particularity of the economic field that it authorizes and fosters the calculating vision and the strategic dispositions that go with it, one does not have to choose between a purely structural vision and a strategic vision: the most consciously elaborated strategies can be implemented only within the limits and in the directions assigned to them by the structural constraints and by the practical or explicit knowledge – always unequally distributed – of those constraints (the informational capital afforded to the occupants of a dominant position – particularly through presence on company boards or, in the case of banks, through the data provided by those requesting credit – is, for example, one of the resources which make it possible to choose the best strategies for capital management). Neoclassical theory, which refuses to take structural effects, and, *a fortiori,* objective power relations, into account, is able to explain the advantages accorded to those with the highest capital by the fact that, being more diversified, having greater experience and a greater reputation (and hence more to lose), they offer the guarantees that enable capital to be provided to them at a lower cost, all simply for reasons of economic calculation. And it will no doubt be objected that it is more parsimonious and rigorous to invoke the 'disciplinary' role of the market as an agency ensuring optimal coordination of preferences (by virtue of individuals being forced to submit their choices to the logic of profit maximization on pain of being eliminated) or, more simply, the price effect.

Now, the notion of the field breaks with the abstract logic of the automatic, mechanical and instantaneous determination of prices in markets in which unfettered competition prevails:[8] it is the structure of the field, that is to say, the structure of relations of force (or power relations) among firms that determines the conditions in which agents come to decide (or negotiate) purchase prices (of materials, labour, etc.) and selling prices (we see also in passing that, overturning entirely the usual image of 'structuralism', conceived as a form of 'holism' implying adherence to a radical determinism, this vision of action restores a certain free play to agents, without forgetting, however, that decisions are merely choices among possibles, defined, in their limits, by the structure of the field, and that actions owe their orientation and effectiveness to the structure of the objective relations between those engaging in them and those who are the objects of those actions). The structure of the relations of force among firms, which do not just interact indirectly, by way of prices, contributes, in most essential respects, to determining prices by determining, through the position occupied within this structure, the differential chances of influencing price formation – for example, through the economy-of-scale effect resulting from the fact that bargaining positions with suppliers improve with size or investment costs per unit of capacity diminish as total capacity increases. And it is this specific social structure that governs the trends immanent in the mechanisms of the field and, thereby, the degrees of freedom left for the strategies of the agents. It is not prices that determine everything, but everything that determines prices.

Thus, field theory stands opposed to the atomistic, mechanistic vision which hypostasizes the price effect and which, like Newtonian physics, reduces agents (shareholders, managers or firms) to interchangeable material points, whose preferences, inscribed in an exogenous utility function or even, in the most extreme variant (formulated by Gary Becker, among others), an immutable one, determine actions mechanically. It also stands opposed, though in a different way, to the interactionist vision, which is, by virtue of the representation of the agent as a calculating atom, able to cohabit with the mechanistic vision, and according to which the economic and social order can be reduced to a host of interacting individuals, most often interacting on a contractual basis. Thanks to a series of postulates fraught with consequences, notably the decision to treat firms as isolated decision-makers maximizing their profits,[9] some industrial organization theorists transfer to the collective level, such as that of the firm (which, in reality, itself functions as a field), the model of individual decision-making on the basis of a conscious calculation, consciously oriented towards profit maximization (some readily accept that the model is unrealistic, recognizing, for example, that the firm is a 'nexus of contract', though without deriving any consequences from this). In this way, industrial organization theory reduces the structure of the relations of force constitutive of the field to a set of interactions that in no respect transcend those engaged in the field at a particular moment and can therefore be described in the language of game theory. Being perfectly congruent in its basic postulates with the intellectualist theory that also underlies it, neoclassical theory, which, as is often forgotten, was explicitly and expressly constructed against the logic of practice – on the basis of postulates lacking any anthropological underpinning, such as the postulate that the system of preferences is already constituted and transitive[10] – tacitly reduces the effects which take place in the economic field to a play of reciprocal anticipations.

Similarly, those who, in order to avoid the representation of the economic agent as an egoistic monad confined to the 'narrow pursuit of his interests' and as an 'atomized actor taking decisions outside of any social constraints', remind us, as Mark Granovetter does, that economic action remains embedded in networks of social relations 'generating trust and discouraging malfeasance'[11] avoid 'methodological individualism' only to fall back into the interactionist vision which, ignoring the structural constraint of the field, will (or can) acknowledge only the effect of the conscious and calculated anticipation each agent may have of the effects of its actions on the other agents (precisely what a theorist of interactionism, like Anselm Strauss, referred to as 'awareness context'[12]); or the effect, conceived as 'influence', which 'social networks', other agents or social norms have on it. These are so many solutions which, eliminating all structural effects and objective power relations, amount to proposing a false supersession of the (itself spurious) alternative between individualism and holism.[13] Though there is no question here of denying the economic efficacy of 'networks' (or, better, of social capital) in the functioning of the economic field, the fact remains that the economic practices of agents and the very potency of their 'networks', which a rigorously defined notion of social capital takes into account, depend, first and foremost, on the position these agents occupy in those structured microcosms that are economic fields.

It is not certain, then, that what is usually called the 'Harvard tradition' (that is to say, the industrial economics developed by Joe Bain and his associates) does not deserve better than the somewhat condescending attitude 'industrial organization theorists' usually accord it. It is perhaps better to move in the right direction with 'loose theories', stressing the empirical analysis of industrial sectors, than to go off, with all the appearances of rigour, down a cul-de-sac, from a concern to present an 'elegant and general analysis'. I refer here to Jean Tirole who writes: 'The first wave, associated with the names of Joe Bain and Edward Mason and sometimes called the "Harvard tradition", was empirical in nature. It developed the famous "structure-conduct-performance paradigm" according to which market structure (the number of sellers in the market, the degree of product differentiation, the cost structure, the degree of vertical integration with suppliers, and so on) determines conduct (which consists of price, research and development, investment, advertising and so forth) and conduct yields market performance (efficiency, ratio of price to marginal cost, product variety, innovation rate, profits and distribution). This paradigm, although plausible, often rested on loose theories, and it emphasized empirical studies on industries.'[14]

Edward Mason does indeed have the merit of laying the foundations of a true structural (as opposed to interactionist) analysis of the functioning of an economic field: first, he argues that only an analysis capable of taking account both of the structure of each firm, which underlies the disposition to react to the particular structure of the field, and the structure of each industry, both of which are disregarded by advocates of game theory (a theory which, in passing, he criticizes in advance of its actual emergence: 'Elaborate speculation on the probable behavior of A on the assumption that B will act in a certain way, seems particularly fruitless'), can account for all the differences between firms in terms of competitive practices, particularly in their pricing, production and investment policies.[15] He subsequently strives to work out, both theoretically and empirically, the factors that determine the relative strength of the firm within the field: absolute size, number of firms, and product differentiation. Reducing the structure of the field to the space of possibles as they appear to the agents, he attempts, lastly, to draw up a 'typology' of 'situations' defined by 'all those considerations which . . . [the seller] takes into account in determining his business policies and practices'.[16]

The economic field as a field of struggles

The field of forces is also a field of struggles, a socially constructed field of action in which agents equipped with different resources confront each other in order to gain access to exchange and to preserve or transform the currently prevailing relation of force. Firms undertake actions there which depend, for their ends and effectiveness, on *their position in the field of forces*, that is to say, in the structure of distribution of capital in all its species. Far from being faced with a weightless, constraint-free world in which to develop their strategies at leisure, they are oriented by the constraints and possibilities built into their position and by the representation they are able to form of that position and the positions of their competitors as a function of the information at their disposal and their cognitive structures. The amount of free play afforded to them is undoubtedly greater than in other fields, on account of the particularly high degree to which the means and ends of action, and hence strategies, are made explicit, avowed, declared, if not indeed cynically proclaimed, particularly in the form of 'native theories' of strategic action (management) expressly produced to assist the agents, and particularly business leaders, in their decisions, and explicitly taught in the schools where they are trained, such as the major business schools.[17] ('Management theory', a literature produced by business schools for business schools, fulfils a function identical to that of the writings of the European jurists of the sixteenth and seventeenth centuries who, in the guise of describing the state, contributed to building it: being directed at current or potential managers, that theory oscillates continually between the positive and the normative, and depends fundamentally on an overestimation of the degree to which conscious strategies play a role in business, as opposed to the structural constraints upon, and the dispositions of, managers.)

This kind of instituted cynicism, the very opposite of the denial and sublimation which tend to predominate in the worlds of symbolic production, means that in this case the boundary between the native representation and the scientific description is less marked: for example, one treatise on marketing refers to the 'product market battlefield'.[18] In a field in which prices are both stakes and weapons, strategies, both for those who produce them and for others, have spontaneously a *transparency* they never achieve in such worlds as the literary, artistic or scientific fields, where the potential sanctions remain largely symbolic, that is to say, both vague and subject to subjective variations. And, in fact, as is attested by the work which the logic of the gift has to perform to mask what is sometimes known in French as *'la vérité des prix'* [literally: the truth of prices] (for example, price-tags on presents are always carefully removed), the money price has a kind of brutal objectivity and universality that allows little scope for subjective appreciation (even if one can say, for example: 'it's expensive for what it is' or 'it's well worth the price you paid for it'). It follows that conscious or unconscious bluffing strategies, such as strategies of pure pretension, have less chance of succeeding in economic fields – though they also have their place in those fields, but rather as strategies of deterrence or, more rarely, strategies of seduction.

Strategies depend, first, on the particular configuration of powers that confers structure on the field and which, defined by the degree of concentration, that is to say, the distribution of market share among a more or less large number of firms, varies between the two poles of perfect competition and monopoly. If we are to believe Alfred D. Chandler, between 1830 and 1960 the economies of the large industrialized countries saw a process of concentration (particularly through a wave of mergers) that gradually eliminated the world of small competing firms to which the classical economists referred: 'The profile of American industry delineated in the McLane Report and other sources is, then, one of production being carried out by a large number of small units employing less than 50 workers and still relying on traditional sources of energy ... Investment decisions for future output, as well as those for current production, were made by many hundreds of small producers in response to market signals, in much the way Adam Smith described.'[19] Now, at the end of a period of development characterized, particularly, by a long series of mergers and a profound transformation of corporate structures, we see that, in most fields of industry, the struggle is confined to a small number of powerful competing firms which, far from passively adjusting to a 'market situation', are able to shape that situation actively.

These fields are organized in a relatively invariant manner around the main opposition between those who are sometimes called 'first movers' or 'market leaders' and the 'challengers'.[20] The dominant firm usually has the initiative in terms of price changes, the introduction of new products, and distribution and promotion; it is able to impose the representation most favourable to its interests of the appropriate style of play and rules of the game, and hence of participation in the game and the perpetuation of that game. It constitutes an essential reference point for its competitors who, whatever they do, are called upon to position themselves, either actively or passively, in relation to it. The threats it constantly faces – either of the appearance of new products capable of supplanting its own or of an excessive increase in costs such as to threaten its profits – force it to be constantly vigilant (particularly in the case of shared market dominance, where coordination designed to limit competition is the order of the day). Against these threats, the dominant firm has a choice of two quite different strategies: it can work to improve the overall position *of* the field, by attempting to increase overall demand; or it can defend or improve its established positions *within* the field (its market share).

The interests of the dominant are indeed bound up with the overall state of the field, defined, in particular, by the average opportunities for profit it offers, which also define the attraction it exerts (by comparison with other fields). It is in their interest to work for increased demand, from which they derive a particularly substantial benefit, since it is proportionate to their market share, by attempting to recruit new users and stimulate new uses or a more intensive utilization of the products they offer (by acting, where applicable, on the political authorities). But, above all, they have to defend their position against the challengers by permanent innovation (new products and services, etc.) and by price reductions. By virtue of all the competitive advantages they enjoy (foremost among them the economies of scale linked to their size), they can lower their costs and, at the same time, reduce their prices, while limiting any reduction in their margins, making life very difficult for new entrants and eliminating the least well-equipped competitors. In short, by virtue of the determining contribution they make to the structure of the field (and the price formation in which that structure expresses itself), a structure whose effects manifest themselves in the form of barriers to entry or economic constraints, the 'first movers' enjoy decisive advantages both in relation to already established competitors and to potential new entrants.[21]

The forces of the field orient the dominant towards strategies whose end is the perpetuation or reinforcement of their domination. In this way, the symbolic capital they have at their disposal, by virtue of their pre-eminence and also their seniority, enables them successfully to resort to strategies intended to intimidate their competitors, such as putting out signals to deter them from attacking (for example, by organizing leaks about price reductions or the building of a new factory) – strategies which may be pure bluff but which their symbolic capital renders credible and hence effective. It may even happen that these dominant firms, confident in their strength and aware they have the resources to sustain a long offensive which puts time on their side, choose to abstain from any riposte and allow their opponents to mount attacks that are costly and doomed to failure. Generally speaking, the hegemonic firms have the capacity to set the tempo of transformation in the various areas of production, marketing, research, etc., and the differential use of time is one of the main levers of their power.

The appearance of a new and effective agent modifies the structure of the field. Similarly, the adoption of a new technology or the acquisition of a greater market share modifies the relative positions and field of all the species of capital held by the other firms. But the second-rank firms in a field can also attack the dominant firm (and the other competitors), either frontally, for example by attempting to reduce their costs and prices (particularly by technological innovation), or laterally, by attempting to fill the gaps left by the action of the dominant firm and to occupy niches at the cost of a specialization of their production, or by turning the dominant firm's strategies back against it. In this case, success seems to depend on the relative position in the structure of capital distribution and, thereby, in the field: whereas very large firms can make high profits by achieving economies of scale, and small firms can obtain high profits by specializing to devote themselves to a limited market segment, medium-size firms often have low rates of profit because they are too big to benefit from tightly targeted production and too small to benefit from the economies of scale of the largest firms.

Given that the forces of the field tend to reinforce the dominant positions, one might well wonder how real transformations of relations of force within a field are possible. In fact, *technological capital* plays a crucial role here, and we may cite a number of cases in which dominant firms have been supplanted through a technological change which, thanks to ensuing cost reductions, handed the advantage to smaller competitors. But technological capital is effective only if it is associated with other kinds of capital. This no doubt explains the fact that victorious challengers are very seldom small, emerging firms and, where they are not the product of mergers between existing firms, *they originate in other nations or, particularly, from other subfields*. It most often falls to the large firms to effect revolutions – firms which, by diversifying, can take advantage of their technological competences to present a competitive proposition in new fields. So the changes within a field are often linked to changes in the relations with the exterior of that field.

To these boundary crossings must be added also *redefinitions of boundaries* between fields: some fields may find themselves segmented into smaller sectors, the aeronautics industry dividing up, for example, into producers of airliners, fighter planes and tourist aircraft; or, conversely, technological change may lower the barriers between industries that were previously separated: for example, computing, telecommunications and office technology are increasingly coming to be merged, with the result that firms previously present in only one of the three subfields are increasingly tending to find themselves in competition in the new space of relationships that is forming – the field of the audio-visual industry undergoing drastic change as a result of new entrants breaking into it from telecommunications and computing, where firms have resources greatly exceeding those of the traditional agents. In this case, a single firm may come into competition not merely with other firms in its field, but also with firms belonging to various other fields. We can see, in passing, that in economic fields, as in all other categories of field, the *boundaries* of the field are at stake in the struggles within the field itself (most notably, through the question of possible substitutes and the competition they introduce); and that, in each case, empirical analysis alone can determine these. (It is not uncommon for fields to have a quasi-institutionalized existence in the form of branches of activity equipped with professional organizations functioning at one and the same time as clubs for the managers of the industry, defence groups for the prevailing boundaries, and hence for the principles of exclusion underlying them, and as representative bodies for dealing with the public authorities, trade unions and other similar bodies, in which capacity they are equipped with permanent organs of action and expression.)

However, of all exchanges with the exterior of the field the most important are those established with the state. Competition among firms often takes the form *of competition for power over state power* – particularly over the power of regulation and property rights[22] – and for the advantages provided by the various state interventions: preferential tariffs, trade licences, research and development funds, public sector contracts, funding for job-creation, innovation, modernization, exports, housing, etc. In their attempts to modify the prevailing 'rules of the game' to their advantage, and thereby to exploit some of their properties which can function as capital in the new state of the field, dominated firms can use their social capital to exert pressures on the state and to have it modify the game in their favour.[23] Thus what is called the market is the totality of relations of exchange between competing agents, direct interactions that depend, as Simmel has it, on an 'indirect conflict' or, in other words, on the socially constructed structure of the relations of force to which the different agents engaged in the field contribute to varying degrees through the modifications they manage to impose upon it, by drawing, particularly, on the state power they are able to control and guide. The state is not simply the regulator put there to maintain order and confidence, the arbiter responsible for 'overseeing' firms and their interactions, as commonly conceived. In the quite exemplary case of the field of production of single-family houses, as in many other fields, it contributes quite decisively to the construction of both demand and supply, each of these two forms of intervention occurring under the direct or indirect influence of the parties most directly concerned.[24]

Other external factors capable of contributing to a transformation of relations of force within the field include transformations of sources of supply (for example, the great petroleum finds of the early twentieth century) and changes in demand determined by demographic changes (such as the fall in the birth-rate or increased life expectancy) or in lifestyles (women's increased participation in the labour force, which leads to a fall in demand for certain products linked to the traditional definition of women's roles and creates new markets, such as those for frozen foods and microwave ovens). In fact, these external factors exert their effects on the relations of force within the field only through the logic of those relations of force, that is to say, only to the extent that they provide an advantage to the challengers: they enable the challengers to gain a position in specialized niche markets when it is difficult for 'first movers', focused on standardized, volume production, to satisfy the very particular demands of these markets – those of a particular category of consumer or a specific regional market – and the footholds gained by the challengers may constitute bridgeheads for subsequent development.

The firm as a field

It is clear that decisions on prices or in any other area of activity do not depend on a single actor, a myth which conceals the power games and stakes within the firm functioning as a field or, to put it more precisely, within the field of power specific to each firm. In other words, if we enter the 'black box' that is the firm, we find not individuals, but, once again, a structure – that of the firm as a field, endowed with a relative autonomy in respect of the constraints associated with the firm's position within the field of firms. Though the surrounding field affects its structure, this embedded field, as a specific relation of force and area of free play, defines the very terms and stakes of the struggle, giving a particular cast to them which often renders them unintelligible, at first sight, from the outside.

If the strategies of firms (most notably with regard to prices) depend on the positions they occupy within the structure of the field, they depend also on the structure of power positions constitutive of the internal governance of the firm or, more exactly, on the (socially constituted) dispositions of the directors [*dirigeants*] acting under the constraint of the field of power within the firm and of the field of the firm as a whole (which may be characterized in terms of indices such as the hierarchical composition of the labour force, the educational and, in particular, scientific capital of the managerial staff, the degree of bureaucratic differentiation, the weight of the trade unions, etc.). The system of constraints and inducements that is built into the position within the field and inclines the dominant firms to act in the direction most likely to perpetuate their domination has nothing inevitable about it, nor does it even represent a kind of infallible instinct orienting firms and managers towards the choices most favourable to the maintenance of acquired advantages. Reference is often made, in this connection, to the example of Henry Ford who, after his brilliant success in production and distribution had made him the manufacturer of the world's cheapest automobiles, destroyed his firm's competitive capacities in the period after the First World War by driving out almost all his most experienced and competent managers, who subsequently brought about the success of his competitors.

This being said, though it enjoys relative autonomy from the forces of the overall field, the structure of the field of power within the firm is itself closely correlated with the position of the firm in that field, principally through the *correspondence* between, on the one hand, the volume of the firm's capital (itself linked to the age of the firm and its position in the life-cycle – hence, roughly speaking, to its size and integration) and the structure of that capital (particularly, the relative proportions of financial, commercial and technical capital) and, on the other, the structure of the distribution of the capital among the various directors [*dirigeants*] of the firm, that is, between owners and 'functionaries' – managers – and, among these latter, between the holders of different species of cultural capital: predominantly financial, technical or commercial, that is to say, in the French case, between the various elite corps and the schools where they received their training: the École Nationale d'Administration, the École Polytechnique or the École des Hautes Études Commerciales.[25]

Undeniable trends can be identified over the long term in the evolution of the relations of force between the major agents in the field of power within firms: most notably one sees, first, a preeminence of entrepreneurs with a mastery of new technologies, capable of assembling the funds required to exploit them, then the increasingly inevitable intervention of bankers and financial institutions, and finally the rise of managers.[26] However, apart from the fact that one must analyse the particular form the configuration of the distribution of powers among firms assumes at each state of each field, it is by analysing, for each firm at every moment, the form of the configuration of powers within the field of power *over* the firm that one can fully understand the logic of the struggles in which the firm's goals are determined. It is, in fact, clear that these goals are the stakes in struggles and that, for the rational calculations of an enlightened 'decision-maker', we have to substitute the political struggle among agents who tend to identify their specific interests (linked to their position in the firm and their dispositions) with the interests of the firm and whose power can no doubt be measured by their capacity to identify, for better or for worse (as the Henry Ford example shows), the interests of the firm with *their interests within the firm* (see appendix I, p. 217).

Structure and competition

To take into account the structure of the field is to say that competition for access to exchange with clients cannot be understood as being oriented solely by conscious, explicit reference to direct competitors or, at least, to the most dangerous of them, according to Harrison White's formula: 'Producers watch each other within a market.'[27] The same point is made even more explicitly by Max Weber, who sees here a 'peaceful conflict' to seize 'chances or advantages also wanted by others'. He writes: 'the potential partners are guided in their offers by the potential action of an indeterminately large group of real or imaginary competitors rather than by their own actions alone.'[28] Weber is here describing a form of rational calculation, but a calculation quite different in its logic from that of economic orthodoxy: not agents who make their choices on the basis of information furnished by prices, but agents taking account of the actions and reactions of their competitors and 'evolv[ing] roles on the basis of each others' behavior'; hence they are equipped with information about their competitors and capable of acting with or against them, as in the action of bargaining, the 'most consistent form of market formation', and the 'compromise of interests' which seals it. However, though he has the virtue of substituting the *relationship with the totality of producers* for the transaction with the partner or client alone, he reduces that relationship to a conscious, considered interaction between competitors investing in the same object ('all parties potentially interested in the exchange'). And it is the same with Harrison White who, though he sees the market as a 'self-reproducing social structure', seeks the underlying principle behind the strategies of the producers not in the constraints inherent in their structural position, but in the observation and deciphering of signals given out by the behaviour of other producers: 'Markets are self-reproducing social structures among specific cliques of firms and other actors who evolve roles from observations of each other's behavior.'[29] Or elsewhere: 'Markets are tangible cliques of producers watching each other. Pressure from the buyer side creates a mirror in which producers see themselves, not consumers.'[30] The producers, armed with the knowledge of the cost of production, attempt to maximize their income by determining the right volume of production 'on the basis of observed positions of all other producers' and seek a niche in the market.

The point is, in fact, to subordinate this 'interactionist' description of strategies to a structural analysis of the conditions that delimit the space of possible strategies – while, at the same time, not forgetting that competition among a small number of agents in strategic interaction for access (for some of them) to exchange with a particular category of clients is also, and above all, an encounter between producers occupying different positions within the structure of the specific capital (in its different species) and clients occupying positions in social space homologous to the positions those producers occupy in the field. What are commonly called *niches* are simply those sections of the clientele which structural affinity assigns to the different firms, and particularly to second-rank firms: as I have shown for cultural goods and goods with a high symbolic content such as clothes or houses, one can probably observe in each field a homology between the space of the producers (and products) and the space of the clients distributed according to the pertinent principles of differentiation. We may note, in passing, that this amounts to saying that the sometimes lethal constraints the dominant producers impose on their current or potential competitors are invariably mediated by the field: consequently, competition is never other than an 'indirect conflict' (in Simmel's sense) and is not targeted directly against the competitor. In the economic field, as elsewhere, the struggle does not need to be inspired by any intention to destroy for it to produce destructive effects. (We may deduce an 'ethical' consequence from the vision of the worlds of production as fields: just as we can say with Harrison White that 'each firm is distinctive', as a position in a field, a point in a space, without being obliged to suppose that all its strategies are inspired by a pursuit of distinction – the same thing being true of every undertaking of cultural production, for example on the part of an artist, a writer or a sociologist – so we can assert that every agent committed to a field is engaged in an 'indirect conflict' with all those engaged in the same game: his or her actions may have the effect of destroying them, without being in the least inspired by any destructive intent, or even any intention to outdo them or compete with them.)

The economic habitus

Homo oeconomicus, as conceived (tacitly or explicitly) by economic orthodoxy, is a kind of anthropological monster: this theoretically minded man of practice is the most extreme personification of the scholastic fallacy,[31] an intellectualist or intellectualocentric error very common in the social sciences (particularly in linguistics and ethnology), by which the scholar puts into the heads of the agents he is studying – housewives or households, firms or entrepreneurs, etc. – the theoretical considerations and constructions he has had to develop in order to account for their practices.[32] It is one of the virtues of Gary Becker, who is responsible for the boldest attempts to export the model of the market and the (supposedly more powerful and efficient) technology of the neoclassical firm into all the social sciences, that he declares quite openly what is sometimes concealed within the implicit assumptions of scholarly routine: 'The economic approach ... now assumes that individuals maximize their utility from basic preferences that do not change rapidly over time and that the behavior of different individuals is coordinated by explicit or implicit markets ... The economic approach is not restricted to material goods and wants or to markets with monetary transactions, and *conceptually* does not distinguish between major or minor decisions or between "emotional" and other decisions. Indeed, the economic approach provides a framework applicable to all human behavior – to all types of decisions and to persons from all walks of life.'[33] Nothing now escapes explanation in terms of the maximizing agent – structural organizations, firms or contracts, parliaments and municipal authorities, marriage (conceived as the economic exchange of services of production and reproduction) or the household, and relations between parents and children or the state. This mode of universal explanation by an explanatory principle that is itself universal (individual preferences are exogenous, ordered and stable and hence without contingent genesis or evolution) no longer knows any bounds. Gary Becker does not even recognize those bounds Pareto himself was forced to assume in the founding text in which, identifying the rationality of economic behaviour with rationality as such, he distinguished between strictly economic behaviour, which is the outcome of 'a series of logical reasonings' based on experience, and behaviour determined by 'custom', such as the act of raising one's hat on entering a room[34] (thus acknowledging another principle of action – usage, tradition or custom – unlike methodological individualism which recognizes only the alternative between conscious and deliberate choice, satisfying certain conditions of efficacy and coherence, and the 'social norm', which also requires a choice for it to become effective).

It is perhaps by recalling the arbitrary nature of the founding distinction (a distinction still present today in the minds of economists, who leave the *curiosa* or failings of economic operations to sociologists) between the economic order, governed by the effective logic of the market and a place of logical behaviours, and the uncertain 'social' order, shot through with the 'non-logical' arbitrariness of custom, passions and powers, that we can best contribute to the integration, or 'hybridization', of the two disciplines of sociology and economics – disciplines which have undergone a dramatic separation, in spite of the efforts to the contrary on the part of some of their great founders (Pareto and Schumpeter, for example, in the direction of sociology, and Durkheim, Mauss, Halbwachs, and, above all, Weber, in the direction of economics).[35] One can reunify an artificially divided social science only by becoming aware of the fact that economic structures and economic agents or, more exactly, their dispositions, are social constructs, indissociable from the totality of social constructs constitutive of a social order. But this reunified social science, capable of constructing models that cannot easily be assigned to either of the two disciplines alone, will undoubtedly find it very hard to win acceptance, both for political reasons and reasons relating to the specific logic of scientific worlds. There are undoubtedly many who have an interest in obscuring the connections between economic policies and their social consequences or, more precisely, between so-called economic policies (the political character of which asserts itself in the very fact of their refusing to take account of the social) and the social, and economic, costs – which would not be so difficult to calculate if there were any will to do so – of their short- and long-term effects (I have in mind, for example, the increase in economic and social inequalities resulting from the implementation of neoliberal policies, and the negative effects of those inequalities on health, delinquency, crime, etc.). But if strong reasons exist for the cognitive hemiplegia currently afflicting sociologists and economists to perpetuate itself, in spite of the increasing efforts to overcome it, this is also because the social forces that weigh on the supposedly pure and perfect worlds of science, particularly through the systems of penalties and rewards embodied in scholarly publications, caste hierarchies, etc., promote the reproduction of separate spaces, associated with different, if not indeed irreconcilable dispositions and structures of opportunity, which are the product of the initial separation.

It is the primary function of the concept of habitus to break with the Cartesian philosophy of consciousness and thereby overcome the disastrous mechanism/finalism alternative or, in other words, the alternative of determination by causes and determination by reasons; or, to put it another way, between so-called methodological individualism and what is sometimes called (among the 'individu-alists') holism – a semi-scientific opposition that is merely the euphemistic form of the alternative (undoubtedly the most powerful in the political order) between, on the one hand, individualism or liberalism, which regards the individual as the ultimate autonomous elementary unit, and, on the other, collectivism or socialism, which are presumed to regard the collective as primary.

In so far as he or she is endowed with a habitus, the social agent is *a collective individual or a collective individuated by the fact of embodying objective structures.* The individual, the subjective, is social and collective. The habitus is socialized subjectivity, a historic transcendental, whose schemes of perception and appreciation (systems of preferences, tastes, etc.) are the product of collective and individual history. Reason (or rationality) is 'bounded' not only, as Herbert Simon believes, because the human mind is generically bounded (there is nothing new in that idea), but because it is socially structured and determined, and, as a consequence, limited. Those who will be first to point out that this, too, is nothing new should ask themselves why economic theory has remained so solidly deaf to all reminders of these anthropological findings. For example, even in his day Veblen defended the idea that the economic agent is not a 'bundle of desires' but 'a coherent structure of propensities and habits',[36] and it was James S. Duesenberry who observed that the explanation for consumer choices was to be found not in rational planning, but rather in 'learning and habit formation', and who established that consumption was as dependent on past income as on present.[37] And it was Veblen again, anticipating the idea of 'interactive demand', who, like Jevons and Marshall, long ago enunciated the effects of structure, or of position within a structure, on the definition of needs and hence on demand. In short, if there is a universal property, it is that agents are not universal, because their properties, and in particular their preferences and tastes, are the product of their positioning and movements within social space, and hence of collective and individual history. The economic behaviour socially recognized as rational is the product of certain economic and social conditions. It is only by relating it to its individual and collective genesis that one can understand its economic and social conditions of possibility and, consequently, both the necessity and the sociological limits of economic reason and of apparently unconditioned notions such as needs, calculation or preferences.

This said, habitus is in no sense a mechanical principle of action or, more exactly, of reaction (it is not a 'reflex'). It is *conditioned and limited spontaneity.* It is that autonomous principle which means that action is not simply an immediate reaction to a brute reality, but an 'intelligent' response to an actively selected aspect of the real: linked to a history fraught with a probable future, it is the inertia, the trace of their past trajectory, which agents set against the immediate forces of the field, that means that their strategies cannot be deduced directly from either the immediate position or the immediate situation. It produces a response, the directing principle of which is not pre-given in the stimulus and which, without being entirely unpredictable, cannot be predicted on the basis of knowledge of the situation alone; a response to an aspect of reality which is distinguished by a selective and (in both senses of the term) partial – but not strictly 'subjective' – apprehension of certain stimuli, by an attention to a particular side of things of which it can be said, without distinction, either that it 'arouses interest' or that interest arouses it; an action which one can describe non-contradictorily as being both determined and spontaneous, since it is determined by *conventional, conditional* stimuli that exist as such only for an agent disposed to perceive them and capable of perceiving them.

The screen that the habitus introduces between stimulus and reaction is a screen of time in so far as, being itself the product of a history, it is relatively constant and durable, and hence *relatively* independent of history. As a product of past experiences and a whole collective and individual accumulation, it can be understood adequately only by a genetic analysis applying both to collective history – with, for example, the history of tastes, as illustrated by Sidney Mintz's demonstration of how the taste for sugar, originally an exotic luxury product reserved for the well-to-do, gradually became an indispensable element in the ordinary diet of the working classes[38] – and to individual history – with the analysis of the economic and social conditions of the genesis of individual tastes in terms of diet, decoration, clothing and also songs, theatre, music or cinema, etc.,[39] and, more generally, of the *dispositions* (in the dual sense of capacities and propensities) to perform economic actions adapted to an economic order (for example, calculating, saving, investing, etc.).

The concept of habitus also enables us to escape the dichotomy between finalism – which defines action as determined by the conscious reference to a deliberately set purpose and which, consequently, conceives all behaviour as the product of a purely instrumental, if not indeed cynical, calculation – and mechanism, which reduces action to a pure reaction to undifferentiated causes. The orthodox economists and philosophers who defend rational action theory swing, sometimes in the space of a single sentence, between these two logically incompatible theoretical options: on the one hand, a finalist decisionism, in which the agent is a pure rational consciousness acting in complete awareness of the consequences, the principle of action being a reason or rational decision determined by a rational evaluation of probable outcomes; and on the other hand, a physicalism which regards the agent as an inertia-less particle, reacting mechanically and instantaneously to a combination of forces. But the task of reconciling the irreconcilable is made easier here by the fact that the two branches of the alternative are really only one: in each case, yielding to the scholastic fallacy, the scientific subject, endowed with a perfect knowledge of causes and probable outcomes, is projected into the active agent, presumed to be rationally inclined to set as his goals the opportunities assigned to him by the causes (it hardly needs saying that the fact that economists subscribe quite consciously to this fallacy in the name of 'the right to abstraction' is not sufficient to obviate its effects).

Habitus is a highly economical principle of action, which makes for an enormous saving in calculation (particularly in the calculation of costs of research and measurement) and also in time, which is a particularly rare resource when it comes to action. It is, therefore, particularly well suited to the ordinary conditions of existence which, either because of time pressure or an insufficiency of requisite knowledge, allow little scope for the conscious, calculated evaluation of the chances of profit. Arising directly out of practice and linked to it in both its structure and functioning, this practical sense cannot be assessed outside of the practical conditions of its implementation. This means that the tests to which 'judgmental heuristics'[40] subjects individuals are doubly inadequate, since they attempt, in an artificial situation, to assess an aptitude to conscious and calculated evaluation of probable outcomes, the implementation of which itself presupposes a break with the inclinations of practical sense (this is, in fact, to forget that the calculus of probabilities was developed to counter the spontaneous tendencies of primary intuition).

The relation of the habitus to the field – a relationship that is obscure in practice because it lies below the level of the dualism of subject and object, activity and passivity, means and ends, determinism and freedom – in which the habitus determines itself in determining what determines it, is a calculation without calculator and an intentional action without intention, for which there is much empirical evidence.[41] In the particular (and particularly frequent) case in which the habitus is the product of objective conditions similar to those under which it operates, it generates behaviours that are particularly well suited to those conditions without being the product of a conscious, intentional search for adaptation (it is for this reason that we should beware of taking Keynes's 'adaptive expectations' for 'rational expectations', even if the agent with a well-adjusted habitus is, in a sense, a replica of the agent as producer of rational expectations). In this case, the effect of the habitus remains, so to speak, invisible, and the explanation in terms of habitus may seem redundant in relation to explanation in terms of the situation (one may even have the impression that we are dealing with an ad hoc explanation along the lines of the explanation of sleep by some 'dormitive property'). But the specific efficacy of habitus can be clearly seen in all the situations in which it is not the product of the conditions of its actualization (increasingly frequent as societies become differentiated): this is the case when agents formed in a precapitalist economy run up, in some disarray, against the demands of a capitalist cosmos;[42] or when old people quixotically cling to dispositions that are out of place and out of time; or when the dispositions of an agent rising, or falling, in the social structure – a *nouveau riche*, a *parvenu* or a *déclassé* – are at odds with the position that agent occupies. Such effects of hysteresis, of a lag in adaptation and counter-adaptive mismatch, can be explained by the relatively persistent, though not entirely unchangeable, character of habitus.

To the (relative) constancy of dispositions there corresponds a (relative) constancy of the social games in which they are constituted: like all social games, economic games are not games of chance; they present regularities and a finite number of similar patterns recur, which confers a certain monotony on them. As a result, the habitus produces *reasonable* (not rational) expectations, which, being the product of dispositions engendered by the imperceptible incorporation of the experience of constant or recurring situations, are immediately adapted to new but not radically unprecedented situations. As a disposition to act that is the product of previous experiences of similar situations, habitus provides a practical mastery of situations of uncertainty and grounds a relation to the future which is not that of a project, as an aiming for possible outcomes which equally well may or may not occur, but a relation of *practical anticipation*: discovering in the very objectivity of the world what is, apparently, the only course of action, and grasping time-to-come as a quasi-present (and not as a contingent future), the anticipation of time-to-come has nothing whatever in common with the purely speculative logic of a calculus of risk capable of attributing values to the various possible outcomes. But habitus is also, as we have seen, a principle of differentiation and selection that tends to conserve whatever confirms it, thus affirming itself as a potentiality which tends to ensure the conditions of its own realization.

Just as the intellectualist vision of economic orthodoxy reduces the practical mastery of situations of uncertainty to a rational calculus of risk, so, drawing on game theory, it construes the anticipation of the behaviour of others as a kind of calculation of the opponent's intentions, conceived hypothetically as intentions to deceive, particularly with regard to intentions themselves. In fact, the problem that economic orthodoxy resolves by the ultra-intellectualist hypothesis of 'common knowledge' (I know that you know that I know) is resolved in practice by the *orchestration of habitus* which, to the very extent that they are congruent, permit a mutual anticipation of the behaviour of others. The paradoxes of collective action have their solution in practices based on the implicit assumption that others will act responsibly and with that kind of constancy and truth-to-self that is inscribed in the durable character of habitus.

A well-founded illusion

Thus the theory of habitus allows us to *explain the apparent truth of the theory that it shows to be false*. If a hypothesis as unrealistic as the one that founds rational action theory or rational expectation theory may seem to be validated by the facts, this is because, by virtue of an empirically established statistical correspondence between dispositions and positions, in the great majority of cases (the most noticeable exceptions being subproletarians, *déclassés* and renegades, which the model does in fact enable us to explain nonetheless) agents form reasonable expectations, that is to say, expectations matching up to the objective probabilities – and almost always adjusted and reinforced by the direct effect of collective controls, particularly those exercised by the family. And the theory of habitus even enables us to understand why a theoretical construct such as the 'representative agent', based on the hypothesis that the choices of all the different agents in a single category – consumers, for example – can, in spite of their extreme heterogeneity, be treated as the choice of a standard 'representative individual' maximizing his utility, is not visibly invalidated by the evidence. Alan Kirman has shown not only that this fiction rests on very restrictive and special hypotheses, but that there are no grounds for asserting that the aggregated set of individuals, even if they were all maximizers, itself behaves as an individual maximizing its utility and, conversely, that the fact that a community presents a certain degree of rationality does not entail that all the individuals are acting rationally; Kirman consequently suggests that we may found a global demand function not on the homogeneity, but the heterogeneity, of agents, as highly dispersed demand behaviour on the part of individuals is capable of producing very unified and highly stabilized overall aggregated demand behaviour.[43] Now, there is a realist grounding for such a hypothesis in the theory of habitus and in the representation of consumers as a set of heterogeneous agents with dispositions, preferences and interests that are very different (just as they have very different conditions of existence) but adjusted, in each case, to conditions of existence involving different chances, and subject, as a result, to the inbuilt constraints of the structure of the field – the structure of the overall economic field – and also of the more or less limited subspaces in which they interact with a limited subgroup of agents. There is little room in the economic field for 'madcap behaviour' and those who indulge in it pay the price for defying the immanent rules and regularities of the economic order by failure or disappearance.

In giving an explicit, systematic form to the philosophy of the agent and of action which economic theory most often accepts tacitly (because, among other reasons, with notions such as 'preference' or 'rational choice', economic orthodoxy is merely rationalizing a common-sense 'theory' of decision-making), the advocates of rational action theory (who include a number of economists such as Gary Becker) and of methodological individualism (such as James Coleman, Jon Elster and their French epigones) will undoubtedly have rendered a great service to research: by its very excess and its unconcern for experience, their narrowly intellectualist (or intellectualocentric) ultra-rationalism directly contradicts the best-established findings of the historical sciences of human practices. If it has seemed necessary to demonstrate that many of the established findings of economic science are perfectly compatible with a philosophy of agents, action, time and the social world quite different from the one normally accepted by the majority of economists, this has, therefore, not been done here to satisfy some philosophical point of honour, but solely in an attempt to reunify the social sciences by working to restore economics to its true vocation as a historical science.

APPENDIX I

THE FIELD OF THE FIRM: A CASE STUDY

In 1986, I carried out research in a large cement production firm which, on the occasion of relocating some of its Paris-based departments to the provinces, was looking to redirect its financial and commercial policy through an exercise in 'staff participation' (which included, among other things, the organization of an internal seminar);[44] During the course of this research, it was observed that the various members of the management had standpoints on the firm, and particularly on its future, which were very closely related to their position within the firm and their educational capital. The clashes, which were most often indirect and muffled in nature, between the various members of the 'senior management' – the chairman of the board, by tradition a *polytechnicien* [a graduate of the École Polytechnique]; the chief executive who, at the time of the observation, was a graduate of the École des Hautes Études Commerciales (HEC), known for his financial management skills; the deputy chief executive, also known as the 'works director', a *polytechnicien* who, given his seniority and his position as personnel director, possessed an enormous capital of information and contacts; the director of industrial installations, another *polytechnicien*; the commercial director who, in spite of his title, showed no great commitment to communication; and, lastly, the director of research and development, a young *polytechnicien* – always related, in the last analysis, to questions of definition.

Battles over definitions are clearly associated with battles over priorities, that is to say, battles over the pre-eminence to be accorded, in future plans, and the restructurings they necessitate, to a particular function (for example, the financial, commercial or 'communicative' function) or to a particular officer of the firm: in those battles, some may invoke the very special characteristics of the cement market – namely, the situation of duopoly which meant there were no price wars in the market – and the very particular characteristics of distribution, to reject a genuine policy of communication; others argue for developing the firm on the basis of a financial strategy, such as buying up firms within the sector, or on the basis of an industrial strategy, but a strategy of a new type, which involves extending and diversifying the market on the basis of investment in chemical research (this is dependent on the different definitions of the product which are given: for some, cement is seen as a relatively simple product, involving technical operations performed 'to a straightforward industrial recipe'; for others, it is a kind of adhesive, and hence belongs to the sphere of chemical engineering, where it is associated with all kinds of potentially marketable derivatives). Given that the possible options are never entirely exclusive, and that partial combinations of these options are not to be excluded, then various, most often tacit, alliances can be formed to advance the interests of one or other of the potential competitors. In the struggles in which they engage to press their own 'views', which it would be naive (or spuriously subtle) to reduce to conflicts of career interests, in so far as each of them in a sense embodies the 'tendency to persevere in being', the *conatus*, of the position he or she occupies and which his or her entire social being, his or her habitus, expresses and realizes, the protagonists commit the capital they hold, in its different species and its different states: they bring a specific bureaucratic capital to the struggle, a capital linked to their position in the corporate hierarchy and also to their length of service, together with an informational capital, which may run from commercial know-how or a knowledge of chemistry to familiarity with the history of the firm and of each of its members, and, lastly, a social capital of useful relations.

Although the conditions of confidentiality in which the research was carried out prevent us from chronicling in detail the countless interventions (including, in particular, what one informant called the 'billiard games', in which one person was played off against another) and the negotiations, or even from listing the strategies deployed – particularly to impose a policy or win acceptance for it by inducing the chief executive to decide in its favour – we can at least speak of the logic of the struggle within the field of power in the firm, that is to say, the competition between those holding one of the relevant powers. Everything took place as if the structure of the field of power was organized at every moment in terms of different oppositions which, particularly in moments of crisis, could crystallize into strategic alliances among the holders of the various different forms of power: for example, at the time of the observation, the chief executive, an advocate of a *financial* policy of expansion through buying up the small firms in the sector (supported in this by the young R&D director, who favoured a policy of product diversification – based on primacy accorded to 'adhesives' and 'chemical engineering'), was meeting with resistance from one of the technical managers in the new plant, a civil engineer, who, fired by a futuristic vision of the firm, saw the new industrial site as a kind of Silicon Valley (a typical example of total self-commitment, not reducible to mere careerist opportunism), from the director of information technology, and from the deputy chief executive, a *polytechnicien* with a virtual monopoly of information on the firm and its staff: between these extremes, though closer to the latter faction, were those known as the 'cement men', that is, the directors most directly involved with production, who were willing to accept a policy of diversification, but one that consisted in 'selling an industrial know-how or the products of that know-how'.

In this battle over the definition of the firm, its goals and its future, three principles of legitimacy were in conflict. Two of these were forms of 'cement men's' legitimacy, to use the internal idiolect: the one, a traditional form, saw cement as the firm's primary concern, cement here being conceived as a primitive form of adhesive, produced by relatively routine industrial techniques; the other, just as technical, but modernist, focused more on 'concrete', a product which, being less standardized than cement and capable of adaptation to user needs, provided opportunities for profiting from commercial know-how, and, above all, on 'adhesive', a product of chemical research which also opens the door to all kinds of derivative products. Lastly, there was a third form of legitimacy, a financial form, possessed by the chief executive, a product of HEC, who, from the standpoint of corporate orthodoxy ('normally this company is run by a *polytechnicien*'), was regarded as having in some way usurped power. It was this same movement (or this same *conatus*) which brought this latter man to seek the chairmanship of the company (held at the time by a somewhat discredited *polytechnicien*) and to change the financial and commercial policy of his predecessor. These two inseparable and objectively indistinguishable objectives could really be achieved only if he could win the support of two *polytechniciens*, the one enthusiastically bringing him the technical modernism of organic chemistry, the other meeting the modernizing plans which threatened his hold over the firm's personnel with the inertia of a neutralizing, disarming assent. In fact, this latter, without ever openly declaring a position of resistance to the chief executive's attempts to transform the company, seemed the embodiment of corporate inertia, that is to say, the embodiment of the tendencies immanent in the institutional structures and the dispositions of the agents. (An analysis of the distribution of the employees of all levels among the various working groups formed at the long-range planning seminar reveals that those who chose the group focusing on 'the reorganization of the production process' had been with the company longer, had less educational capital and were more often from the factories than from headquarters, whereas those who chose the groups working on distinctly more forward-looking themes, such as the group on the future of product differentiation, possessed higher educational qualifications – particularly in organic chemistry.)

These different orientations, which may be expressed, out of unconscious mimicry or with an intention of veiled resistance, in the same word 'diversification', were constantly clashing. And not just in open confrontations within the board or in the deliberations of the working groups, led more or less by the innovative executives who had taken the initiative within them, but also, as one informer put it, 'in people's heads and in bilateral discussions'. And it was from these countless interactions, always oriented by the structure of the relations of force between the agents or agencies among which the interactions were established, that there eventually emerged what, in the end, could appear as a policy freely deliberated on and determined by a management identified as a rational agent.

APPENDIX II

AN IMAGINARY ANTHROPOLOGY

The difficulty with any attempt freely to rethink the foundations of economics arises from the fact that economic orthodoxy is doubtless one of the most powerful discourses for speaking about the social world, particularly because mathematical formalization confers on it an ostentatious appearance of rigour and neutrality. Although economic theory is far from being unified, and although one can distinguish within it a sociologically dominant hard core, organized around the isolated individual and the abstract market, complementary or corrective theories (such as game theory, theory of institutions and evolutionary theory) and antagonistic theories, it is organized socially after the model of the great chain of being dear to Arthur Lovejoy with, at the one extreme, the pure, unblemished mathematicians of the theory of general equilibrium and, at the other, the authors of small-scale models of applied economics, the former serving as a legitimating guarantee to the latter, whereas the latter provide the former with the semblance of a grasp of the realities of the world as it is.

Keeping to essentials, we can first submit to examination the eclectic theoretical construction, more socially than scientifically grounded, that goes by the name of Rational Action Theory or Methodological Individualism, and which is based, ultimately, on a Cartesian philosophy of science, the agent (conceived as subject) and the social world.

This is, first, a *deductivist epistemology*, which, equating rigour with mathematical formalization, sets out to deduce significant 'theorems' or 'laws' from a set of fundamental axioms that are rigorous, but silent on the real functions of the economy. We may cite Durkheim here: 'Political economy ... remained an abstract, deductive science, concerned not with the observation of reality, but with the construction of a more or less desirable ideal. For this abstract man, this systematic egoist whom it describes, is solely a creature of reason. Real man – the man whom we all know and whom we all are – is much more complex: he is of a time, of a country; he has a family, a city, a fatherland, a religious belief and political ideas.'[45]

Second, it is an *intellectualist* philosophy that conceives agents as pure consciousnesses without history, capable of determining their ends freely and instantaneously and acting in complete awareness of what they do (or, in a variant that cohabits with the foregoing without contradicting it: as isolated atoms, without autonomy or inertia, and mechanically determined by causes). We may here call on Veblen and his argument that the hedonistic philosophy which underpins economic theory leads to crediting agents – atoms without inertia and 'lightning calculators' – with a 'passive and substantially inert and immutably given ... nature': 'The hedonistic conception of man is that of a lightning calculator of pleasures and pains, who oscillates like an homogeneous globule of desire of happiness under the impulse of stimuli that shift him about the area, but leave him intact. He has neither antecedent nor consequent. He is an isolated, definitive human datum, in stable equilibrium except for the buffets of the impinging forces that displace him in one direction or another. Self poised in elemental space, he spins symmetrically about his own spiritual axis until the parallelogram of forces bears down upon him, whereupon he follows the line of the resultant. When the force of the impact is spent, he comes to rest, a self-contained globule of desire as before.'[46]

Last, and most important, it is a strictly *atomistic and discontinuist* (or instantaneist) view of the social world that provides the basis for the model of perfect competition or the perfect market. This typically Cartesian philosophy simply excludes history altogether. Just as, by locating the principle of action in explicit intentions and in reasons (or, more simply, as Friedrich Hayek has it, in psychology), the philosophy of consciousness of economic orthodoxy excludes the history of agents, whose preferences, which owe nothing to past experience, are immune from historical fluctuations and variations, the individual utility function being decreed immutable or lacking in analytic pertinence,[47] so the philosophy of the economic order inherent in the notion of 'market' evokes very directly the physical world as described by Descartes, that is to say, it is a world devoid of immanent force and hence doomed to radical discontinuity (in Descartes's work the discontinuity of the acts of the divine creator). As a mathematical fiction, referring back to the abstract mechanism of price formation described by the theory of exchange (at the cost of consciously and avowedly bracketing out legal and state institutions), the perfect market, characterized by perfect competition and information, is merely the idealized designation of the abstract mechanism charged with ensuring the *instantaneous* adjustment of prices in the limit case of a frictionless world, that is to say, the market equilibrium which is supposed to coordinate individual actions through variations of price.[48]

Coming back to the model of the 'great chain of being', we can understand why a notion like that of 'market' – the economic mechanism characteristic of 'market economies' – is ideally suited to play the role of 'scholarly myth', available, at whatever level of the chain one places oneself, for any ideological ends. It is possible, by appealing to the ambiguous, polysemic notion of 'market' (the scientific shortcomings and weaknesses of which are only too easy to demonstrate[49]), to evoke, either as alternatives or simultaneously, the abstract, mathematical meaning, with all its associated 'science effects', or any one of the term's concrete meanings, which all have some proximity to ordinary experience, whether it be as the place where trade takes place ('the marketplace'), outlets for products ('gaining market share') or the range of transactions open to a particular good ('the oil market').[50] Thus, at the 'divine' end of the chain, the Chicago School, and Milton Friedman in particular,[51] were able to base their efforts to rehabilitate the market (chiefly against intellectuals, whom they assumed to be hostile to it[52]) on the identification of the market with freedom, summarily making economic freedom the condition for political freedom.

Postscript: From the National to the International Field

Historically, the economic field was constructed within the framework of the national state, with which it is intrinsically linked. The state contributes in many ways to unifying the economic space (which in its turn contributes to the emergence of the state). As Karl Polanyi shows in *The Great Transformation*, the emergence of national markets was not the mechanical product of the gradual extension of economic exchange, but the effect of a deliberately mercantilist state policy aimed at increasing domestic and foreign trade (particularly by fostering the commercialization of land, money and labour). However, far from leading to a process of homogenization, as one might think, unification and integration are accompanied by a concentration of power, which may reach monopoly proportions, and, at the same time, by the dispossession of part of the population thus integrated. This means that integration into the state and the territory it controls is in fact the precondition for domination (as can be readily seen in all situations of colonization). As I was able to observe in Algeria, the unification of the economic field tends, particularly through monetary unification and the extension of monetary exchanges that ensues, to pitch all social agents into an economic game for which they are not equally prepared and equipped, culturally and economically; by the same token it tends to subject them to the norm objectively imposed by competition from more efficient productive forces and modes of production, as can clearly be seen with small rural producers, who are increasingly wrenched from a state of autarky. In short, *unification benefits the dominant*, with the difference between the two being turned into capital by the mere fact of their being brought into relation. (To take a recent example, in the 1930s, Roosevelt had to lay down common social rules on employment, such as the minimum wage, the limitation of working hours, etc., to avoid the integration of unequally developed regions into a single national unit producing a fall in wages and a deterioration in working conditions.)

But, in other respects, the process of unification (and concentration) remained confined within national borders: it was limited by all the barriers, especially juridical ones, to the free movement of goods and persons (customs duties, exchange controls, etc.) and limited also by the fact that the production, and particularly the movement, of goods remained narrowly bound to geographical place (owing, in part, to transport costs). It is these – both technical and juridical – limits on the extension of economic fields that are tending today to weaken or disappear under the impact of various factors: on the one hand, purely technical factors, such as the development of new means of communication (air transport, the internet); on the other, more properly political or juridical-political factors, such as liberalization and deregulation. In this way, the formation of a *global economic field* is fostered, particularly in the financial sector (where computerized means of communication are tending to eliminate the *time differentials* that separated the various different national markets).

The double meaning of 'globalization'

We must return here to the word 'globalization': we have seen that, in a rigorous sense, it could refer to the unification of the global economic field or to the expansion of that field to the entire world. But it is also made to mean something quite different, in a surreptitious slide from the descriptive meaning of the concept, as I have just formulated it, to a normative or, more exactly, performative one: in this second sense, 'globalization' refers to an *economic policy* aimed at unifying the economic field by a whole set of juridical-political measures, designed to remove all the limits to that unification, all the obstacles to that extension, most of which are linked to the nation-state. And this very precisely defines neoliberal policy, inseparable as it is from the outright economic propaganda that lends it some of its symbolic force by playing on the ambiguity of the notion.

Economic globalization is not a mechanical effect of the laws of technology or the economy, but the product of a policy implemented by a set of agents and institutions, and the result of the application of rules deliberately created for specific ends, namely, trade liberalization (that is, the elimination of all national regulations restricting companies and their investments). In other words, the 'global market' is *a political creation* (as the national market had been), the product of a more or less consciously concerted policy. And, as was the case with the policy which led to the emergence of national markets, the effect of this policy (and perhaps also its *aim*, at least among the most lucid and cynical of neoliberalism's advocates) is to create the conditions for domination by starkly confronting agents and firms hitherto confined within national limits with competition from more powerful and more efficient forces and modes of production. In the emerging economies, for example, the disappearance of protection spells ruin for national enterprises and, for countries like South Korea, Thailand, Indonesia or Brazil, the removal of all obstacles to foreign investment leads to the collapse of local enterprises, which are bought up, often at ridiculously low prices, by the multinationals. For these countries, public procurement contracts remain one of the only methods that enable local companies to compete with the big Northern concerns. While they are presented as necessary for the creation of a 'global field of action', World Trade Organization directives on competition and public procurement policies would have the effect, by establishing competition 'on an equal footing' between the big multinationals and small national producers, of wiping out an enormous number of the latter. We know that, as a general rule, formal equality in a situation of real inequality favours the dominant.

The word 'globalization' is, as we can see, *a simultaneously descriptive and prescriptive pseudo-concept* that has supplanted the term 'modernization', long used by American social sciences as a euphemistic way of imposing a naively ethnocentric evolutionary model by which to classify different societies in terms of their distance from the most economically advanced society, that is to say, American society, established as the end-point and goal of all human history (this is the case, for example, when the criterion adopted for the level of development is one of the typical, but apparently neutral and unquestionable, properties of that society, such as energy consumption per inhabitant, as criticized by Lévi-Strauss in *Race and History*). The term (and the model it expresses) embodies the most complete form of the *imperialism of the universal*, the form which consists in universalizing a society's own particularity by establishing it implicitly as a universal model (as French society did for a long time when, as the supposed embodiment of human rights and of the heritage of the French Revolution, it was enshrined as the model, especially through the Marxist tradition, of any possible revolution).

By way of this word, then, it is the process of the unification of the global economic and financial field, that is, the integration of hitherto compartmentalized national economic universes, now organized along the lines of an economy rooted in the historical particularities of a particular social tradition – that of American society – that is established as an inevitable destiny and a political project of universal liberation, as the end-point of a *natural evolution* and the civic and ethical ideal which, in the name of the connection postulated between democracy and the market, promises political emancipation for the peoples of all countries. The most fully developed form of this *utopian capitalism* is undoubtedly the myth of the 'stockholder democracy', that is to say, of a world of wage-earners who, receiving income in the form of shares, would collectively become 'the owners of their companies', thereby bringing about the perfect association between capital and labour. And the triumphant ethnocentrism of 'modernization' theories reaches sublime heights with the most inspired prophets of the new economic religion who see the United States as the new homeland of 'achieved socialism' (we see here, in passing, that a certain scientistic madness currently triumphant in Chicago today is in every respect the equal of the wildest ravings about 'scientific socialism' that flourished in another age and place with consequences that are well known).

We should pause here to demonstrate, first, that what is universally proposed and imposed as the norm of all rational economic practice is, in reality, the universalization of the particular characteristics of an economy embedded in a particular history and social structure – those of the United States; and that, by the same token, the United States is, by definition, the fully realized form of a political and economic ideal which is for the most part the product of the idealization of its own economic and social model, characterized, among other things, by the weakness of the state. But we should also demonstrate, secondly, that in the global economic field the United States occupies a dominant position which it owes to the fact that it possesses an exceptional set of competitive advantages: *financial advantages*, with the exceptional position of the dollar, which enables it to drain off from all over the world (that is, from countries with a high savings rate like Japan, but also from the ruling oligarchies of poor countries or from global trafficking networks) the capital it needs to finance its enormous deficit and to compensate for an exceedingly low rate of savings and investment, and which enables it to implement the monetary policy of its choice, without worrying about the repercussions on other countries, especially the poorest, which are objectively tied to American economic decisions and which have contributed to American growth not merely by the fact of the low costs in money terms of their labour and products (particularly raw materials), but also by the levies they have paid from which the American banks and stock exchange have benefited; *economic advantages*, with the strength and competitiveness of the capital goods and investment sector and, in particular, of industrial micro-electronics, or the role of banking in the private financing of innovation; *political and military advantages*, its diplomatic weight allowing the United States to impose economic and commercial norms favourable to its interests; *cultural and linguistic advantages*, with the exceptional quality of the public and private system of scientific research (measurable by the number of Nobel Prize winners), the power of lawyers and the big law firms, and, lastly, the effective universality of English which dominates telecommunications and the whole of commercial cultural production; *symbolic advantages*, with the imposition of a quasi-universally recognized lifestyle, or at least a lifestyle universally recognized by adolescents, particularly through the production and diffusion of representations of the world, especially cinematic ones, that have an image of modernity attaching to them. (We can see, in passing, that the superiority of the American economy, which is moving further and further away from the model of perfect competition in the name of which it is being thrust on the rest of the world, *is due to structural effects and not to the particular efficacy of a given economic policy*, even if the effect of the intensification of work and the extension of working hours, combined with very low wages for the least skilled, and also the role of a new technologically and scientifically led economy, have played a part.)

One of the most unquestionable manifestations of the relations of force being established within the global economic field is undoubtedly the asymmetry and the logic of double standards that allows, for example, the dominant powers, and particularly the USA, to resort to the protectionism and subsidies they deny to developing countries (which are prohibited from limiting imports of a product inflicting serious damage on their industry or from regulating flows of foreign investment). And it takes a great deal of goodwill to believe that concern for welfare rights in the countries of the South (or, for example, for the prevention of child labour) is wholly without protectionist motives, when we see that concern emanating from countries like the USA which are engaged in deregulating and flexibilizing their labour markets, and curbing wages and trade union rights. And the policy of 'globalization' is no doubt in itself the best illustration of this asymmetry, since it aims to extend to the entire world, though on a one-way basis and without reciprocity (that is, combining it with isolationism and particularism), the model most favourable to the dominant.

The unification of the global economic field by imposing the absolute rule of free exchange, the free movement of capital and export-led growth is marked by the same ambiguity as integration into the national economic field was in another age. While bearing all the outward signs of a boundless universalism, a kind of ecumenism which finds its justification in the universal spread of the 'cheap' lifestyles of the 'civilization' of McDonald's, jeans and Coca-Cola, or in a 'juridical harmonization' that is often regarded as an indicator of positive 'globalization', this 'societal project' serves the dominant, that is, the big investors, who, while standing above states, can count on the major states, particularly the most politically and militarily powerful of them, the USA, and on the major international institutions – the World Bank, the International Monetary Fund and the World Trade Organization – which those states control, to ensure conditions favourable to the conduct of their economic activities. *The effect of domination linked to integration within inequality* can be clearly seen in the fate of Canada (which could well be the fate of Europe also, if it moves towards a kind of customs union with the USA): as a result of the lowering of its traditional protective barriers, which has left it defenceless, particularly in cultural matters, that country is undergoing virtual economic and cultural integration into the United States.

Like the old national states, the dominant economic forces are in effect capable of making (international) law and the great international organizations, which are exposed to the influence of the lobbyists, operate to their advantage. The lobbies work to clothe the economic interests of companies or nations in juridical justifications (for example, by guaranteeing industrial investors maximum rights and prerogatives); and they devote a very substantial part of their intellectual energies to dismantling national laws, such as consumer protection legislation and regulations. Without fulfilling all the functions ordinarily assigned to national states (such as those pertaining to social welfare), the international institutions invisibly govern the national governments which, being increasingly reduced to managing secondary matters, now constitute

a political smokescreen that effectively masks the true sites of
decision-making. They reinforce at the symbolic level the quasi-
mechanical action of economic competition that compels national
states to vie with each other in terms of both taxation (by granting
tax breaks) and competitive advantage (by providing free infrastructures).

The state of the global economic field

The global economic field presents itself as a set of global subfields,
each of which corresponds to an 'industry', understood as a set of
firms competing to produce and commercialize a homogeneous
category of products. The almost always oligopolistic structure of
each of these subfields corresponds to the structure of the
distribution of capital (in its different species) between the different
firms capable of acquiring and maintaining the status of efficient
competitor at the global level, the position of a firm in one country
being dependent on the position occupied by that firm in all the
other countries. The global field is highly polarized. By the mere fact
of their weight within the structure (which functions as a barrier to
entry), the dominant national economies tend to concentrate the
assets of companies and to appropriate the profits they produce, as
well as to orient the tendencies immanent in the functioning of the
field. The position of each firm in the national and international field
depends not only on its own specific advantages, but on the
economic, political, cultural and linguistic advantages that ensue
from its membership of a particular nation, with this kind of
'national capital' exerting a positive or negative 'multiplier effect' on
the structural competitiveness of the different firms.

Today these different fields are structurally subordinated to the
global financial field. That field was abruptly released (through
measures such as the French financial deregulation law of 1985–6)
from all the regulations that had been imposed upon it for almost
two centuries and which had been particularly reinforced after the
major string of banking collapses of the 1930s. Having achieved
almost complete autonomy and integration in this way, it has
become one site among others for generating returns on capital. The
concentrations of money effected by the big investors (pension funds,
insurance companies, investment funds) have become an autonomous force, controlled solely by bankers, who increasingly favour
speculation – financial operations for ends that are purely financial –
over productive investment. The international speculation economy

thereby finds itself freed from the control of the national institutions, such as central banks, which used to regulate financial operations, and long-term interest rates tend now to be determined not by national bodies, but by a small number of international operators who set the trends on the financial markets.

The concentration of finance capital in the pension and mutual funds that attract and manage collective savings enables the trans-state managers of those savings to impose on firms, in the name of shareholder interests, demands for financial profitability that gradually come to direct their strategies. And to direct those strategies, in particular, by restricting their scope for diversification, by imposing 'downsizing' or mergers and acquisitions in which all the risks are borne by the employees, who (at least the higher-ranking among them) are sometimes given a – fictitious – part in the profits through remuneration in the form of shares. The increased freedom to invest and, perhaps more crucially, to divest capital, so as to obtain the highest financial profitability promotes the mobility of capital and the generalized delocalization of industrial or banking enterprises. *Direct investment abroad* makes it possible to exploit the differences between nations or regions in terms of capital and labour costs and to move closer to the most favourable markets. Just as nascent nations transformed autonomous fiefs into provinces subordinate to the central power, in a market that is both internal and international 'network firms' find the means for 'internalizing' transactions, as Oliver Williamson puts it, that is, for organizing them within production units that incorporate the firms absorbed and thereby reduce them to the status of 'subsidiaries' of a 'parent company'; while others look to outsourcing as another way of establishing relations of subordination within relative independence.

Integration into the global economic field thus tends to weaken all regional or national powers, and, by discrediting all other models of development, particularly national models, which are condemned from the outset as nationalistic, the formal cosmopolitanism in which that integration cloaks itself leaves citizens powerless in the face of the great transnational economic and financial forces. The so-called policies of 'structural adjustment' aim at ensuring the incorporation through subordination of the dominated economies by reducing the role of all the so-called 'artificial' or 'arbitrary' mechanisms of political regulation of the economy associated with the welfare state (the only body capable of opposing the transna-tional companies and the international financial institutions) in favour of the so-called free market through a series of convergent measures of deregulation and privatization, such as abolishing all protection for the domestic market and relaxing controls on foreign investment (in the name of the Darwinian tenet that exposure to competition will make firms more efficient). In so doing, they tend to grant concentrated capital almost total freedom and allow free rein to the big multinationals that more or less directly inspire these policies. (Conversely, they contribute to neutralizing the attempts of the so-called 'emerging' nations, that is to say, those nations capable of mounting effective competition, to rely on the national state in order to construct an economic infrastructure and to create a national market by protecting national production and fostering the development of real demand, linked to the access of peasants and workers to consumption by way of increased purchasing power, itself promoted by state policies such as agrarian reform or the introduction of progressive income taxation.)

The relations of force of which these policies are a barely euphemized expression, tending, as they do, increasingly to reduce the poorest nations to an economy based almost exclusively on the extensive or intensive exploitation of natural resources, are also manifested in the asymmetrical treatment meted out to the various nations by the global institutions, depending on the position they occupy within the structure of the distribution of capital: the most typical example is no doubt the way that IMF requests to the USA to reduce its persistent deficit have long gone unheeded, whereas the same body has forced many an African economy, already greatly at risk, to reduce its deficit at the cost of increasing levels of unemployment and poverty. And we know also that the same countries that preach open frontiers and the dismantling of the state to the whole world can practise more or less subtle forms of protectionism through import quotas, voluntary export restrictions, the imposition of quality or safety standards, and enforced currency revaluations, not to mention certain self-righteous calls for the universal enforcement of workers' rights; or through state assistance via what are called 'mixed oligopolies', based on state intervention to divide up markets through Voluntary Restraint Agreements, or through production quotas for foreign subsidiaries.

Unlike the unification that took place at national state level in Europe in the past, globalization is being carried out without the state – counter to Keynes's wish to see the creation of a world central bank issuing a neutral reserve currency which would be able to guarantee trade on an equal footing between all countries – and solely to serve the interests of the dominant, who, unlike the jurists who presided over the origins of the European states, do not really need to dress up the politics which suits their interests in the trappings of universalism. It is the logic of the field and the intrinsic force of concentrated capital that impose relations of force favourable to the interests of the dominant. And they have the means to transform these relations of force into an apparently universal set of rules through the falsely neutral interventions of the great international bodies they dominate (IMF, WTO), or under cover of the representations of the economy and politics they are able to inspire and impose – and which have found their most thorough formulation in the draft 'Multilateral Agreement on Investment'. This quasi-utopia of a world freed from all state constraints and surrendered to the arbitrary whim of investors enables us to form an idea of the really 'globalized' world that the conservative International of heads and executives of the industrial and financial multinationals of all nations is aiming to impose, with support from the political, diplomatic and military power of an imperial state that is gradually being reduced to a role of merely maintaining internal and external order.[1] It is, then, vain to hope that this unification produced by the 'harmonization' of national legal provisions will lead, of itself, to a genuine universalization, under the aegis of a universal state. But it is doubtless not unreasonable to expect that the effects of the policy of a small oligarchy, concerned only for its own short-term economic interest, may promote the progressive emergence of political forces, themselves also global, capable of gradually imposing the creation of transnational bodies with a remit to control the dominant economic forces and subordinate them to genuinely universal ends.

Notes

Introduction

1 I am grateful to Mr Loïc Wacquant for his assistance with Bourdieu's terminology. It is essentially at his behest that 'maison individuelle' has, in all theoretical contexts, been rendered as 'single-family house', and 'atout' as 'strength'. [Trans.]

2 Strategies aimed at 'correcting' the shortcomings or inadequacies of a paradigm without ever really challenging it — Herbert Simon speaking of 'limited rationality' or Mark Granovetter reintroducing 'social networks' — are reminiscent of the painstaking constructions with which Tycho Brahe sought to rescue Ptolemy's geocentric model from the Copernican revolution.

3 For an analysis of the difference between the concept of cultural capital, as used in P. Bourdieu and J.-P. Passeron, *Les Héritiers. Les étudiants et la culture* (Paris: Minuit, 1964), and the notion of 'human capital' proposed by Gary Becker, see P. Bourdieu, 'Avenir, de classe et causalité du probable', *Revue française de sociologie*, 15 (Jan.–Mar. 1974), pp. 3–42, and *The State Nobility* (Cambridge: Polity, 1998), pp. 275–6. On social capital, see P. Bourdieu, 'Le capital social. Notes provisoires', *Actes de la recherche en sciences sociales*, 31 (Jan. 1980), pp. 2–3; on symbolic capital, see P. Bourdieu, *Distinction. A Social Critique of the Judgement of Taste* (London: Routledge, 1986), *Pascalian Meditations* (Cambridge: Polity, 2000) and, for a recent clarification of my position, 'Scattered remarks', *European Journal of Social Theory*, 2: 3 (Aug. 1999), pp. 334–40.

4 On the 'discovery of work', see P. Bourdieu, with A. Darbel, J.-P. Rivet and C. Seibel, *Travail et travailleurs en Algérie*, part 2 (Paris/The Hague: Mouton, 1963). See also P. Bourdieu and A. Sayad, *Le Déra-*

cinement. La crise de l'agriculture traditionnelle en Algérie (Paris: Minuit, 1964).

5 On the economic conditions for access to economic calculation, see P. Bourdieu, *Travail et travailleurs en Algérie* and *Algérie 60* (Paris: Minuit, 1977), trans. as *Algeria 1960* (Cambridge: Cambridge University Press, 1979). On the cultural conditions for that access, a description of the progressive emergence of 'market culture' – a spontaneous social theory which describes 'social relationships exclusively in terms of commodities and exchanges when they continued to involve so much more' – can be found in William M. Reddy, *The Rise of Market Culture: The Textile Trades and French Society 1750–1900* (Cambridge: Cambridge University Press, 1984). [The passage quoted here is to be found on p. 3, Trans.]

6 For further development of this analysis, see Bourdieu, *Pascalian Meditations*, pp. 17–24, 50–60.

7 See M. Allais, 'Le comportement de l'homme rationnel devant le risque. Critique des postulats et axiomes de l'école américaine', *Econometrica*, 21 (1953), pp. 503–46.

8 We might, from this point of view, agree with Max Weber that the theory of marginal utility is a 'historico-cultural fact' which manifests that fundamental aspect of contemporary societies that is the tendency towards – formal – rationalization, a tendency correlative, *inter alia*, with the spread of monetary exchange.

9 The fact that practices which may be termed *reasonable* because they have a reason to them or are *meaningful* are not fundamentally underpinned by reason or rational calculation has very real consequences: the problems and the ways of resolving them are quite different from what they would be if they were made explicit and treated methodically.

10 'Governance' is one of those many new terms made fashionable by the think tanks and other technocratic circles of that kind, and given currency by trendy journalists and 'intellectuals', which are contributing to the 'globalization' of language and thinking.

11 See D. Ross, *The Origins of American Social Science* (Cambridge: Harvard University Press, 1988). See also P. Bourdieu and L. Wacquant, 'Les ruses de la raison impérialiste', *Actes de la recherche en sciences sociales*, 121–2 (Mar. 1998), pp. 109–18.

12 Whereas high productivity may be associated with a great degree of flexibility, as is the case in economies like Denmark, but combined with high levels of social provision.

13 For a more in-depth analysis of the long-term consequences of the housing policy analysed below, see P. Bourdieu et al., *The Weight of the World: Social Suffering in Contemporary Society* (Cambridge: Polity, 1999).

14 Ernst Cassirer, *The Philosophy of the Enlightenment* (Princeton: Princeton University Press, 1968), p. 82.

Part I   The House Market

Chapter 1   Disposition of the Agents and the Structure of the Field of Reproduction

For a more detailed exposition of the data on which the analyses presented in this first chapter are based, see two articles which appeared in *Actes de la recherche en sciences sociales*, 81–2 (Mar. 1990): P. Bourdieu, with the collaboration of S. Bouhedja, R. Christin and C. Givry, 'Un placement de père de famille' (pp. 6–33), and P. Bourdieu and M. de Saint Martin, 'Le sens de la propriété' (pp. 52–64).

1 We know, for example, the importance the members of the middle classes and the aristocracy attached, in the nineteenth century, to the social quality of their *address* – which could lead them to choose to rent in a 'good' district rather than to buy in a less fashionable one. And we can see evidence of this awareness of opening oneself to the judgement of others in the names often given to petit-bourgeois suburban houses in France such as 'Ça me suffit' [It'll do for me] or 'Ça me plaît' [I like it].
2 Evidence of this interest is provided by the success of publications devoted to home-improvement which fulfil a function similar to that of manuals of etiquette in another field of practice.
3 By dint of the multiple economic functions it simultaneously fulfils, the dwelling house poses difficult problems of accounting classification.
4 On the model of the 'house', see P. Bourdieu, 'Célibat et condition paysanne', *Études rurales*, 5–6 (Apr.–Sept. 1962), pp. 32–136, and 'Les stratégies matrimoniales dans le système des stratégies de reproduction', *Annales*, 4–5 (July–Oct. 1972), pp. 1105–27, E. Claverie and P. Lamaison, *L'Impossible Mariage. Violence et parenté en Gévaudan, XVIIe, XVIIIe et XIXe siècles* (Paris: Hachette, 1982); and also C. Lévi-Strauss, *Paroles données* (Paris: Plon, 1984), p. 177.
5 It can be seen in this connection that the graph showing the rates of non-financial saving by households (taken as an indicator of property investment) is very similar to that showing the number of marriages (see L. Crétin and P. L'Hardy, 'Les ménages épargnent moins qu'il y a quinze ans', *Économie et statistique*, 219 (Mar. 1989), pp. 21–6).
6 A study of an example of collective mythology particularly linked to the Mediterranean area, though doubtless a constant in the European unconscious, can be found in P. Bourdieu, 'The Kabyle house or the world reversed', in *The Logic of Practice* (Cambridge: Polity, 1990), pp. 271–83.
7 The advertising slogan 'Une maison de maçons' was coined by the Bouygues company to promote 'industrially produced' houses.
8 This point shows up all that is involved in the move, which is being widely encouraged today in the public services – principally, the education and cultural services – from user (listener, viewer, pupil, student) to *client*.

9 A. Martinet, *To Honor Roman Jakobson*, cited by G. Mounin, *La Communication poétique* (Paris: Gallimard, 1971), p. 25.

10 M. Augé, *Demeures et châteaux* (Paris: Seuil, 1989).

11 Ibid., p. 79.

12 One may gain some idea of this formidable labour of appropriation, which has its equivalent in the order of discourse, by looking attentively at the photographs of the internal or external improvements which their owners have made to Phénix houses in *Les Honneurs de la maison. Six photographes dans la maison, témoignages réalisés sous la direction de Lucien Clergue* (Paris: Pandora, 1982).

13 In 1879 the postman Ferdinand Cheval began to build the fairy-tale palace which stands as his monument at Hauterives in the Drôme, using pebbles and other materials garnered on his daily twenty-mile round. The work, one of the longest recorded DIY projects, was completed in 1912. [Trans.]

14 Like the *churingas*, those stone or wooden decorated objects of the Aranda people, representing the physical body of a particular ancestor, which are solemnly attributed in each generation to the living person who is considered the reincarnation of that ancestor, and are brought out periodically to be inspected and honoured, family albums and all the precious goods – family archives, family jewels and family portraits – that are handed down from generation to generation, like the family name, and sometimes certain forenames, owe their sacred character to the fact that, by attesting physically to the ancientness and continuity of the lineage, they consecrate its social unity, which is always indissociable from temporal permanency. See P. Bourdieu, *Un art moyen. Essai sur les usages sociaux de la photographie* (Paris: Minuit, 1965).

15 This is the limiting factor in philosophical anthropology which still survives today, particularly in Germany, and in most of the attempts of ethnologists to transport, without any critical questioning, their instruments and habits of thought outside their traditional fields of application.

16 C. Taffin, 'L'accession à tout prix', *Économie et statistique*, 202 Sept. 1987), pp. 5–16. Direct transmission is, however, much more important than these figures suggest: assistance by the family does in fact take many and varied forms (interest-free loans, gifts of land, part payments, etc.).

17 See Crétin and L'Hardy, 'Les ménages épargnent moins qu'il y a quinze ans'.

18 Literally: beavers. [Trans.]

19 One of the most systematic attempts was made by Pierre Durif, who will be mentioned again below as one of the initiators of housing finance reform, and Sylvie Berniard, on the basis of the 1967 housing survey, which was compared, in particular, with that of 1963 (see P. Durif and S. Berniard, 'Les Français et la maison individuelle',

Économie et statistique, 7 (Dec. 1969), pp. 3–16; P. Durif, 'Propriétaires et locataires en 1967', *Économie et statistique*, 3 (Jul.–Aug. 1969), pp. 41–56). The survey carried out in 1986 by Catherine Bonvalet and her team for the Institut National d'Études Démographiques (INED) on the residential histories of the members of the generation born between 1926 and 1935 living in the Paris region (N = 1,987 individuals) aimed initially to discover the circumstances of arrival in Paris and factors determining that move, 'housing history' and the development of property ownership over the life-cycle, together with retirement plans and further plans to move house. This survey focused primarily on the study of demographic and social factors, devoting much less attention to economic or cultural capital, or the effects of housing policy and supply. See C. Bonvalet, A. Bringé and B. Riandey, *Cycle de vie et changements urbains en région parisienne. Histoire résidentielle d'une génération* (Paris: INED, June 1988), 179 pages plus appendices. The study of geographic and family origins, careers, residence and styles of life which was carried out at Credoc by Nicole Tabard and her team on 1,000 households in the Essonne département having at least one child under 20, was focused initially on the construction of a socio-professional typology of the communes and districts of that département and on the analysis of the relations between, on the one hand, the morphology of the communes or districts of residence and the behaviour and practices of households in terms of housing and, on the other, between the social and geographical trajectories of those surveyed and their specific location within the Essonne département. See N. Tabard et al., *Relations entre la structure socio-économique de l'espace, la production de l'environnement et les conditions de logement. Analyse de l'enquête Essonne* (Paris: Credoc, Jan. 1987), 124 pages.

20 The interpretation of the statistics was informed throughout by indications and hypotheses drawn from a number of in-depth interviews (N = 45) which we carried out with owners of single-family houses in the Paris region and in the south of France (see appendix I to this chapter).

21 M. Villac, G. Balland and L. Touchard, 'Les conditions de logement des ménages en 1978', *Les Collections de l'INSEE*, série Ménages, 85 (1980).

22 SOFRES, *Les Français et l'immobilier*, Mar. 1986.

23 Within this category, the proportion of homeowners is also independent of age.

24 The CEP and the CAP are, respectively, the Certificat d'Études Primaires and the Certificat d'Aptitude Professionnel. The former is the primary school leaving certificate, while the latter was roughly equivalent at the time of the study to a British City and Guilds certificate. The BEPC (below is the Brevet d'Études du Premier Cycle, equivalent to the General Certificate for Secondary Education (GCSE) in the UK; the BEP is the Brevet d'Études Professionnelles. [Trans.]

25 Rates of flat ownership seem more closely linked to educational qualifications than house ownership, at least in certain categories. However, this is surely to be seen as an effect of urbanization, flat owners being more common in the large conurbations where there are more people with educational qualifications.

26 The foremen with the lowest incomes (less than 65,000 francs per year) own their own homes much more often (39.5% of cases) than do white-collar workers (16.5%) or middle managers (8.2%) with the same resources.

27 See G. Ballester, *Maison préfabriquée* (Paris: Institut Français de Démoscopie, Nov. 1984).

28 Villac, Balland and Touchard, 'Les conditions de logement des ménages en 1978', pp. 161–6. Apart from size of settlement, we should also be able to take into account region. Pierre Durif has shown that there were in 1968 very marked regional variations, particularly between western and eastern France: in that year, the proportion of single-family houses was above average throughout western France and was particularly high in the north. By contrast, there were more collective dwellings in central and eastern France, and particularly in the south east (Durif and Berniard, 'Les Français et la maison individuelle', esp. pp. 5–7).

29 Tabard et al., *Relations entre la structure socio-économique* ...

30 Bonvalet, Bringé and Riandey, *Cycle de vie et changements urbains en région parisienne*, p. 121.

31 Ibid., pp. 125–6.

32 On the link between restriction of fertility and ambition to move up the social scale, see P. Bourdieu and A. Darbel, 'La fin d'un malthusianisme?' in Darras, *Le Partage des bénéfices* (Paris: Minuit, 1966, pp. 117–29) and P. Bourdieu, *Distinction: A Social Critique of the Judgement of Taste* (London: Routledge and Kegan Paul, 1984).

33 This hypothesis finds confirmation in the first published results of the survey Nicole Tabard carried out in the Essonne, which should enable us to develop more detailed knowledge of the effects of social trajectory. In particular, it brings out the links between social origin, particularly for managers and professionals, and the fact of living in a more or less well-to-do locality.

34 See P. Culturello, *De la location à l'accession* (Nice/Marseille: GERM-CERCOM, 1989), report of research for the CNAF (Caisse Nationale des Allocations Familiales – National Family Allowance Fund).

35 C. Topalov, *Le Logement en France* (Paris: Presses de la FBSP, 1987), see esp. pp. 305–14. The proportion of farmers and industrial and commercial employers who owned their own dwellings, which was already very high at the beginning of this period, increased much more slowly.

36 The logic of the increasingly intensive 'mining' of a failing seam undoubtedly led the banks to push back the limits of reasonable risk. As

a result, the recession hit working-class borrowers hard. Thus, between 1981 and 1983, 21 of the 51 cases in which a verdict was delivered at the *tribunaux de grande instance* (equivalent of the county courts) of Rennes and St Malo on a dispute between a lender and a new entrant to the property market concerned blue-collar workers, nine of whom worked in the construction and civil engineering industries. Five of the other cases concerned white-collar workers and three were farmers, with socio-professional categories being unknown in 20 of the cases (see Agence d'Urbanisme et de Développement Intercommunal de l'Agglomération Rennaise, 'Les accédants à la propriété en difficultés financières', Rennes, Feb. 1986).

37 See Bonvalet, Bringé and Riandey, *Cycle de vie et changements urbains en région parisienne*, p. 31.

38 See M. Eenschooten, 'Le logement de 1978 à 1984. Toujours plus grand et toujours mieux', *Économie et statistique*, 206 (Jan. 1988), pp. 33–43.

39 N. Tabard, *Consommation et inscription spatiale. Synthèses et perspectives* (Paris: Credoc, 1984).

40 This set of negative collateral effects of the change of housing explains the fact, paradoxical in appearance, that access to ownership of a modern flat is often experienced, very logically, as a regression, in spite of all the effort made to '*be happy with it*' (this paradoxical discrepancy between the experience of agents and the apparent improvement in their housing conditions – relating to their moving from shanty towns to the equivalent of a council flat – came home to me very clearly in the investigation I carried out in Algeria in the 1960, see Bourdieu, *Algérie 60*, pp. 83–114).

41 See Topalov, *Le Logement en France*, p. 315.

42 Since the survey on which this work is based was carried out at the end of the 1980s, the data gathered relate to a period before the 1990s. The decision to focus on this period is justified by the scope and significance of the structural transformations which characterize it and by the fact that an economics that is in its essence historical cannot reason outside of a definite spatio-temporal framework.

43 'Maison individuelle: promoteurs et constructeurs résistent bien', *Le Moniteur des travaux publics et du bâtiment*, 9 (2 Mar. 1984), p. 37. It follows from this that the 'sector' is characterized by the employment of a large workforce, staff costs in building and civil engineering companies with more than 50 employees representing 38% of pre-tax turnover in 1981 and 90% of added value. See J. J. Granelle and M. Pelège, *Construction, croissance et crise. Réflexions pour une relance* (Paris: Éditions du Moniteur, 1985). Having said this, advances in total or partial industrialization (with regard to the components employed) mean that building costs in the strict sense are a decreasing factor in the cost of buildings (particularly luxury residences or apartment blocks), whereas the proportion of incidental costs – the cost of the land, notaries' fees and, most importantly, marketing and financial costs – is

increasing. See P. Madelin, *Dossier I comme immobilier* (Paris: A. Moreau, 1974), pp. 265–8. See also *Le Moniteur des travaux publics et du bâtiment*, magazine supplement 17 (28 Apr. 1980).

44 Union de Crédit pour le Bâtiment de la Compagnie Bancaire.

45 Union de Crédit pour le Bâtiment, *Regards sur une profession. Les constructeurs de maisons individuelles* (Paris: UCB, 1983). The reality is much more complex than this classification suggests. Into what category, for example, do associations of architects such as architect-builders fall?

46 Though much has been published on the building of single-family houses, there is no study covering all the relevant building concerns (apart from confidential data such as the 'Baromètre UCB').

47 Control by foreign companies was not taken into account at this stage of the research.

48 Since this first analysis, carried out successively on the 44 construction or development companies and on the 30 building companies, produced only very disappointing – and, in a sense, too predictable – results, it will not be reproduced here. It is presented in detail in *Éléments d'une analyse du marché de la maison individuelle* (Paris: Centre de la Sociologie Européenne, 1987), pp. 53–60.

49 Advertising brochure entitled 'Une maison de maçons, oui, vous pouvez' ('A mason-built house, yes you can'), 1984, 46pp.

50 Francis Bouygues, introductory text to a brochure presenting the Maison Bouygues company, 1984.

51 The same type of effects, which can be understood only in a structural perspective, can be seen in the area of editorial production, in which producers or distributors of 'commercial' literature, industrially produced and targeted at a mass market, can mimic (or ape) the authentic inventions of the avant-garde by way of marketing tricks, which often play on the sincere adherence of certain poorly informed critics, with effects of *allodoxia* also playing their part (See P. Bourdieu, 'Une révolution conservatrice', *Actes de la recherche en sciences sociales*, 126–7 (Mar. 1999), pp. 3–28).

52 E. Panofsky, *Studies in Iconology: Humanistic Themes in the Art of the Renaissance* (Oxford: Oxford University Press, 1939), pp. 9–10.

53 'La maison individuelle se personnalise', *Le Moniteur des travaux publics et du bâtiment*, 2 May 1986, pp. 30–4. See also 'Des constructeurs sur mesure', *Le Moniteur des travaux publics et du bâtiment*, 30 Apr. 1987, pp. i–xviii.

54 Breguet-Construction was found guilty in late 1973 of copying the models of the American company Kaufman and Broad, thus acquiring cheaply many models tried and tested over a long period by Kaufman (see Madelin, *Dossier I comme immobilier*, p. 226; many other instances of trials are quoted here, alongside cases of the poaching of executives and the plagiarizing of models).

55 A commercial secretary in the Bouygues company, who had previously

worked nine years for Phénix, and whose former sales director at Phénix had taken her with him when he himself had moved to Bouygues, explains: 'Bouygues was to some extent got off the ground by my old regional boss at Phénix ... The regional director of Maison Bouygues left Phénix. He started up Maison Bouygues Île-de-France, which was very successful, and he brought in some of the old colleagues he worked well with.' She went on to recall that several salespeople she knew from Phénix had left to join Bouygues.

56 An analysis of requests for planning permission made to the local council at Taverny (Val-d'Oise) enables us to verify directly the pre-eminence of small and medium-sized local builders. Of the 32 requests for permission to build single-family houses presented in 1984, and the 30 presented in 1985 (which represent less than 20% of requests of all kinds – the rest being made up of requests to build blocks of flats or offices, shops, to carry out demolition, etc.), only a fraction (less than 25%) were made by national construction companies (Phénix, Bâti-Service, Maison Bouygues, Nouveaux Constructeurs and Alskanor).

57 The Crédit Foncier is a semi-public credit establishment specializing in the medium- and long-term financing of land and property operations. [Trans.]

58 Ricardo Bofill is a Spanish architect with a reputation for adventurous design. [Trans.]

59 A reference to seaside-chalet-style building at that location (Vendée). [Trans.]

60 This is a 'crawl space' extending for a metre or so above ground level. It provides space for plumbing and ventilation beneath the ground floor slab and to some extent prevents the transmission of humidity from the ground to the ground floor. [Trans.]

Chapter 2   The State and the Construction of the Market

This chapter draws on the article by the author and R. Christin, 'La construction du marché', which appeared in *Actes de la recherche en sciences sociales*, 81–2 (Mar. 1990), pp. 65–85.

1 Crédit Commercial de France.

2 Association of Builders of Detached Houses. [Trans.]

3 National Union of Builders of Detached Houses. [Trans.]

4 Joint Committee for Detached Housing. [Trans.]

5 The HLM is the major French form of public housing provision and is roughly equivalent to British 'council housing'. [Trans.]

6 Before the 1977 law, which implemented recommendations made by the Barre Commission, these loans were made at fixed rates for a period of 45 years. After 1977, the rates were indexed, the annual repayments became progressive and the repayment period was reduced to 34 years, with a compensatory increase in *aide à la personne*.

7 Housing allowance. [Trans.]
8 Since 1977, every new dwelling built has created an entitlement to APL (*aide personnalisé au logement* [personalized housing assistance]). The provision also applies to the purchase of certain existing dwellings.
9 See Y. Carsalade and H. Lévy-Lambert, Note to the *Rapport du groupe 'Interventions publiques' de la Commission de l'habitation du 6e plan*, vol. 2, pp. 175ff.; see also H. Lévy-Lambert, 'Modèle de choix en matière de politique du logement', *Revue d'économie politique*, 6 (1968), p. 938, and H. Lévy-Lambert, *La Vérité des prix* (Paris: Seuil, 1969).
10 i.e. a kind of departmental staff. [Trans.]
11 Graduate of the École Nationale d'Administration. [Trans.]
12 Graduates of the École Polytechnique. [Trans.]
13 Directorate of Building, Public Works and Construction. [Trans.]
14 i.e. by the office of the President of France. [Trans.]
15 Thanks to the 'neutralization' which remoteness in time brings, it has been possible here to conceal an investigation into permanent structures and issues – hence structures and issues which are still present and topical – in the garb of a historical inquiry into past struggles. We have nonetheless resolved, both in the text and the diagrams, to cite only the names of the higher civil servants whose participation in the reform project was publicly known, the others being referred to simply by their initials.
16 Housing and Social Life Group. [Trans.]
17 Economic and International Affairs Department. [Trans.]
18 Directorate of Land Development and Town Planning. [Trans.]
19 These are, respectively, the General Planning and Productivity Authority, the Central Group on New Towns and the National Commission for Property Operations and Architecture. [Trans]
20 Delegation for Regional Development and Regional Action. [Trans.]
21 The Caisse des Dépôts et Consignations is a state-owned financial institution which manages the funds French savers deposit in their National Savings Bank (Caisse d'Épargne) accounts and 'Livret A' accounts in the French Post Office Savings Scheme. It is the body that provides the cheap long-term loans to the specialist agencies which build social housing. [Trans.]
22 The publishing house most directly connected with the French Communist Party. [Trans.]
23 See H. Rouanet and B. Le Roux, *Analyse des données multi-dimensionnelles* (Paris: Dunod, 1993).
24 The French school of Political Sciences, known familiarly as Sciences Po. [Trans.]
25 Respectively, the Association for Social Housing, Association of Mayors of France, National Family Allowance Fund, General Housing Confederation, National Building Federation, Union of Savings Banks, National Union of Family Associations, National Union of HLM Federations, National Joint Housing Union. [Trans.]

26 The equivalent of the Audit Office (UK) or Government Accounting Office (US). [Trans.]
27 After the *arbitrages* of March and July 1976, there were profound changes in the personnel responsible for the reform (among other things, GRECOH broke up). The fact remains, however, that the new people in charge (in the *cabinet* of the Housing Minister, Jacques Barrot, or in the Construction Directorate) presented characteristics very similar to those of their predecessors: they were to a very great extent from research departments of the Economic Plan or DATAR and had spent some part of their careers abroad or with international bodies.
28 The Nora Commission was undoubtedly the most impeccably bureaucratic of the three commissions. Originating in the heart of the bureaucracy itself (the Finance Ministry) and presided over by a high-ranking career civil servant, it was made up almost entirely of relatively young, innovative civil servants and its conclusions seemed to be accepted unreservedly by the upper reaches of the public service.
29 The opposition between these two logics can be clearly seen in the case studied by Bernard Guibert in *L'Intervention de l'état dans l'obligation alimentaire. Premières leçons de la loi de 1984* (Paris: CNAF, 1987), where the '*logique du forfait*', which characterizes the *maintenance obligation* in the 1804 Civil Code, contrasts with the '*logique du quotient*' characteristic of income tax, the cost of the child being regarded as a proportion of the income of its parents (ibid., pp. 10–11). This opposition is homologous to the one we find in the field of housing rights, with building subsidies (*aide à la pierre*) on one side and, on the other personal assistance (*aide à la personne*) and, more generally, the whole policy of 'personalized credit' implemented in the 1960s by the banks, which tends to make the current and potential monetary value of economic agents the absolute measure of their value, and of the *credit* (in the strong sense of the term) to be accorded to them, both socially and economically.
30 On the role of 'Sciences Po' in the codification and inculcation of the 'liberal' vulgate, see P. Bourdieu and L. Boltanski, 'La production de l'idéologie dominante', *Actes de la recherche en sciences sociales*, 2–3 (1976), pp. 4–73.
31 The French 'workers' gardens' are similar to British allotments or North American community gardens. [Trans.]
32 The National Building Council. [Trans.]
33 The National Estate Agents' Federation. [Trans.]
34 The National Chamber of Property Administrators. [Trans.]
35 The National Real Estate Union. [Trans.]

Chapter 3   The Field of Local Powers

1 The phantasm of the apparatus, originating in the most mechanistic Marxist tradition, has been applied with particular force to the state,

which has in this way been invested with a kind of divine or demonic power of manipulation. And, by a strange quirk of fate, it has often been applied to the Communist Party and state by all the anti-communist proponents of 'theories' of 'totalitarianism', who have, in this way, prevented themselves from seeing (though did they want to?) and understanding the changes the countries of Eastern Europe have constantly undergone, changes of which the 'Gorbachev phenomenon' is the expression and culmination. See P. Bourdieu, 'A long trend of change', *Times Literary Supplement*, 12–18 August 1988, pp. 875–6 (review of M. Lewin, *The Gorbachev Phenomenon: A Historical Interpretation*).

2 This uncertainty is constitutive of the very logic of play. A game in which one of the players is able to win at will (for example, an adult 'playing' against a child) is no game at all ('no contest'). It is a game not worth playing.

3 See B. Reynaud, 'Types of rules, interpretation and collective dynamics: reflections on the introduction of a salary rule in a maintenance workshop', *Industrial and Corporate Change*, 5: 3 (1996), pp. 699–721.

4 The charisma of the teacher-prophet, analysed elsewhere, is another example of this process.

5 All these mechanisms come fully into play where the subjects of the bureaucratic rulings in question are particularly bereft of resources or remedies, as is so with immigrants or, in the extreme case, with those 'without documents', the hypocrisy of the central decisions consisting in their leaving matters to the discretionary powers of the executive agencies and their tendencies to be repressive rather than accommodating.

6 A body which exists to provide legal information in the field of housing. [Trans.]

7 Created to provide architectural and environmental advice to private individuals and communes. [Trans.]

8 Communes, headed by mayors elected by the 'conseil municipal', are the basic unit of the French political and administrative system; 90% of them have fewer than 2,000 inhabitants. [Trans.]

9 That is to say, the graduate of ENA, i.e. the Prefect. [Trans.]

10 See P. Grémion, *Le Pouvoir périphérique. Bureaucrates et notables dans le système politique français* (Paris: Seuil, 1976).

11 This interview, together with all the interviews quoted here, was carried out within the framework of research conducted in a département of the Île-de-France, namely the Val-d'Oise, which involved interviews with a variety of actors: departmental architects (CAUE, DDE, etc.), lawyers (ADIL), a notary; agents of the various offices of the DDE-Argenteuil (planning permission division), Cergy Préfecture (town planning disputed claims department); and the mayor and officials from the technical services of the town planning department at Taverny. We also conducted lengthy observations in the technical service of the town

planning department of Taverny town hall, particularly relating to planning permissions in 1984 and 1985, to the establishment of the ZAC des Lignières at Taverny and to the marketing by AFTRP (Agence Foncière et Technique de la Région Parisienne) of a first tranche of building plots offered for sale in Taverny. Lastly, we carried out observations at Moisselles, a 'show village' of detached houses, conducted interviews with local builders and systematically collected advertising material. For comparative purposes, we also carried out a similar research project in the Loiret département.

Chapter 4   A Contract under Duress

This article draws on an article by the author (with the collaboration of S. Bouhedja and C. Givry), entitled 'Un contrat sous contrainte', *Actes de la recherche en sciences sociales*, 81–2 (Mar. 1990), pp. 34–51.

1 The use made of technical language, in alternation with ordinary language, by the members of the medical profession (doctors of various levels, nurses, etc.) essentially follows this same pattern.
2 In 1963, *only* 0.06% of *clients* of the Compagnie Bancaire gave cause for litigation. Various studies show that problems of excessive mortgage debt have increased considerably in the last few years, largely on account of the deflation which has compromised the solvency of those holding loans with rising repayments made in the years 1981–4, thus transforming the structure in relation to which dispositions and strategies were formed (cf. Comité consultatif, 'Rapport du groupe de travail sur l'endettement et le surendettement des ménages', Paris, July 1989).
3 On the calculability and predictability associated with the career (as opposed to the insecurity and uncertainty of the existence of the subproletariat) as the condition of emergence of the calculating disposition, see Bourdieu, *Algérie 60*.
4 On the theory of contracts and the concepts of 'adverse selection' or 'moral hazard', see, *inter alia*, O. Hart and B. Holmström, 'The theory of contracts', in T. Bewdley (ed.), *Advances in Economic Theory* (Cambridge: Cambridge University Press, 1987).
5 According to an analysis of the family allowance authority in Mâcon, the proportion of mortgages involving a housing expense ratio above 30% decreased slightly between 1985 and 1987, moving from 30% to 20% of the property owners receiving assistance. However, in 1987, almost 7% of loans still involved a housing expense ratio above 40% and in February 1988 10.5% had a ratio above 37% (cf. Comité Consultatif, *Rapport*, p. 17).

Conclusion

1 'For in a contract not everything is contractual. The only undertakings worthy of the name are those that are desired by individuals, whose sole origin is this free act of the will. Conversely, any obligation that has not been agreed by both sides is not in any way contractual.' Emile Durkheim, *The Division of Labour in Society* (London: Macmillan Education, 1984), p. 158. [Trans.]
2 Christiane Olivier, *Les Enfants de Jocaste* (Paris: Denoel/Gonthier, 1980). [Trans.]
3 The French television channel TF1, which has the highest viewing figures, was bought by Francis Bouygues in 1987. It devotes a large part of its schedules to entertainment programming, such as game shows offering domestic appliances as prizes, and to variety shows hosted by presenters with very high popular audience ratings.

Part II Principles of an Economic Anthropology

The translator thanks Richard Nice and Loïc Wacquant for their assistance in the preparation of this section.

1 In the absence, as yet, of any formalization along the lines laid down by these principles, we can call on correspondence analysis (the theoretical foundations of which are very similar) to help us bring out the structure of the economic field or, in other words, the true *explanatory principle* of economic practices.
2 W. H. Hamilton, *Price and Price Policies* (New York: McGraw Hill, 1938).
3 M. R. Tool, 'Contributions to an institutional theory of price determination', in G. M. Hodgson and E. Screpanti (eds), *Rethinking Economics: Markets, Technology and Economic Evolution* (Cheltenham: European Association for Evolutionary Political Economy/Edward Elgar, 1991), pp. 29–30
4 This conception of social capital differs from the definitions which have subsequently been given in American sociology and economics in that it takes into account not only the network of relations, characterized as regards its extent and viability, but also the volume of capital of different species which it enables to be mobilized by proxy (and, at the same time, the various profits it can procure: promotion, participation in projects, opportunities for participation in important decisions, chances to make financial or other investments). See Bourdieu, 'Le capital social. Notes provisoires'.
5 Cultural capital, technical capital and commercial capital exist both in objectivized form (equipment, instruments, etc.) and in embodied form (competence, skills, etc.). One can see an anticipation of the distinction between the two states of capital, the objectivized and the embodied, in the work of Thorstein Veblen, who criticizes the orthodox theory of

capital for overestimating tangible assets to the detriment of intangible ones. See T. Veblen, *The Instinct of Workmanship* (New York: Augustus Kelley, 1964).

6 B. Mintz and M. Schwartz, *The Power Structure of American Business* (Chicago: University of Chicago Press, 1985).

7 J. A. Kregel, 'Markets and institutions as features of a capitalistic production system', *Journal of Post-Keynesian Economics*, 3: 1 (Fall 1980).

8 As R. H. Coase has pointed out, it is on the basis of the assumption, tacitly made in orthodox theory, of zero transaction costs that acts of exchange can be rendered instantaneous: 'Another consequence of the assumption of zero transaction costs, not usually noticed, is that, when there are no costs of making transactions, it costs nothing to speed them up, so that eternity can be experienced in a split second.' R. H. Coase, *The Firm, the Market and the Law* (Chicago: University of Chicago Press, 1988), p. 15.

9 J. Tirole, *The Theory of Industrial Organization* (Cambridge: MIT Press, 1988), p. 4.

10 The classic work of Amos Tversky and Daniel Kahneman has shown up the shortcomings of agents, and the mistakes they make, with regard to probability theory and statistics. See A. Tversky and D. Kahneman, 'Availability, a heuristic for judging frequency and probability', *Cognitive Psychology*, 2 (1973), pp. 207–32; see also S. Sutherland, *Irrationality, the Enemy Within* (London: Constable, 1972). There is a danger that the intellectualist assumption which underlies this research may lead us to miss the fact that the logical problem one infers from a real situation is not posed as such by the agents (friendship as a social relation is not informed by the principle that 'my friends' friends are my friends') and the logic of dispositions means that agents are capable of responding in practice to situations involving problems of anticipation of opportunity which they cannot resolve abstractly. See P. Bourdieu, *The Logic of Practice* (Cambridge: Polity, 1990).

11 M. Granovetter, 'Economic action and social structure, the problem of embeddedness', *American Journal of Sociology*, 91: 3 (Nov. 1985), pp. 481–510.

12 A. Strauss, *Continual Permutations of Action* (New York: Aldine de Gruyter, 1993).

13 See M. Granovetter, 'Economic institutions as social constructions: a framework for analysis', *Acta Sociologica*, 35 (1992), pp. 3–11. Granovetter presents here a modified version of the alternative between 'individualism' and 'holism', which is rampant in economic (and sociological) orthodoxy, in the form of the opposition, borrowed from Dennis Wrong ('The oversocialized conception of man in modern sociology', *American Sociological Review*, 26 (1961), pp. 183–93) between the 'undersocialized view' dear to economic orthodoxy and the 'oversocialized view', which assumes that agents are 'so sensitive to the

opinions of others that they automatically [obey] commonly held norms for behavior' ('Economic institutions', p. 5) or that they have so profoundly internalized the norms or constraints that they are no longer affected by existing social relations (wholly erroneously, the notion of habitus is sometimes understood in this way). Hence the conclusion that, ultimately, this oversocialization and undersocialization have much in common, both of them regarding agents as closed monads, uninfluenced by 'concrete, ongoing systems of social relations' (ibid., p. 6) and 'social networks'.

14 Tirole, *The Theory of Industrial Organization*, pp. 2–3. A little further on, the author gives some hints regarding the costs and benefits associated with the different categories of product (mainly, theoretical and empirical) on the economics market, which enables us to understand the comparative destinies of the 'Harvard tradition' and the 'new theory of industrial organization' he is defending: 'Until the 1970s, economic theorists (with a few exceptions) pretty much ignored industrial organization, which did not lend itself to elegant and general analysis the way the theory of competitive general equilibrium analysis did. Since then, a fair number of top theorists have become interested in industrial organization.'

15 E. S. Mason, 'Price and production policies of a large-scale enterprise', *American Economic Review*, 29: 1 (Mar. 1939), supplement, pp. 61–74, esp. p. 64.

16 'The structure of a seller's market includes all those *considerations* which he takes into account in determining his business policies and practices' (ibid., p. 68; my italics, to point up the oscillation between the language of structure and structural constraint and that of consciousness and intentional choice).

17 Max Weber observes that commodity exchange is quite exceptional in that it represents the most instrumental, most calculating of all forms of action, this 'archetype of rational action' representing 'an abomination to every system of fraternal ethics', *Economy and Society*, vol. I (Berkeley/Los Angeles/London: University of California Press, 1978), p. 637.

18 P. Kotler, *Marketing Management, Analysis, Planning, Implementation, and Control* (Englewood Cliffs: Prentice Hall, 1988), p. 239.

19 Alfred D. Chandler, *The Visible Hand: The Managerial Revolution in American Business* (Cambridge: Harvard University Press, 1977), p. 62.

20 Although this vision has sometimes been contested in recent years on the grounds that the recession has seen a constant overturning of hierarchies, and that mergers and acquisitions allow small firms to buy up large ones, or to compete effectively with them, the world's 200 largest firms have nonetheless remained relatively stable.

21 A. D. Chandler, *Scale and Scope: The Dynamics of Industrial Capitalism* (Cambridge: Harvard University Press, 1990), pp. 598–9.

22 See J. Campbell and L. Lindberg, 'Property rights and the organization of economic action by the state', *American Sociological Review*, 55 (1990), pp. 634–47.

23 Neil Fligstein has shown that one cannot understand the transformation of corporate control without dissecting the state of firms' relations over the long term with the state. And he has done this in the case most favourable to liberal theory, that of the United States, where the state remains a decisive agent in the structuring of industries and markets. See N. Fligstein, *The Transformation of Corporate Control* (Cambridge: Harvard University Press, 1990). Further evidence of the decisive importance of central regulation is provided by the organized lobbying activity European firms carry on in Brussels.

24 The state, which plays a clear role in the case of the economy of house building, is far from being the only mechanism for coordinating supply and demand. Other institutions, such as networks of interpersonal relations in the case of crack cocaine, the 'communities' formed by auction-goers, or 'matchmakers' in the economy of boxing, also play their part in the creative regulation of markets. See P. Bourgois, *In Search of Respect: Selling Crack in El Barrio* (Cambridge: Cambridge University Press, 1996), C. Smith, *Auctions* (Berkeley: University of California Press, 1990) and L. Wacquant, 'A flesh peddler at work: power, pain and profit in the prizefighting economy', *Theory and Society*, 27: 1 (Feb. 1998), pp. 1–42.

25 Among France's major employers I have elsewhere demonstrated a close homology between the space of firms and the space of their directors, as characterized by the volume and structure of their capital. See P. Bourdieu, *The State Nobility: Elite Schools in the Field of Power* (Cambridge: Polity, 1996), pp. 300–35.

26 See Fligstein, *The Transformation of Corporate Control*, which describes how the control of firms comes successively under the sway of the directors in charge of production, marketing and, ultimately, finance. See also N. Fligstein and L. Markowitz, 'The finance conception of the corporation and the causes of the reorganization of large American corporations, 1979–1988', in W. J. Wilson (ed.), *Sociology and Social Policy* (Beverly Hills: Sage, 1993); N. Fligstein and K. Dauber, 'Structural change in corporate organization', *Annual Review of Sociology*, 15 (1989), pp. 73–96; and 'The intraorganizational power struggle: the rise of finance presidents in large corporations', *American Sociological Review*, 52 (1987), pp. 44–58.

27 H. White, 'Where do markets come from?', *American Journal of Sociology*, 87: 3 (1981), pp. 517–47, esp. p. 518.

28 M. Weber, *Economy and Society*, vol. 1, p. 636.

29 White, 'Where do markets come from?', esp. p. 518.

30 Ibid., p. 543.

31 Phrase in English in original. [Trans.]

32 See Bourdieu, *Pascalian Meditations*, pp. 49–50.

33 G. S. Becker, *Treatise on the Family* (Cambridge: Harvard University

Press, 1981), p. ix; see also *The Economic Approach to Human Behavior* (Chicago: University of Chicago Press, 1976).

34 V. Pareto, *Manual of Political Economy* (London: Macmillan, 1972), pp. 29–30.

35 See J.-C. Passeron, 'Pareto, l'économie dans la sociologie', in C. Malandrino and R. Marchionatti (eds), *Economia, sociologia e politico nell'opera di Vilfredo Pareto* (Florence: Leo S. Olschki, 2000), pp. 25–71.

36 T. Veblen, 'Why is economics not an evolutionary science?', *Quarterly Journal of Economics* (July 1898), p. 390.

37 J. S. Duesenberry, *Income, Saving and the Theory of Consumer Behavior* (Cambridge: Harvard University Press, 1949).

38 S. Mintz, *Sweetness and Power: The Place of Sugar in Modern History* (New York: Penguin Books, 1985).

39 Bourdieu, *Distinction*; L. Levine, *High Brow/Low Brow: The Emergence of Cultural Hierarchy in America* (Cambridge: Harvard University Press, 1988). As we see from the analysis of the economic and social determinants of preferences for buying a house or renting, we may repudiate the ahistorical definition of preferences without condemning ourselves to a relativism – which would rule out all rational knowledge – of tastes consigned to pure social arbitrariness (as the old formula *de gustibus non est disputandum*, invoked by Gary Becker, suggests). We are led, rather, to establish empirically the necessary statistical relations which form between tastes in the various fields of practice and the economic and social conditions of the formation of those tastes, that is to say, the present and past position of the agents in (or their trajectory through) the structure of the distribution of economic and cultural capital (or, if the reader prefers, the state at the given moment and the development over time of the volume and structure of their capital).

40 See Tversky and Kahneman, 'Availability'.

41 We may call in evidence here the findings of the behaviourist tradition, represented most notably by Herbert Simon, though without accepting this philosophy of action. Herbert Simon has stressed, on the one hand, the degree of uncertainty and incompetence that affects the process of decision-making, and, on the other, the limited capacity of the human brain. He rejects the general maximization hypothesis, but retains the notion of 'bounded rationality': agents may not be capable of gathering and processing all the information required to arrive at overall maximization in their decision-making, but they can make a rational choice within the bounds of a limited set of possibilities. Firms and consumers do not maximize, but, given the impossibility of gathering and processing all the information required to achieve a maximum, they do seek to achieve acceptable minima (a practice Simon calls 'satisficing'). H. Simon, *Reason in Human Affairs* (Stanford: Stanford University Press, 1984).

42 See Bourdieu, *Algeria 1960*.

43 A. P. Kirman, 'Whom or what does the representative individual represent?', *Journal of Economic Perspectives*, 6 (Spring 1992), pp. 117–36.

44 I was assisted in this investigation by Pierre Delsaut.

45 *Émile Durkheim on Institutional Analysis*, ed. M. Traugott (Chicago: Chicago University Press, 1978), pp. 43–70 (trans. modified); originally published as 'Cours de science sociale. Leçon d'ouverture', *Revue internationale de l'enseignement*, 15 (1888), pp. 23–48.

46 Veblen, 'Why is economics not an evolutionary science?', pp. 373–97.

47 G. J. Stigler and G. S. Becker, 'De gustibus non est disputandum', *American Economic Review*, 67 (Mar. 1977), pp. 76–90.

48 A critique of this supposed idealization is to be found in A. Hirschman, 'Rival interpretations of market society: civilizing, destructive or feeble?', *Journal of Economic Literature*, 20: 4 (1982), pp. 1463–84.

49 Douglas North observes, for example: 'It is a peculiar fact that the literature on economics ... contains so little discussion of the central institution that underlies neo-classical economics – the market' (D. North, 'Markets and other allocation systems', *Journal of European Economic History*, 6 (1977), pp. 703–16). We may here recall the two transgressions of this law of silence that are always cited: A. Marshall, *Principles of Economics*, 1890 (the chapter entitled 'On markets') and Joan Robinson's *Encyclopaedia Britannica* article 'Market', republished in her *Collected Economic Papers*. Moreover, we know that the conditions that have to be fulfilled for any market equilibrium to be optimal (quality of the product clearly defined; symmetrical information; buyers and sellers sufficiently numerous to prevent the formation of monopolistic cartels) are practically never achieved and that the rare markets that do conform to the model are artificial social constructs based on quite exceptional conditions of viability, such as networks of public regulation or of organizations. And one still finds quite unambiguous admissions of this in the very heart of the orthodoxy – for example, in a reference work of Industrial Organization Theory (see Tirole, *The Theory of Industrial Organization*, p. 12).

50 French has also the expression 'conclure un marché' – to strike a bargain – so that the term 'market' comes additionally to cover the notion of making an agreement on the terms of a transaction.

51 M. Friedman, *Capitalism and Freedom* (Chicago: Chicago University Press, 1962).

52 G. Stigler, *The Intellectual and the Marketplace* (Cambridge, Mass.: Harvard University Press, 1963). See especially pp. 143–58.

Postscript   From the National to the International Field

1 Cf. François Chesnais, *La Mondialisation du capital* (Paris: Syros, 1994) and M. Freitag and E. Pineault (eds), *Le Monde enchaîné* (Montreal: Nota Bene, 1999).

Index